The Adam Smith Review

Volume 1

The Adam Smith Review is a multidisciplinary scholarly annual review that covers all aspects of research relating to Adam Smith, his writings, and his significance for the modern world. It is the only publication of its kind and it aims to facilitate debate between scholars working across the humanities and social sciences.

This first volume contains contributions from a multidisciplinary range of specialists, including Stephen Darwall, Samuel Fleischacker, Willie Henderson, Takashi Negishi, Ian Simpson Ross, Emma Rothschild, Richard B. Sher, Ernst Tugendhat, Gloria Vivenza and Patricia H. Werhane, who discuss such themes as:

- the reception of the *Wealth of Nations*
- the classics and Adam Smith
- Adam Smith and Kant
- Adam Smith and disequilibrium economic theory

Under the editorship of Vivienne Brown, this first volume sets the standard at an impressively high level. Readers from a wide variety of backgrounds will want to add this volume to their bookshelves.

Vivienne Brown is Professor of Intellectual History at The Open University, UK.

The Adam Smith Review

Published in association with the International Adam Smith Society

Edited by Vivienne Brown

Faculty of Social Sciences, The Open University, UK

Book Reviews

Edited by James R. Otteson

Department of Philosophy, University of Alabama, USA

Books available in this series

The Adam Smith Review (Volume 1)

Edited by Vivienne Brown

The Adam Smith Review

Volume 1

Edited by
Vivienne Brown

Routledge
Taylor & Francis Group
LONDON AND NEW YORK

IASS

First published 2004
by Routledge
2 Park Square, Milton Park, Abingdon, Oxon, OX14 4RN

Simultaneously published in the USA and Canada
by Routledge
270 Madison Ave, New York, NY 10016

Routledge is an imprint of the Taylor & Francis Group

Transferred to Digital Printing 2009

Published in association with the International Adam Smith Society

Typeset in Times New Roman by
Newgen Imaging Systems (P) Ltd, Chennai, India

British Library Cataloguing in Publication Data
A catalogue record for this book is available
from the British Library

Library of Congress Cataloging in Publication Data
A catalog record for this book has been requested

ISSN 1743–5285
ISBN10: 0–415–27863–5 (hbk)
ISBN10: 0–415–49348–X (pbk)

ISBN13: 978–0–415–27863–8 (hbk)
ISBN13: 978–0–415–49348–2 (pbk)

Editorial

The Adam Smith Review is a multidisciplinary annual review sponsored by the International Adam Smith Society. It aims to provide a unique forum for vigorous debate and the highest standards of scholarship on all aspects of Adam Smith's works, his place in history, and the significance of his writings for the modern world. *The Adam Smith Review* aims to facilitate interchange between scholars working within different disciplinary and theoretical perspectives, and to this end it is open to all areas of research relating to Adam Smith. The Review also hopes to broaden the field of English-language debate on Smith by occasionally including translations of scholarly works at present available only in languages other than English.

The Adam Smith Review is intended as a resource for Adam Smith scholarship in the widest sense. The Editor welcomes comments and suggestions, including proposals for symposia or themed sections in the Review. Future issues are open to comments and debate relating to previously published papers.

For details of membership of the International Adam Smith Society and reduced rates for purchasing the Review, please contact the Membership Secretary, Ryan Patrick Hanley (ryan.hanley@yale.edu).

Contents

Notes on contributors

Fonna Forman-Barzilai is Assistant Professor of Political Science at the University of California, San Diego. She works primarily in the history of modern political thought and is currently completing a manuscript entitled *Adam Smith and the Circles of Sympathy*.

Lauren Brubaker is a visiting assistant professor at the United States Air Force Academy and holder of the Lyons Chair in Professional Ethics. His dissertation for the Committee on Social Thought at the University of Chicago was *Religious Zeal, Political Faction and Moral Corruption: Adam Smith and the Limits of Enlightenment* (2002).

Kenneth E. Carpenter is recently retired from Harvard University Library. He is now an associate of Eliot House, Harvard University, Cambridge, Massachussets, USA.

Henry C. Clark is Professor of History at Canisius College in Buffalo, NY. He is author of *La Rochefoucauld and the Language of Unmasking in Seventeenth-Century France* (1994, Droz) and editor of *Commerce, Culture and Liberty: Readings on Capitalism Before Adam Smith* (2003, Liberty Fund). He is completing a book on the idea of commercial society in old-regime France.

Stephen Darwall is the John Dewey Collegiate Professor of Philosophy at the University of Michigan. He is the author of many works on the foundations and history of ethics, including *Impartial Reason, The British Moralists and the Internal 'Ought', Philosophical Ethics*, and *Welfare and Rational Care*.

Samuel Fleischacker is an Associate Professor of Philosophy at the University of Illinois at Chicago. His work includes *On Adam Smith's* Wealth of Nations: *A Philosophical Companion* (Princeton, 2004) and *A Third Concept of Liberty: Judgment and Freedom in Kant and Adam Smith* (Princeton, 1999).

Christel Fricke has held visiting professorships at UFRGS, Porto Alegre, RS, Brazil and at Emory University, Atlanta, GA, USA, and is currently chair of philosophy at the University of Oslo, Norway. Publications on the history of modern philosophy, on philosophical aesthetics, philosophy of language, ethics.

Ryan Patrick Hanley is Assistant Professor of Political Science at Marquette University. His recent articles have appeared in *History of Political Thought, The Review of Politics* and *The American Political Science Review*, and he is currently working on his first book, a study of *The Theory of Moral Sentiments*.

Willie Henderson is Professor of Continuing Education in the University of Birmingham. His interests include the history of economic thought including economics education. He has published work on women economists (*Economics as Literature*, 1995, Routledge) and John Ruskin (*John Ruskin's Political Economy*, 2000, Routledge).

Peter McNamara teaches political science at Utah State University. He has written on Alexander Hamilton, John Locke and Adam Smith.

Takashi Negishi is a member of the Japan Academy, Professor Emeritus of University of Tokyo, Former President of Econometric Society and Former President of Japanese Society for History of Economic Thought. Major publications include *General Equilibrium Theory and International Trade* (1972) and *History of Economic Theory* (1989).

Ian Simpson Ross is Professor Emeritus of English, The University of British Columbia, and Fellow of the Royal Society of Canada. Author of *Lord Kames and the Scotland of his Day* (1972), *William Dunbar* (1981) and *The Life of Adam Smith* (1995); co-editor with E.C. Mossner of *The Correspondence of Adam Smith* (2nd edn. 1987); and editor of *Contemporary Responses to Adam Smith: On the Wealth of Nations* (1998). He is now preparing a second edition of the Smith biography.

Emma Rothschild is Director of the Centre for History and Economics at King's College, Cambridge, and a Visiting Professor of History at Harvard University. She is the author of *Economic Sentiments: Adam Smith, Condorcet, and the Enlightenment*.

Richard B. Sher is Distinguished Professor of History at New Jersey Institute of Technology and NJIT Chair of the Federated History Department of Rutgers University-Newark and NJIT. He is completing a book on Scottish authors and publishers in the Enlightenment.

Ernst Tugendhat, formerly Professor of Philosophy at Heidelberg and the Free University of Berlin; Honorary Professor at Tübingen. His books include *Traditional and Analytical Philosophy* (1982, Cambridge University Press), *Vorlesungen über Ethik* (1993, Suhrkamp), *Self-consciousness and Self-determination* (1986, MIT) and *Egozentrizität und Mystik* (2003, Beck Munich).

Gloria Vivenza is Professor in History of Economic Thought at the University of Verona, Italy. She is interested in the influence of the ancient classics on modern economic thought, especially on Adam Smith. Her main work on this subject has recently been translated into English under the title *Adam Smith and the Classics* (2001, Oxford University Press).

Jack Russell Weinstein is an Assistant Professor in the Department of Philosophy and Religion at the University of North Dakota. He is the author of *On MacIntyre*, which, like *On Adam Smith*, is a volume in the Wadsworth Philosophers Series.

Patricia H. Werhane is the Wicklander Chair of Business Ethics and Director of the Institute for Business and Professional Ethics at DePaul University and Peter and Adeline Ruffin Professor of Business Ethics and Senior Fellow at the Olsson Center for Applied Ethics in the Darden School at the University of Virginia. She is the author or editor of fifteen books including *Ethical Issues in Business* (with T. Donaldson and Margaret Cording, seventh edition), *Persons, Rights and Corporations, Adam Smith and His Legacy for Modern Capitalism*, and *Moral Imagination and Managerial Decision-Making* with Oxford University Press. Her latest book is *Employment and Employee Rights* (with Tara J. Radin and Norman Bowie) with Blackwell's.

Articles

New light on the publication and reception of the *Wealth of Nations*

Richard B. Sher

I

Since the bicentennial of the *Wealth of Nations* (WN) in 1976, significant contributions have been made to our biographical and bibliographical knowledge of Adam Smith and his most famous book. Yet, important aspects of the story of the publication and reception of the WN remain untold or misunderstood, despite the appearance of a number of stimulating revisionist studies during the past two decades (Teichgraeber 1987, 2000; Rashid 1982, 1998). This article will revisit this subject, using new documents as well as new interpretations of previously known evidence. It will also attempt to show how the emerging discipline of book history can throw new light on this topic.

I shall begin with some commonly accepted facts about the book's earlier publication history in Great Britain. *An Inquiry into the Nature and Causes of the Wealth of Nations* was published in London in two quarto volumes on 9 March 1776 by the printer William Strahan and the bookseller Thomas Cadell, whose publishing partnership was pre-eminent in its day. Although the Strahan printing ledgers in the British Library contain no record of the first edition, subsequent eighteenth-century editions are listed there, and some of that information is reproduced in the Glasgow Edition of the WN (Smith 1976; 'Text and Apparatus': *61–4*). Contemporary advertisements reveal that the price of the first edition was £1.16s. in boards (temporary covers that would hold the pages in place until the book's owner arranged to have it properly bound), which is to say, eighteen shillings per volume, but it could also be purchased for two guineas (£2.2s.) bound. The second edition appeared in London in February 1778, also in two quarto volumes, and sold for the same price as the first. However, the third edition contained significant revisions and was published in London in November 1784 in the more economical format of three octavo volumes; this allowed the price to be reduced to one half of the previous quarto editions, to eighteen shillings in boards per set, or one guinea bound. The title pages of the first three editions of the WN are shown in Figure 1.

The Adam Smith Review, 1: 3–29 © 2004 The International Adam Smith Society, ISSN 1743–5285, ISBN 0–415–27863–5

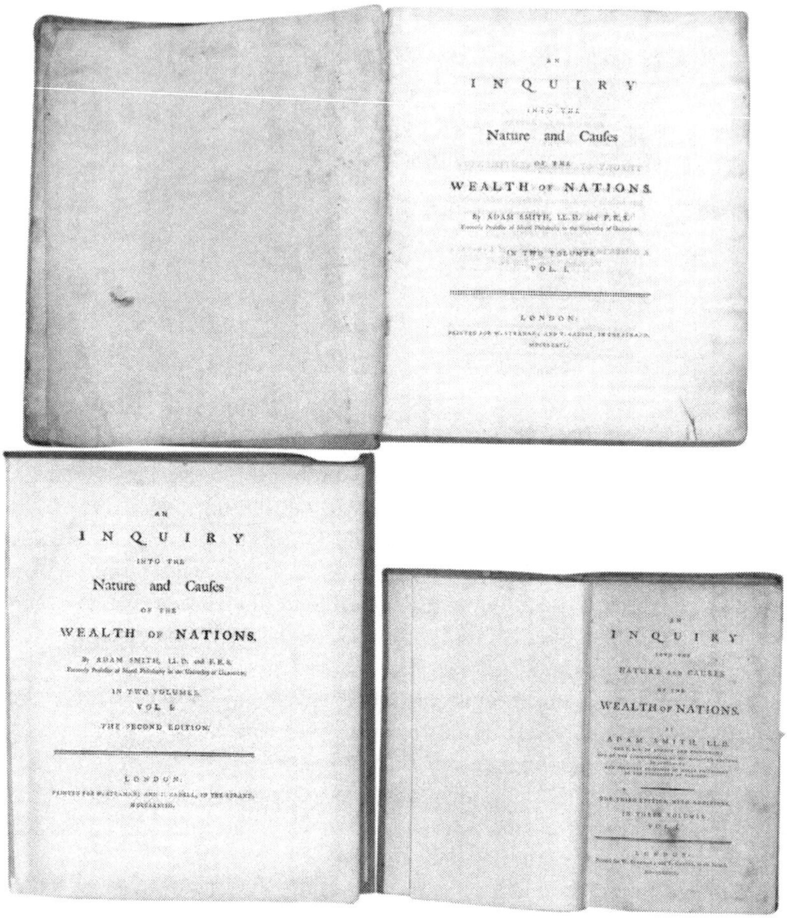

Figure 1 Title pages of the earliest authorized editions of the WN: the first edition, published in two quarto volumes in 1776 (top); the second edition of 1778, in the same format as the first edition (bottom left); and the three-volume octavo third edition of 1784 (bottom right). Courtesy of the Thomas Fisher Rare Book Library, University of Toronto.

November 1784 also saw the publication of a separate quarto volume of *Additions and Corrections to the First and Second Editions of Dr. Adam Smith's Inquiry into the Nature and Causes of the Wealth of Nations*, intended exclusively for the purchasers of the quarto editions. The fourth edition of the WN, published in 1786, continued with the format of three octavo volumes, as did the fifth edition of 1789 – the last edition to be published during Smith's lifetime. A sixth edition, again in three octavo volumes, appeared in 1791. No printing information for subsequent editions of the WN is reproduced or discussed in the Glasgow Edition.

Against this backdrop of basic bibliographical facts, this article argues that the WN was a more successful book during its author's lifetime than recent revisionist accounts would lead us to believe. This claim is based chiefly on the reinterpretation of two interrelated issues, using approaches grounded in book history. First, Section II reconsiders both the modes and the amounts of 'copy money', or payment that Smith received from his publishers, and shows that the matter was more complicated and more significant – and for Smith far more lucrative – than has previously been thought. Second, Sections III and IV analyse the way the WN was produced, marketed and consumed by the public, including a comparison with Sir James Steuart's *Inquiry into the Principles of Political Economy* and other works on political economy from the same era. Taken together, Sections II–IV demonstrate that the *Wealth of Nations* was an exceptionally popular book of its kind in Smith's day. Section V reflects on the broader implications of this conclusion for understanding the relationship between book history and intellectual history as complementary methodologies for investigating the reception of books.

II

Financial arrangements between authors and publishers in late eighteenth-century Britain were often complex, and none more so than those concerning the WN. Several pieces of evidence exist, but they are not always easy to reconcile with each other. First, there is an exchange of letters between Smith and fellow-Scot William Strahan, beginning about eight months after publication. In the first of these letters, dated 13 November 1776, Smith tells Strahan that he has 'received £300 of the copy money of the first edition of my book' and wonders 'what balance may be due to me' after the cost of the 'good number of copies' that he sent as gifts has been deducted from his earnings. He also suggests that the second edition 'should be printed in four vol. octavo; and I would propose that it should be printed at your expense, and that we should divide the profits' (*Corr*. Letter 179: 221–2). Strahan replies on 26 November: 'Your Proposal to print the next Edition of your Work in 4 vols Octavo, at *our* Expence, and to divide the Profits, is a very fair one, and therefore very agreeable to Mr Cadell and me' (*Corr*. Letter 180: 223).

In an ingenious analysis of these passages, Smith's late nineteenth-century biographer, John Rae, reasoned that the first edition could not have been undertaken on the basis of 'half-profits' (i.e. an arrangement in which half the profits went to the author and half to the publisher), because Smith seems to be proposing that arrangement for the second edition 'as if it were a new one, and [it] is accepted in the same way by Strahan'. Another possible arrangement was for books to be printed 'for the author', who paid the cost of paper, printing and advertising and then received all the profits, if there were any, but risked losing his investment if the book did not sell well. Rae argued that the first edition of the WN could not have been published under those terms either because 'the presentation copies [Smith] gave away were deducted from the copy money he received'. Having eliminated both of these options to his satisfaction, Rae determined that Smith had sold the rights to the book – which is to say, the copyright – to Strahan and Cadell 'for a definite sum'. Since Smith mentioned receiving £300 and seemed to allude to a further balance due to him once the cost of his presentation copies had been deducted, Rae concluded that 'one may reasonably conjecture that the full sum was £500 – the same sum Cadell's firm had paid for the last economic work they had undertaken, Sir James Steuart's *Inquiry into the Principles of Political Economy*', published in 1767 (Rae 1895: 285). Like Rae, Smith's modern biographer, Ian Simpson Ross, has interpreted Smith's letter of 13 November 1776 to mean that Smith sold the copyright of the WN to his publishers in advance for a fixed sum, which he gives as £300 rather than £500. Although his choice of words – 'Smith was paid £300 *from* copy money, that is, the price paid by the booksellers for the copyright of the book' (Ross 1995: 270; emphasis added) – does not explicitly rule out the possibility that £300 was merely a partial payment, nothing more is said of the matter.

Both biographers were on the wrong track, not only about the total amount of copy money that Smith received for his book but also about the manner in which he received it. Crucial evidence appears in a portion of the Strahan ledgers that was not cited by the editors of the Glasgow Edition or Smith's biographers, and in a letter from Thomas Cadell of 21 December 1792, which refers to those ledgers. The key sentence in Cadell's letter occurs in the context of an offer being made by Cadell and Andrew Strahan (William's son and successor) to Henry Mackenzie (representing Smith's executors) to purchase the copyright of Smith's posthumous *Essays on Philosophical Subjects* for £300, and to pay £200 more in the event of a second edition. Cadell writes: 'On referring back to our former agreement with Mr Smith we find that we shared the profits of the Quarto Edition with the Author; that when the Book was established we paid for the property £300 for the term of 14 Years, and a further sum of £300 in case the Author lived to assign his second term of 14 Years which you know he did' (Mackenzie 1989: 177). This sentence is quoted in full in Ross's biography, but it is thought to refer to the *Theory of Moral Sentiments* rather than the WN (Ross 1995: 410, 426, n. 1). However, since the *Theory of Moral Sentiments* never appeared in quarto and was not originally published under the imprint of the Strahan–Cadell publishing partnership, there can be no doubt that the reference is actually to the WN.

More detailed evidence can be found in Andrew Strahan's record of the WN from the time of the fourth edition of 1786 (the first edition to appear after Andrew assumed control of the family firm upon the death of his father in July 1785) until 1821 (Strahan Ledgers, Add. MS 48,814A, f. 8). The ledger reveals that in April 1786 Strahan paid Cadell £100 'for $\frac{1}{2}$ Copy Money for 4th. Edit.', that on 16 July 1788 he paid Cadell £150 'for $\frac{1}{2}$ Copy Money for the Wealth of Nations (in full)', and that on 3 April 1790 he paid 'Adam Smith Esqr. my $\frac{1}{2}$ of £300 for the Copy Right of the 2^{d}. 14 Years' (see Figure 2). It would seem, then, that Smith negotiated separately for the first, second, third and fourth editions, after which, in July 1788, he sold the copyright outright to Strahan and Cadell for £300.

According to the terms of the Statute of Anne – the copyright act of 1710 that was upheld as the law of the land on appeal to the House of Lords in 1774 – the renewal of a copyright for a second period of fourteen years could only occur if

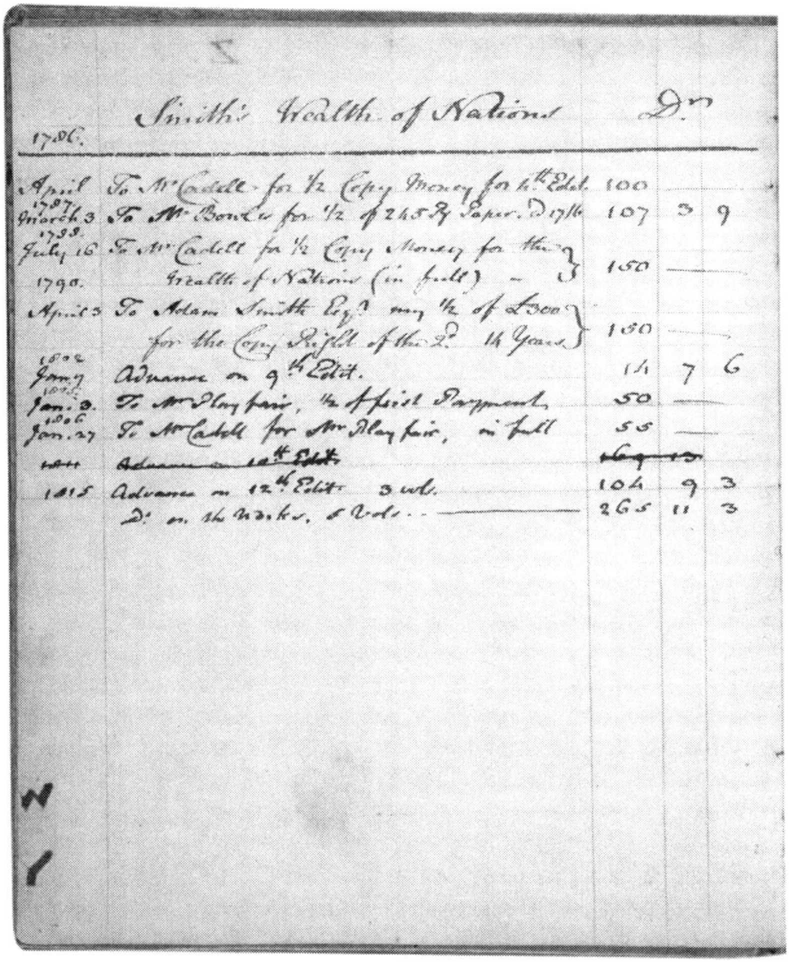

Smith's Wealth of Nations Dr

1786. April	To Mr Cadell for ½ Copy Money for 4th Edit.	100		
1787 March 3	To Mr Bowles for ½ of 245 Rm Paper. D 1786	107	3	9
1788 July 16	To Mr Cadell for ½ Copy Money for the Wealth of Nations (in full) —	150	—	
1790. April 5	To Adam Smith Esqr my ½ of £300 for the Copy Right of the 2d 14 Years	150	—	
1802 Jany 7	Advance on 9th Edit.	14	7	6
1805 Jan. 9	To Mr Playfair, ½ of first Payment	50	—	
1806 Jan. 27	To Mr Cadell for Mr Playfair, in full	55	—	
[illegible]	~~Advance on 10th Edit.~~	[illegible]		
1815	Advance on 12th Edit. 3 vols.	104	9	3
	Do on the works, 5 vols.	265	11	3

Figure 2 Andrew Strahan's account of copy money payments for the WN, 1786–1815. The recto page, not shown, records Strahan's income from sales of the book from August 1790 to 1821 (Strahan Ledgers, Add. MS 48,814A, f. 7). By permission of the British Library.

the author were still alive fourteen years after the original date of publication (Rose 1993: 46–7). In this case, Smith became eligible to renew the copyright on 9 March 1790 and effected the renewal by early April, scarcely three months before his death in mid-July. So Smith lived just long enough to ensure that his publishers would receive a fourteen-year extension on the copyright, until April 1804, and that he himself would receive a second copyright payment of £300. Cadell's use of the phrase 'which you know he did' in his letter to Mackenzie is probably a reference to the fact that Smith was failing rapidly during the first half of 1790, and Mackenzie and the executors, along with Strahan and Cadell and presumably Smith himself, were apprehensive about whether he would live long enough to execute the copyright extension. We know from another letter that Henry Mackenzie sent to Cadell on 2 August 1792 that Smith's camp was very concerned about receiving as much copy money as possible for *Essays on Philosophical Subjects* because Smith's nephew and heir, David Douglas, was not well off (National Library of Scotland, Acc 9546). The same concern would have been present when the copyright renewal of the WN was in doubt two years earlier.

Although these clues do not tell us everything we would like to know about the publishing arrangements for the WN, they provide the foundation for a re-examination of that subject. First we need to reconsider the initial terms. Contrary to Rae, to whom we shall return shortly, the first edition of the WN was apparently published on a shared basis by the publishers and the author: that is, they divided equally both the expenses of publishing and, as Andrew Strahan remarked in his letter to Mackenzie of 21 December 1792, the profits. This arrangement reflected the fact that William Strahan and Thomas Cadell did not expect the book to sell very well, and therefore did not wish to risk an outright purchase of the copyright. As the Edinburgh bookseller William Creech told James Beattie in a letter of 17 May 1787:

> It is often…the case that the first rate literary abilities, and labour, are but ill rewarded. A Bookseller estimates the merit of a Book merely by the sale of it. When a new work is offered, he considers what has been the success of similar publications, and hence endeavours to make an estimate in his own mind. Sheridan for writing a Sing, Song opera of three Acts[1] received much more money, than D[r]. Smith did for writing his Wealth of Nations 2 Vols Quarto which I have been told cost him fifteen years labour.
>
> (James Beattie Papers, 30/2/545)

We know from other sources, such as Strahan's letters to Creech of 9 September 1774 (William Creech Letterbooks) and to William Robertson of 6 December 1776 (National Library of Scotland, MS 3,942, ff. 299–300), that in the mid-1770s Strahan was feeling uneasy about Scottish authors puffing each other in order to secure better publishing terms than they deserved, and he was displeased about losing money on at least two books that were recommended to him in this manner. And we know that Strahan was pleasantly surprised at the commercial success of the WN, for in a letter of 12 April 1776, scarcely a month after publication, he told David Hume that the sale, while not nearly so rapid as the first volume of Edward Gibbon's *Decline and Fall of the Roman Empire*, 'has been more than I could have expected from a Work, that requires much Thought and Reflection (Qualities that do not abound among modern Readers) to peruse to any Purpose' (National Library of Scotland, MS 23,157, no. 67).

On 20 May 1776 Strahan wrote to Creech: 'I know not what Dr. Smith expects for his second Edit. or when it will be wanted; but we shall be able pretty well to judge of its Value from the Sale of the first, and the Call that shall appear to be for another, of which you shall hear in due time' (William Creech Letterbooks). Besides indicating that Creech was somehow involved in the publication of the

WN, even though his name does not appear in the imprint,[2] this passage is of interest for two reasons. First, it shows that just a month and a half after publication of the first edition, the publishers were beginning to plan for an encore. Although it was still too soon to determine the timing and 'Value' of the second edition, its existence was already given. Second, this passage confirms that Smith was expected to name his price for the second edition, because he still owned the copyright and was in a position to renegotiate the terms of publication.

As the first edition of the WN continued to sell, Smith acknowledged receipt of a payment of £300 in his letter to Strahan of 13 November 1776. As Rae pointed out, the wording of the letter suggests that this may not have been the final payment. A partial accounting of this kind, occurring eight months after publication, was characteristic of a conditional publishing arrangement, in which publishers periodically sent payments to authors. Smith's letter then turned to the question of a second edition, and made the suggestion that 'it should be printed at your expense, and that we should divide the profits'. Recall that Rae ruled out the possibility that the first edition of the WN had been published on the basis of 'half-profits' because he thought Smith proposed this arrangement for the second edition, and Strahan accepted it, 'as if it were a new one'. It seems to me, however, that besides the change from quarto to octavo, what is new in Smith's proposal for the second edition is not how the profits would be divided but the way the publication expenses would be paid. Smith presents this part of the proposed arrangement first, and Strahan puts special emphasis on it when he accepts Smith's proposal 'to print the next Edition of your Work in 4 vols Octavo, at *our* Expence, and to divide the Profits'. Why would Strahan have placed emphasis on the word 'our' unless he was underlining the feature of the arrangement that would differentiate the second edition from the first?

Despite the fact that Strahan and Smith were in agreement, the second edition turned out to be not a more affordable octavo but another two-volume quarto. This was almost certainly the work of Cadell, who was more sensitive than Strahan to the bookselling end of the publishing business. Although quartos cost considerably more to produce than octavos, and were therefore riskier in the event of poor sales, their profit margins were much higher. The trick was determining how many copies would satisfy the quarto market without overprinting. Cadell had started his career as a Scottish Enlightenment publisher by making a similar decision in 1767, when he followed up the unexpectedly strong sales of the first edition of Adam Ferguson's *Essay on the History of Civil Society* with a second quarto edition of 500 copies, even though doing so enraged his Edinburgh co-publisher, John Bell (of the firm Kincaid and Bell), who knew he would be able to sell octavo copies to the book-buying public in Scotland, including Ferguson's students at the University of Edinburgh, but did not have access to the large market for expensive quartos that Cadell enjoyed in London (John Bell Letterbooks; Sher, forthcoming). In the case of the WN, publishing the second edition in quarto was probably the right move from a commercial standpoint, even though this decision slowed down the pace of dissemination. It is likely that the author and the publishers stuck to the half-profits agreement for the second edition that Smith and Strahan made when they had projected it to be a four-volume octavo; such an arrangement can be inferred from Cadell's letter to Henry Mackenzie of 21 December 1792, and it is also consistent with Smith's reference, in a letter to Strahan of 26 October 1780, to debiting his presentation copies 'at our final settlement' (*Corr*. Letter 207: 249). We do not know how much money Smith received for his share of the profits of the second edition by the time of that final settlement. Considering, on the one hand, the small size of the print run, and on the other, the profitability of quartos and the fact that the author evidently did not have to contribute to the publishing expenses, I do not believe the amount could have been less than £200.

It is particularly unfortunate that no hard evidence exists about the pecuniary arrangements for the expanded and revised third edition of 1784, the first British edition to appear in a three-volume octavo format. In all likelihood, Smith published that edition on the same terms as the second edition: half-profits, but all expenses paid by the publishers. The author could have profited handsomely from such an arrangement. The third edition had a respectable print run, as we shall see, and the total price for the set, although much lower than that of the quarto editions, was high enough to generate substantial profits if the edition sold out, as it did. It is also possible that Smith received something for the quarto volume of *Additions and Corrections* for the use of purchasers of the first and second editions.

The mode of compensation changed with the fourth edition of 1786, for which Smith received a fixed payment of £200. The terms of the fourth edition were apparently offered in an untraced letter from Cadell of 25 March 1785 that is alluded to in Smith's reply of 21 April 1785: 'Your letter of the 25th of March was extremely agreeable to me, as you may well imagine, and I am very much obliged to you for it. I shall be very glad to hear that a new edition [of the *Wealth of Nations*] is called for and we shall have no difference about the terms of Publication' (*Corr*. Letter 244: 281). On 13 February 1786 Smith wrote to Andrew Strahan in regard to this edition: 'I should likewise be glad to know when I may draw for the money; I wish to conclude the transaction, least Mr Cadell should take another fit of the ague and make another request which may not be so well received as the former' (*Corr*. Letter 256: 293). As is so often the case with Smith, the fundamental information we would like to know is not clearly presented. Yet what exists is sufficient to suggest a plausible hypothesis. Since the fourth edition was not published until 6 November 1786 (WN, 'Text and Apparatus': *63*), Smith would not have been asking in February of that year about when he could draw for the money if his payment was to be dependent on sales and profits. An offer of a fixed payment in advance of publication would have made sense for the publishers only if they were confident that a substantial print run of the fourth edition was going to sell out completely, and that they would have to pay the author more in the long run by publishing it for half-profits. For Smith, on the other hand, selling the rights to the fourth edition for £200 free and clear would have been advantageous in two respects: he would get his money sooner that way, and he would be sure of it, in the event that sales turned out to be disappointing. The fact that the previously cited ledger kept by Andrew Strahan reveals that he paid Cadell his share of the copy money for the fourth edition in April 1786 – six months before printing and seven months before publication – seems to clinch this argument.

To summarize this scenario, Smith received (1) at least £300 for the first edition of the WN, as a result of an arrangement that seems to have called for sharing of both expenses and profits; (2) an undetermined amount for the second quarto edition of 1778, as a result of an arrangement which apparently allowed Smith to share the profits but did not require him to contribute anything to the expenses; (3) an undetermined amount for the third edition of 1784, probably published on the same profit-sharing terms as the second; (4) £200 for the fourth edition of 1786, paid in advance of publication as a fixed fee; (5) £300 for the sale of the copyright in 1788, retroactive to March 1776; and (6) another £300 when the copyright was renewed for a second period of fourteen years while Smith was dying in the spring of 1790. That makes £1,100 certain, in addition to whatever the author received for the second and third editions and whatever he got (if anything) beyond the £300 payment he is known to have received for the first edition. For purposes of estimating the full amount of Smith's income, let us suppose that Smith earned a total of £300–400 for the first edition and £200–300 for each of the next two editions. Using these numbers, Smith would have received a grand total of £1,500–1,800 in copy money from his publishers for the WN – the equivalent of more than £100,000 in the early twenty-first century.[3] This estimate is a far cry from Rae's conjecture of £500, which to the best of my knowledge is the highest amount that anyone has ever suggested. Thus, Smith earned much more copy money for the WN than has previously been thought, and he did so in the period of just fourteen years.

I shall try to put this information into perspective. In 1783 William Creech boasted that during the past two decades 'the value of literary property was carried higher by the Scots than ever was known among any people' (Creech 1793: 12). The three best-selling authors whom Creech mentioned by name in support of this assertion – Hugh Blair, David Hume and William Robertson – each made thousands of pounds from their major publications, the equivalent of hundreds of thousands today. Of course, not every author who participated in what is now called the Scottish Enlightenment benefited from this trend, and relatively few made their fortunes from it. At the low end were books that yielded modest amounts of copy money, such as the £50 paid to Thomas Reid for his *Inquiry into the Human Mind, on the Principles of Common Sense* and to Alexander Gerard for his *Essay on Genius*. Yet more than half of the seventy-six Scottish Enlightenment books about which I have been able to acquire information on copy money brought their authors £300 or more from all known editions (Sher, forthcoming). Although modest in comparison with the £4,000 that Robertson received for the copyright of his *History of the Reign of Charles V* (1769), a sum of several hundred pounds was a substantial amount of money at the time – more, for example, than many professors or clergymen earned in a year, or sometimes two.

The WN ranks towards the top of this copy money calculus. Until the time of Smith's death in 1790, few original scholarly works are known to have brought their authors more income, and most of the ones that did so were written in the popular genre of history by the likes of Hume, Robertson and James Macpherson, joined by Gibbon and Catharine Macaulay among English authors. Moreover, unlike books whose copyrights were sold in advance of publication, such as Robertson's histories, the WN generated its copy money in direct response to the work's success in the marketplace.

III

In a 1987 article on the reception of the WN, Richard F. Teichgraeber III raised serious doubts about the traditional view that Smith's book was 'an immediate success' – a belief that he labels 'one of the enduring clichés in Western historiography' (Teichgraeber 1987: 338, n. 4). Against this view, Teichgraeber argues:

> A close inspection of the earliest responses to Smith's work shows that the arrival of the *Wealth of Nations* had no immediate impact on Britain or its colonies. But it shows too that the book was not simply overlooked or dismissed out of hand. During the last five years of Smith's life, the *Wealth of Nations* enjoyed some limited but still notable success.
>
> (Teichgraeber 1987: 339)

Teichgraeber recognizes that the WN initially sold well and was warmly received by most reviewers. Nevertheless, a reader of his article might conclude that it was a book of modest or uncertain popularity during the late eighteenth century. After noting, for example, that 'the rapid sale and warm reception of the first edition of the *Wealth of Nations* may have been remarkable', Teichgraeber adds, without any regard for formats or circumstances: 'Almost two years would pass before Strahan published a second edition of just five-hundred copies; then another six before a third edition of one thousand' (Teichgraeber 1987: 341). This sceptical language is in keeping with his contention that 'the *Wealth of Nations* went from being a book of very limited interest during the first several years after its publication to one whose public audience and intellectual authority were broadening at the time of Smith's death on 17 July 1790' (Teichgraeber 1987: 340). There is a reference to 'the public indifference' that greeted the book, and there is an attempt to explain why it was 'that the first edition of the *Wealth of Nations* did not enjoy a more immediate *éclat*?' (Teichgraeber 1987: 344). Later the author asserts that 'the notion that the *Wealth of Nations* had an immediate impact on its time certainly ought to be put to rest. The book never enjoyed an unrivalled reputation in Smith's lifetime' (Teichgraeber 1987: 364). In another, more recent article, Teichgraeber refers to the book's 'modest early sales' while acknowledging that 'the *Wealth of Nations* did become something of a steady seller by the end of [Smith's] lifetime' (Teichgraeber 2000: 90, 103).

Salim Rashid has pursued a complementary approach (1982; revised as 1998, chapter 7). Like Teichgraeber, Rashid believes that the early fame of the WN has been greatly exaggerated. He builds his case largely by contrasting the popularity of Smith's book with that of Sir James Steuart's *Inquiry into the Principles of Political Economy*. While acknowledging Steuart's own statement that if he had written a book about his dog it would have been 'perhaps as little relished by the public' as the *Principles* had been, Rashid nevertheless argues that Steuart's disappointment at the reception of his book 'seems to reflect more accurately the extent of his ambition than the manner in which the public treated him' (Rashid 1998: 146–7). He claims that the *Principles* 'sold slowly but steadily despite its tortuous style and difficulty of subject matter' (Rashid 1998: 146) and that 'there is no definite evidence to establish Smith's superiority over Steuart in popular estimation before 1790' (Rashid 1998: 154). Nor was Steuart exceptional in this regard. Among other contemporary Scottish writers on political economy, Rashid asserts that David Loch got more attention in the press than Smith for his 'buy Scottish' campaign and that 'in the years after the *Wealth of Nations* was published it was not Adam Smith but the rather "Mercantilist" John Knox or the interventionist James Anderson who were more widely read' (Rashid 1998: 152).

Teichgraeber and Rashid have done valuable service by challenging the claims of careless commentators, who have simply assumed that the WN was an instantaneous best seller, which suddenly and completely changed the way most people thought about political economy. They have rightly drawn attention to the need for careful study of the book's reputation among Smith's contemporaries, in the years before Smith became the object of hagiography and the WN an unassailable – and often unread – 'classic'. My intention is to supplement Teichgraeber's and Rashid's helpful questioning of the reception of the WN in Britain with a more nuanced account of the book's early history, in so far as it can be reconstructed from existing evidence. Since both Teichgraeber and Rashid are chiefly concerned with the history of ideas rather than the history of books, this approach will lead to somewhat different conclusions about the contemporary reception accorded to the WN.

In order to determine the reception of the WN as a book, it will be necessary to review its publication history in greater detail. We have seen that the first two editions were expensive two-volume quartos, and that there is no definite evidence about how many copies of the first edition were printed. On the basis of the extant printing records of other first editions of scholarly quartos that the Strahans printed during this period, I am led to think that 750 copies is the most probable estimate, although 500 and 1,000 are also plausible figures. Strahan and Cadell printed 750 copies of Walter Anderson's *History of France* in 1769 and the same number of John Gillies' *History of Ancient Greece* in 1786 – both two-volume quartos. Gillies, by the way, received £313.14s. for his half of the profits of the first edition of his book (Strahan Ledgers, Add. MS 48,814A, f. 12), which is comparable to the minimum amount that Smith is known to have received for the first edition of the WN. In late summer 1774, Cadell recommended a print run of 750 copies for the first volume of Gibbon's *Decline and Fall of the Roman Empire*, which would be published in quarto in 1776. That number was soon lowered to 500, even though the book was about half the size of the WN, was written in a more popular genre, and dealt with a more widely accessible subject, but at the last moment Strahan decided to print 1,000 copies because he was personally captivated by Gibbon's narrative (Craddock 1989: 39; Gibbon 1966: 157).

Since the print run of the second edition of the WN was definitely 500 copies, the total number of quarto copies that Strahan and Cadell published can be safely estimated at between 1,000 and 1,500 copies, with 1,250 being the most likely number. It is not known when the second edition of 1778 was completely sold out, but the stock must have been dwindling by the early 1780s. The WN then entered a critical phase. The third edition of 1784 would not only be what W.B. Todd has called Smith's 'final version' as a *text*, because it incorporated major new additions and was the last significant revision that the author ever made (WN, 'Text and Apparatus': *63*). It also represented the decisive moment for the work's future as a *book*, when it began to compete in the marketplace in an affordable octavo format.

Although both Teichgraeber and Rashid imply that the six-year gap between the second and third editions was the result of public indifference to the WN, Smith's correspondence with Cadell establishes that the publisher wanted to put out the third edition during the winter of 1782–3, if not sooner, but was prevented from doing so by the time it took Smith to complete his 'additions and corrections'. 'I am happy to hear you are preparing for a new Edition of the Wealth of Nations', Cadell writes in a letter to Smith of 12 December 1782, ' – the delay will I am afraid prevent our publishing this new Edition this Winter – We will however set about it as soon as we receive the Copy' (*Corr.* Letter 223: 264). Yet Cadell responded cheerfully to Smith's plan not only to produce major revisions but also to publish them separately for the benefit of the purchasers of the quarto editions. His actions may not have been entirely altruistic or idealistic. In eighteenth-century Britain, extensive textual revisions constituted one important way that publishers gained an advantage over foreign reprinters and pirates of popular titles (Sher 1999: 54).

Cadell continued to offer encouragement during the following year. However, his eagerness to get on with publishing the third edition increased markedly by 20 November 1783, when Smith tells Strahan in a postscript that 'Cadel…is anxious, on account of something which fell the other day from Mr. Rose that we should set about the new edition immediately' (*Corr.* Letter 232: 270). In a clever piece of detective work, Rashid has traced the mystery surrounding this cryptic reference to 'Mr Rose' to a transcription error in the Glasgow Edition of Smith's correspondence: the name that Smith actually wrote was not 'Mr Rose' but 'Mr Fox' (Rashid 1992: 495–6). It is well known that Charles James Fox had called the WN 'an excellent book' during a debate in the House of Commons just nine days earlier (Willis 1979: 508). It makes sense that Cadell would have told Smith that he was anxious to publish the third edition quickly in order to take full advantage of that fortunate occurrence. According to Rashid, this interpretation obliges us to give serious consideration to an anonymous obituary of Smith which asserted that 'the book was not at first so popular as it afterwards became' and that the 'recommendation of Mr Fox raised the sale of the book' (*The Times*, 6 August 1790, as quoted in Fay 1956: 34–5). In support of this claim, Rashid contends that the second edition of the WN was not selling well by 1780, citing Smith's almost identical remarks, in separate letters to Cadell and Strahan of 25 and 26 October relating to presentation copies, that 'I am afraid I am not only your best, but almost your only customer for this second edition' and 'I suspect I am now almost your only customer for my own book' (*Corr.* Letters 206–7: 248–9; Rashid 1992: 493–7).

Rashid is correct about Fox being the person named in Smith's postscript, and therefore that Fox's actions in Parliament influenced Cadell to push Smith to go to press with the third edition of the WN without further delay. Yet the commercial significance of the Fox episode should not be exaggerated. For one thing, the comments in Smith's letters of 25 and 26 October 1780 do not provide evidence that the second edition was selling poorly. All they show is that Smith himself was anxious about the sales of this edition, just as he was shortly before it was published, when he wrote in a postscript to a letter to Strahan of 20 December 1777: 'Neither you nor Mr Cadell have wrote me anything concerning the new Edition of My Book It is Published? Does it sell well? does it sell ill? does it sell at all?' (*Corr*. Letter 188: 229). Moreover, since Cadell was trying to get Smith to complete the text of the third edition of the WN at least a year before Fox referred to the book in Parliament, the most that can be said about the effect of Fox's remark on publication is that it helped to move along a process that was already well under way (Rae 1895: 288–9). As to whether Fox's public compliment stimulated sales of the third edition once publication had occurred, there is no way to know that with certainty. But considering the fact that the third edition did not make its appearance for another year, I suspect that the commercial effect of this incident was slight.

Cadell's anxiety about publishing the third edition was exacerbated by another factor that he looked upon much less favourably than the free publicity furnished by Fox. By the late spring of 1776, just three months after the initial publication of the *Wealth of Nations* in London, a group of twenty Dublin booksellers, members of an organization that sometimes called itself the Company – or the United Company – of Booksellers, had published a three-volume octavo edition in Ireland (see Figure 3). At a price of 19s.6d. bound, the Dublin edition cost less than half as much as the London quarto, and it was also available for just 16s.3d. with the pages sewed. Yet if the price differential gave the 1776 Dublin octavo its chief marketing advantage, it is worth noting that the Irish reprinters boasted in their newspaper advertisements of using 'fine paper', evidently in order to keep their edition competitive on qualitative grounds (Sher 2002: 24).

Although Irish editions of British books could not legally be imported into Britain during the eighteenth century, Robert Darnton's research on the incessant French thirst for 'philosophical books' printed in Switzerland by the Société typographique de Neuchâtel has shown that when books were in great demand during the late eighteenth century, attempts would be made to smuggle them across borders, even if the risk of detection for the smugglers was 'virtually a matter of life and death' (Darnton 1995: 19). In Britain, where the penalties for smuggling books do not seem to have been nearly so severe as in France, the same temptation existed. It should come as no surprise, therefore, that in August 1776 Scottish customs officials stopped a ship from Dublin carrying fourteen sets of the Irish octavo edition of the WN in unbound sheets – the standard format for smuggling books (McDougall 1997: 161; cf. Darnton 1995: chapters 1–2). Such acts of exportation transformed Dublin editions of British books – which were perfectly legal within Ireland – into piracies. For eight years, the Irish reprinters had no competition in the popularly priced octavo market. During that time

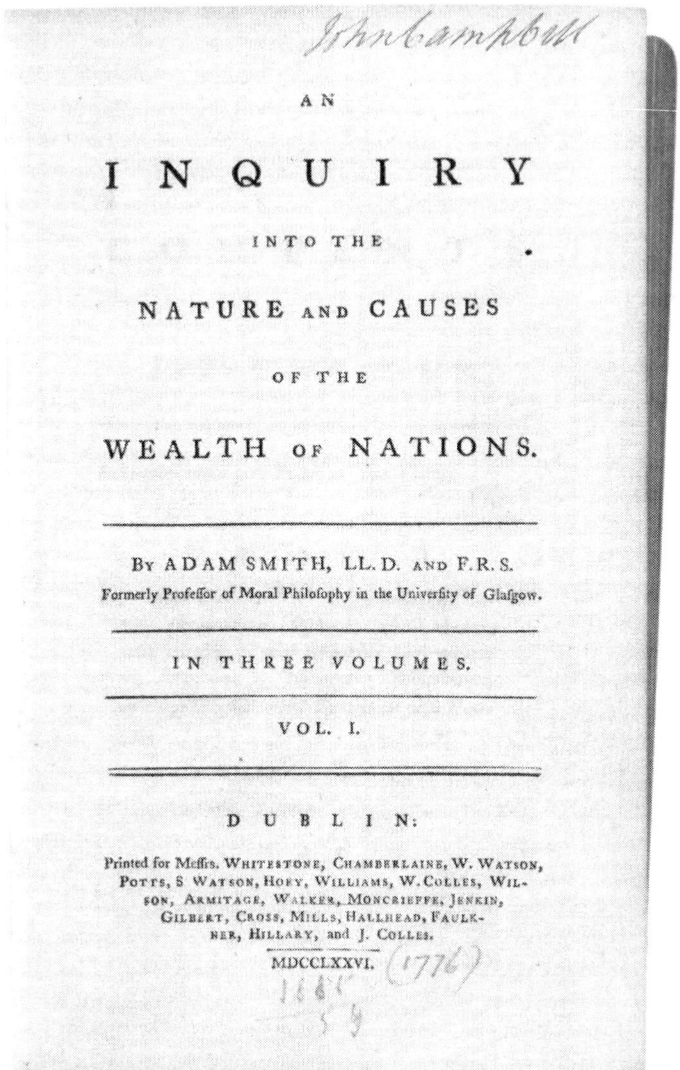

AN

INQUIRY

INTO THE

NATURE AND CAUSES

OF THE

WEALTH OF NATIONS.

By ADAM SMITH, LL.D. AND F.R.S.

Formerly Profeſſor of Moral Philoſophy in the Univerſity of Glaſgow.

IN THREE VOLUMES.

VOL. I.

DUBLIN:

Printed for Meſſrs. WHITESTONE, CHAMBERLAINE, W. WATSON, POTTS, S. WATSON, HOEY, WILLIAMS, W. COLLES, WILSON, ARMITAGE, WALKER, MONCRIEFFE, JENKIN, GILBERT, CROSS, MILLS, HALLHEAD, FAULKNER, HILLARY, and J. COLLES.

MDCCLXXVI.

Figure 3 The title page of the first volume of the 1776 Irish edition of the WN, published in three octavo volumes by twenty booksellers from the Company of Booksellers in Dublin. Courtesy of the Thomas Fisher Rare Book Library, University of Toronto.

another Dublin edition was advertised in the *Dublin Evening Post* for 15 October 1782 (Pollard 2000: 386), although no copies have been located. Irish reprinting must have seriously damaged the market for the London quartos in Ireland itself. Indeed, the wording of a newspaper advertisement for the first Dublin reprint of *The Theory of Moral Sentiments* in April 1777 strongly suggests that this edition was timed to take advantage of the popularity of the WN in Ireland (Sher 2002: 25). It is also probable that Irish copies of the WN permeated the American market to a significant degree towards the end of, and immediately after, the American war of independence. Although it is unlikely that enough copies of Irish editions were smuggled into Britain to make a significant difference there (Pollard 1989), it is worth noting that Strahan and Cadell were deeply troubled by the issue of Irish piracies during this period, and in March 1785 Cadell would testify forcefully on this subject before a parliamentary committee (Sher, forthcoming).

Despite the publishers' fears about Irish piracies, the British market for the WN would ultimately hinge upon the authorized and greatly expanded octavo third edition. From a marketing standpoint, Strahan and Cadell were wise to publish the octavo edition in three volumes, rather than the four volumes that Smith and Strahan had originally agreed upon. A three-volume edition packed more text into each volume. With all the new material that Smith had prepared for the third edition, this meant that each volume would be at least 500 pages long. By pricing the third edition at just six shillings per volume in boards, the publishers effectively quashed the competition from Irish editions of the same size and format. A four-volume edition might have been more elegant, but it also would have been more expensive, and therefore less competitive. Although the Dublin booksellers responded by publishing an even cheaper 'fourth edition' in just two octavo volumes in 1785, and a 'fifth edition' in the same format in 1793 (Sher 2002: 24–5), those cramped editions would not have offered enough financial incentive to risk smuggling large numbers of copies into Britain once an authorized and moderately priced three-volume octavo was available there.

Strahan and Cadell elected to print 1,000 copies of the octavo third edition, which appeared in London on 20 November 1784. By the time of William Strahan's death on 9 July 1785, only 124 copies remained in Cadell's warehouse (Harlan 1968: 160–71, citing British Library, Add Charter 75,424). So 876 copies were in distribution in less than eight months. These promising figures helped to fix the book's future path. Just as Smith would make no major textual revisions in subsequent editions, so would the three-volume octavo format remain standard for many years. What changed, besides some inevitable price increases around the turn of the century,[4] were the number of copies printed, as the publishers began to understand that they had a bona fide hit on their hands. As recorded in the Strahan ledgers, Andrew Strahan printed 1,250 copies of the fourth edition of 1786 and 1,500 copies of the fifth edition of 1789, the last to appear before Smith's death. Thus, not counting foreign editions and piracies, there were approximately 1,250 two-volume quarto sets and exactly 3,750 three-volume octavo sets in circulation with the Strahan–Cadell imprint during the fourteen years that Smith lived after publication.

IV

Was this a little or a lot? Contrasting these five lifetime editions and 5,000 or so lifetime copies with the production of Grub Street hacks and Tom Paine, whose *Rights of Man* (1791–2) sold hundreds of thousands of copies internationally in two years and then disappeared from sight, Teichgraeber suggests that Smith's was a modest achievement (Teichgraeber 2000: 98–101). But this approach is misleading. The WN should be compared with other scholarly books of roughly the same type. This will be done later in regard to works of political economy by Scottish authors, including above all Sir James Steuart's *Inquiry into the Principles of Political Economy*. But more generally, it may be noted that relatively few scholarly quartos published in late eighteenth-century Britain, especially outside the field of history, fared better than the *Wealth of Nations* during their early years. Lord Monboddo's *Antient Metaphysics* (1779–99), James Beattie's *Dissertations, Moral and Critical* (1783), Thomas Reid's *Essays on the Intellectual Powers* (1785) and *Essays on the Active Powers* (1788), William Cullen's *Treatise of the Materia Medica* (1789), James Hutton's *Dissertations on Different Subjects in Natural Philosophy* (1792) and *Investigation of the Principles of Knowledge* (1794) and Smith's own *Essays on Philosophical Subjects* (1795) are just a few of the many quartos by esteemed Scottish authors that were never reprinted in Britain in any format during the late eighteenth or early nineteenth centuries. Many others were fortunate enough to engender a single reprinting, or perhaps two. The fate of the WN was very different, and the large amount of copy money that Smith received for this book was the direct result of its popularity during the fourteen years that he lived after publication.

Furthermore, care must be taken regarding conclusions drawn from two facts about the early reception of the WN that are noted by Teichgraeber: that the print run of the second edition was only 500 copies – in effect, the smallest feasible print run for a book of this size – and that there was a six-year gap between the second and third editions. As we have seen, these circumstances were in large measure the result of deliberate decisions by the author and the publishers. First, the decision to publish the second edition as another expensive quarto, rather than the octavo edition that Smith and Strahan had initially agreed upon, necessitated a smaller print run and a slower process of dissemination because the market for expensive quartos was limited. Second, the decision to delay publication of the third edition until Smith had completed his extensive revisions – along with the decisions to publish the third edition in three rather than four octavo volumes and to put the author's additions into a separate quarto volume for the benefit of the owners of the first and second editions – reflected a comprehensive publishing strategy. The publishers' apparent intention was not to get rich quick but rather to nurture the book over the long haul. Had they shifted to octavo sooner than they did, or insisted that the third edition be published without Smith's revisions, they might have increased their early sales at the expense of their relationship with the author and their plans for developing a work of enduring popularity. These observations remind us that the WN, like any book, has a unique and contingent publishing history (Sher 2000: 58).

The key point is that we cannot attribute either the size of the print run of the second edition or the delay in the publication of the third edition to public indifference. All we can say with confidence is that every Strahan–Cadell edition of the WN seems to have sold well – the second edition not excepted, when the circumstances mentioned earlier are taken into account. Looked at in this way, the

WN can be characterized as a book that started off with surprisingly strong sales, remained competitive in spite of decisions by the author and the publishers which had the effect of delaying its entry into the popular marketplace until 1784, and sold extremely well from that time onwards.

Everyone agrees that after Smith's death in 1790 the WN achieved an extraordinarily high level of popularity and esteem (Tribe 2002: passim). William Creech undoubtedly had in mind this notable increase in the book's fame and stature when he observed in 1802 that 'it was long before its merit was found out' by the public (National Archives of Scotland, RH9/17/195, no. 5). Nine thousand octavo sets were published by the Strahan–Cadell partnership during the 1790s (2,000 copies of the sixth edition of 1791, 2,500 copies of the seventh edition of 1793, 2,500 copies of the eighth edition of 1796 and 2,000 copies of the ninth edition of 1799) and the tenth edition of 1802, the last to be covered under statutory copyright, added 2,000 more (Sher 2002: 20). The Strahans typically printed Hugh Blair's *Sermons*, one of the century's biggest-selling books, in octavo editions of 2,000 copies. When the WN reached that level in 1791, it was in very fast company indeed. Andrew Strahan's ledgers reveal that the publishers took in more than £3,300 from sales of the book during the period 1790–1811 alone (Strahan Ledgers, Add. MS 48,814A, f. 8).

Although no one in Britain dared to reprint the WN in its entirety while it was protected by statutory copyright, as early as 1797 a small group of booksellers, including the influential London firm headed by George Robinson, published at Cambridge a one-volume octavo abridgement, edited by Jeremiah Joyce. Entitled *A Complete Analysis or Abridgement of Dr. Adam Smith's Inquiry into the Nature and Causes of the Wealth of Nations*, it was expanded from 290 to 324 pages in a second edition of 1804 (reprinted in 1818) and went to a third edition in 1821. The soaring popularity of the WN led William Creech to warn Thomas Cadell, Jr, in a letter of 15 April 1802, of the existence of 'a set of pirates in London' who waited for copyrights to expire in order to commission printers in Scotland to reprint popular books with Scottish imprints, in violation of the booksellers' principle of 'honorary' or *de facto* copyright extending beyond the limits of the law. 'I know that they are now waiting for the expiry of Smith's Wealth of Nations', he added (National Archives of Scotland, RH9/17/195, no. 5). Events after the copyright expired in 1804 suggest that Creech's suspicions were justified. In 1805 alone, two different editions appeared in Glasgow, one in three octavo volumes and the other in four duodecimo volumes, as well as a two-volume octavo edition in London – all in addition to another 2,000 copies printed by Andrew Strahan for Cadell and Davies (successors to Thomas Cadell, Sr, as of 1793) in the 11th Strahan–Cadell edition, edited by William Playfair. The following year, Creech himself published an octavo edition in Edinburgh, as others did in 1808, 1809, 1811, 1814, 1817 and 1819. There were plenty of other London editions, too (Tribe 2002). Honorary copyright depended on a consensus within the book trade rather than legal restrictions (Sher 1998), and it could not be strictly enforced whenever a book generated this much demand (Amory 1984). For their part, Cadell and Davies and Andrew Strahan allowed other London booksellers to purchase shares in the honorary copyright, and a 'new edition' of 1812 contained the names of fifteen firms in the imprint, headed by Cadell and Davies, who used the same impression in volumes 2–4 of the five-volume edition of Smith's *Works* that they published in the same year. With at least twenty full-length British editions by this time, many of them printed in unusually large quantities, in addition to several abridged editions and the *Works* of 1812, the WN was unquestionably one of the best-selling scholarly books of the late eighteenth and early nineteenth centuries.

Meanwhile, booksellers in Europe and America were getting into the act. Besides the Irish editions that have been mentioned, the WN was reprinted in Philadelphia by Thomas Dobson in 1789 and 1796, and regularly in America thereafter; these reprints apparently built upon an early and influential American audience for imported copies of the book (Fleischacker 2002). J. J. Tourneisen and J. L. Legrand reprinted it in English in four octavo volumes in Basel in 1791 and again in 1801, and by the turn of the century it had been translated into Danish, Dutch, French, German, Italian, Spanish, and (in an abridged edition) Swedish, with Polish, Portuguese and Russian to follow soon after (Tribe 2002: 376–89). The WN now had a huge international audience.

However, we must avoid the temptation to underestimate the commercial success of the WN during Smith's lifetime merely because it became even more successful after the author died. The astonishing growth in popularity that occurred after Smith's death constituted an extension of an earlier pattern rather than a new development. From the expanded third edition of 1784 through the seventh edition of 1793, the print run of every octavo edition increased by at least 250 copies, while the time between editions remained more or less constant.

Other evidence, both anecdotal and comparative, serves to establish the popularity of the WN during Smith's lifetime. In early April 1786, a young French nobleman, Alexandre de La Rochefoucauld – son of Louis Alexandre, Duc de La Rochefoucauld-Liancourt, whom Smith knew well – and his travelling companion, Maximilien de Lazowski, met Adam Smith while passing through Edinburgh on their way to the Highlands. Lazowski's travel journal, apparently intended for the eyes of a friend or family member in France, is revealing:

> You will know him through two works (of which one, above all, has earned him his high reputation). But both are extremely well-known: *The Theory of Moral Sentiments* and *The Wealth of Nations*. The second is known in Europe as marking an epoch in the understanding of the principles of trade and finance.
>
> (Scarfe 2001: 121)

Written just ten years after the publication of the first edition of the WN, Lazowski's words indicate not only that Smith was thought to enjoy a 'high reputation' in Europe at this time, mainly on account of the WN, but also that there was widespread recognition of the book's ground-breaking character as a work of political economy.

The Scottish Enlightenment is often considered the birthplace of modern political economy, and not only because of Smith (Sakamoto and Tanaka 2003;

Backhouse 2002, chapter 6; Mair 1990; Thomson 1987; Hont and Ignatieff 1983). It is therefore instructive to compare the publishing history of the WN with other late eighteenth-century Scottish works on this subject that first appeared in quarto. The principal book that contained the economic teachings of Smith's teacher, Francis Hutcheson's *System of Moral Philosophy*, was posthumously published in 1755 but was never reprinted in Britain during the eighteenth century. Neither were Sir James Steuart's *An Inquiry into the Principles of Political Economy* (1767) or James Anderson's *Observations on the Means of Exciting a Spirit of National Industry* (1777), although these two titles were each reprinted once in Dublin, and Steuart's book appeared in his *Works* early in the nineteenth century, as we shall see. George Chalmers' *An Estimate of the Comparative Strength of Britain during the Present and Four Preceding Reigns, and of the Losses of Her Trade from Every War since the Revolution* (1782) had considerable success, passing through several British editions by 1810 (and another in 1812 as *An Historical View of the Domestic Economy of Great Britain*), as well as a French translation in 1789, but it did not rival Smith's book in popularity, especially when one takes into account that the print runs were almost certainly much smaller. John Knox's *A View of the British Empire, More Especially Scotland, with Some Proposals for the Improvement of that Country, the Extension of the Its Fisheries, and the Relief of the People*, originally published in 1784 as a large quarto pamphlet, reached a fourth, greatly expanded edition within five years of publication but was never reprinted after that time. Sir John Sinclair's *The History of the Public Revenue of the British Empire* began appearing in 1785, when it was also reprinted in Dublin, and it reached a second British edition as an expanded octavo in 1790; a third volume would be published as part of the third edition in 1804. John Bruce's *Historical View of Plans, for the Government of British India, and Regulation of Trade to the East Indies* (1793) was never reprinted, and sales were apparently so poor that it was reissued in 1806 with a cancel title page. Of course, many other books on political economy by Scottish authors appeared originally in octavo or duodecimo editions, such as David Loch's *Essays on the Trade, Commerce, Manufactures, and Fisheries of Scotland* (1778–9), William Oglivie's *An Essay on the Right of Property in Land* (1781), James Anderson's *An Account of the Present State of the Hebrides and Western Coasts of Scotland* (1785), George Chalmers' *Opinions on Interesting Subjects of Public Law and Commercial Policy* (1784) and, early in the nineteenth century, James Maitland, earl of Lauderdale's *An Inquiry into the Nature and Origin of Public Wealth, and into the Means and Causes of Its Increase* (1804), which was reprinted in an expanded second edition in 1819. But none of these works went past a second edition, and most were never reprinted at all.[5] These data do not support the view that the reception of the WN was unexceptional for a book of its kind, let alone Rashid's more specific contention that Anderson or Knox was 'more widely read' than Smith after 1776. If that were so, why was the public demand for the books on political economy by Anderson, Knox and other Scottish authors so slight in comparison with the demand for Smith's book on that subject?

Sir James Steuart's *Inquiry into the Principles of Political Economy* is worthy of more detailed consideration because both Rae and Rashid put so much emphasis on it for understanding the publication and reception of the WN. As Rae was aware, Steuart sold the copyright of his book to Andrew Millar for £500. Rae's source was almost certainly a passage in a published biographical sketch by Steuart's son, quoted later, but corroborating evidence is now available. A letter from Steuart to Millar agreeing to these terms, dated 15 April 1766, has survived among Cadell's papers in the Longman Archive at the University of Reading Library (MS 1393/26/2a), as has the formal assignment of copyright, dated 15 June 1767 (MS 1393/26/2d). Millar, then at the end of his long and illustrious career, allowed his young disciple and successor, Thomas Cadell, and his printer, William Strahan, to take one-quarter shares in this publication, although Strahan's name was left off the imprint. In early April 1767, Strahan printed 1,000 copies of Steuart's book in two quarto volumes (Strahan Ledgers, Add. MS 48,803A, f. 71), and the publication was announced 'this day' in the *London Chronicle* for 16–18 April at a retail price of £2.2s. in boards or £2.10s. 'bound and gilt'. It was a very expensive undertaking, aimed at the high end of the book-buying public. The printing alone was charged by Strahan at £203.9s.6d., and the 'fine royal paper' cited in the advertisement undoubtedly cost much more than that. When the author's copy money, the advertising fees, and other expenses are factored in, the publishers' total outlay must have been well over £1,000. To help protect their investment against piracy, the publishers registered the book at Stationers' Hall on 17 April 1767 (Myers 1985: reel 6, pt. 2, 279). Registration constituted yet another significant expense, however, because it required depositing nine bound copies, with a total retail value of £22.10s.

With so much at stake, how did Steuart's book fare in the marketplace? I can discover no grounds for saying that it 'sold slowly but steadily' (Rashid 1998: 146). On the contrary, sales seem to have been quite promising at first, probably owing in part to favourable notices in both the *Monthly Review* and the *Critical Review*. On 4 June 1767, William Rouet, who had apparently served as Steuart's publication agent (Longman Archive, MS 1393/26/2c), informed the author that his book met with 'universal approbation' and that 370 copies had already been sold (quoted in Skinner's Introduction to Steuart 1998: li). Had that rate of sales continued, the first edition would have sold out in a few months, and a second edition would surely have appeared very soon afterwards. Steuart himself made preparations for a second edition, partly in response to contemporary reviews. But a new edition did not appear until General Sir James Steuart edited, for Cadell and Davies, an octavo edition of his father's *Works* in six volumes in 1805, twenty-five years after the author's death. Andrew Strahan printed 750 copies of Steuart's *Works* in January of that year (Strahan Ledgers, Add. MS 48,817, f. 178); it was never reprinted. Excepting a single Dublin edition that was published by subscription in three octavo volumes in 1770, Steuart's *Principles* was not available in English during the eighteenth century in any other form but the expensive quarto first edition. Meanwhile, Goguel prepared a French translation but could not get it published, in contrast to the growing popularity of French translations of Smith's opus during the last quarter of the century (Carpenter 2002: xxi–liv; Tribe 2002: 376–7), achieved in spite of government hostility on account of its support for free trade (Chisick 2004: 246–7). When a five-volume French translation of Steuart's book finally appeared in Paris in 1789–90, it was read largely as a work that complemented Smith's (Faccarello and Steiner 2002: 91).

There can be little doubt, then, that Steuart's disappointment about the public reception accorded to the *Principles* stemmed from real events rather than merely from the author's unrealistically high expectations. Steuart's son admitted as much in the 'Anecdotes of the Life of Sir James Steuart, Bart.' that he included in his edition of his father's works:

> *Inquiry into the Principles of Political Economy*...was the last work, which Andrew Millar purchased, and for which he gave five hundred pounds: but, when the book was published, in 1767, *it did not sell fast*, according to his own phrase; whereby his last bargain was, in the end, found to be the worst. This is one of those books, with regard to which the critics, and the public, differed in opinion.
>
> (Steuart 1805: 3.377)

The contrast in the ways that Smith's WN and Steuart's *Principles* were received by the British public during the last quarter of the eighteenth century could hardly have been more pronounced. Does not this difference constitute 'definite evidence' of Smith's superior reception in popular estimation before 1790?

Andrew Millar died on 8 June 1768, leaving his disciples, Strahan and Cadell, to grapple with the commercial failure of Steuart's *Principles*. Having each invested hundreds of pounds in the venture, they must have lost a great deal of money on it at a vulnerable time in their publishing careers. The printing record shows that Cadell did not pay Strahan his one-quarter share of the printing costs until a full year after publication (15 April 1768), and Millar's one-half share was not paid until eight months after Millar's death (18 February 1769).

All this evidence suggests that Rae was wrong about the way that Sir James Steuart's *Inquiry into the Principles of Political Economy* influenced the publication arrangements for the WN. The weak performance of Steuart's *Principles* in the marketplace worked against Smith in his negotiations with Strahan and Cadell. Earlier we saw that William Creech explained the poor terms that Smith initially received for the WN by invoking a general principle of publishing: 'When a new work is offered, [the bookseller] considers what has been the success of similar publications, and hence endeavours to make an estimate in his own mind' (James Beattie Papers, 30/2/545). Steuart's *Principles* would have been the most prominent of the 'similar publications' to which Creech alluded. Its disappointing sales help to account for the lack of confidence that the publishers placed in the commercial potential of the WN and their unwillingness either to purchase the copyright of Smith's book in advance or to invest as heavily in its production and protection. Unlike Steuart's *Principles*, the WN was not touted in advertisements for its fine royal paper, was not registered at Stationers' Hall at the time of publication, was not offered in a gilt binding, was not given a retail price as high as two guineas in boards, and probably was not printed initially in a quantity as large as 1,000 copies. Yet, whereas Steuart's book failed to live up to the expectations of its author and publishers, Smith's followed the opposite trajectory.

V

All in all, the WN achieved greater commercial success during the last quarter of the eighteenth century than any other comparable work. When set against Teichgraeber's and Rashid's claims about its chequered reception, this conclusion highlights some of the ways that book history may help to fortify and qualify the history of ideas. Historians of ideas typically judge the reception of a book by the things that contemporaries wrote and said about it, as recorded in pamphlets, letters, memoirs, reviews, speeches, newspaper articles, books and any other sources they may find (for example, Lai 2000; Mizuta 1999; Ross 1998), as well as by the things that contemporaries did *not* write and say about it. Teichgraeber and Rashid draw some conclusions about the reception of the WN from contemporary remarks, but their claims that it was greeted indifferently, or that it was not perceived to be a work of singular importance during Smith's lifetime, are founded largely on the *absence* of certain types of contemporary pronouncements. For example, Teichgraeber remarks: 'There is no evidence to show that many people explored [Smith's] arguments with great care before the first two decades of the nineteenth century' (Teichgraeber 1987: 339), and 'despite its rapid sale during the spring and summer of 1776, the first edition of the *Wealth of Nations* provoked no impassioned debates or dramatic confrontations' (Teichgraeber 1987: 341).

But such statements do not tell the whole story. Aside from the possibility that revisionist commentators may have underestimated the impact of the WN on British policy-makers during Smith's lifetime (see Ross 1998: xxii–xxvii, 143–64), the fact that so many thousands of pricey, multi-volume sets of the WN were in circulation during the last quarter of the eighteenth century, first in quarto and then in octavo, constitutes powerful evidence that the public was not indifferent, and that this work was accorded a noteworthy reception. Of course, some of those sets may have gone unread, but others may each have been read by many people, especially if they were purchased by the circulating and subscription libraries that proliferated dramatically during the latter part of the eighteenth century. For example, James Sibbald's circulating library in Edinburgh owned a two-volume quarto copy of the WN, which one could borrow by subscribing for as little as 3s.6d. per quarter (Sibbald (1786): iii, 72) – one-twelfth the price of the book. Moreover, patterns of consumption can tell us something significant about cultural values and beliefs regardless of evidence about reading, and the nature of reading itself may be subject to a wide range of critical interpretations (for example, Rabinowitz 1994 and Lernout 1994). It is unwise to make sweeping generalizations on the basis of relatively few sources when such large numbers of purchasers and readers are involved, or to assume that the absence of certain kinds of contemporary statements and debates about the WN means that it was ignored, misunderstood, or narrowly understood by Smith's contemporaries, or that it did not have much of an impact upon their thinking about political economy and other subjects. At the very least, the findings of the historian of ideas must be tested against those of book history.

Just as book history can enrich our understanding of the reception accorded to the WN, so can the WN help historians of books to gain a better understanding of relations that prevailed between British authors and publishers during the age of the Enlightenment. When a learned work like the WN went to press during the eighteenth century, its publishers sought to balance the copy money paid to the author, the formats in which the book appeared in its different editions, the number of volumes, the prices charged for the book in different formats and in different states of binding, and the quantities printed of each edition in order to stimulate public demand for the book while making a profit for themselves and, at the same time, building their reputations so that authors would choose to publish the most desirable books with them. It will not do to regard the publishers of learned books as cold-blooded profiteers, or to treat intellectual property or copyright as the defining feature of eighteenth-century British book history. Nor can publishing be reduced to a fixed 'logic' of print culture, in which 'systematic economic principles – specialization, the wage-profit ratio, the open marketplace, and its constant pressure for increased efficiency and productivity – determined the life of the book worker, whether writer or printer, as rigidly as they did the coal miner or the weaver' (Kernan 1987: 76). There were too many contingencies and uncertainties, too many choices that had to be made within the context of economic and other constraints, for any such formula to apply. As with coal mining, weaving, and every other historical subject, the more closely one examines the book trade in eighteenth-century Britain, the more it appears complex and variable rather than rigid and formulaic. Neither the process of publishing nor the reception accorded to publications can be understood without taking into account decisions and agreements made by authors and publishers in regard to matters such as the distribution of profits, textual revisions, marketing strategies, and the physical attributes of books.

The publication and reception of the WN illustrate this point. William Strahan and Thomas Cadell, the principal publishers, pursued a careful, conscientious, and ultimately winning strategy that both raised the reputation of the author and kept the book profitable for themselves and their heirs. They first exhausted the high end of the market with two relatively small, expensive, and profitable two-volume quarto editions and then published more affordable octavo editions in three volumes, and in increasingly large print runs, as they and their successors gained confidence in the book's selling power. They drew upon the resources of their Edinburgh colleague William Creech in some as-yet undetermined way, perhaps involving investment in the enterprise as a co-publisher and certainly involving assistance with marketing and sales in Scotland. They maintained warm, close relations with the author and tried to appease him as much as possible. When Smith wished to provide significant additions and corrections to the third edition, they encouraged him (at least until Fox's parliamentary compliment introduced a note of urgency into the process), even though doing so meant delaying the crucial octavo and risking the possibility that demand for the book would wither away in the interim. They were rewarded when the book generated strong sales and growing demand following the appearance of the octavo in 1784, in spite of its difficult subject matter and relatively high price. Throughout this process, they were pleased to share a significant portion of the profits with the author, using several different modes of compensation. Only within the last two years of Smith's life did Andrew Strahan (who had replaced his father at the head of the family firm) and Thomas Cadell purchase, and then renew, the copyright. By that time, the WN had established itself as a work of enduring appeal, poised to receive still greater acclaim in the years ahead.

Acknowledgements

The author would like to thank Anthony Lewis, Warren McDougall, Roger Robinson and Keith Tribe for their assistance with sources, and Vivienne Brown, Sam Fleischacker, Knud Haakonssen, Salim Rashid, Ian Simpson Ross, Doris Sher and Richard Teichgraeber for their helpful comments on earlier drafts.

Notes

1 Creech is undoubtedly referring to *The Duenna*, the extraordinarily successful comic opera which Richard Brinsley Sheridan appeared to compose almost overnight in 1775. Although it is not known exactly how much money Sheridan received for this work, it is believed that £1,300 of his own money that he contributed towards the purchase of the theatre at Drury Lane soon afterwards represented a portion of his earnings (O'Toole 1997: 114). However, Sheridan's income from *The Duenna* came from theatre receipts, not from the book trade.

2 The advertisement in the *Edinburgh Evening Courant* for 20 March 1776 states that the book is 'Published This Day by William Creech', suggesting that Creech was the book's silent co-publisher in Scotland. Furthermore, the postscript to a letter from Dugald Stewart to William Preston (foreman of the Strahan print shop), dated 16 March 1795, concerning the imprint of Smith's posthumous *Essays on Philosophical Subjects*, asserts that 'Mr. Creech wishes his name to be on the Title page of Mr. Smith's Book, *as he is a Proprietor of Mr. Smith's other works*' (Bodleian Library, ff. 115–16; emphasis added). When the *Essays* appeared later that year, Creech's name did in fact appear in the imprint.

3 According to the calculator in 'How much is that worth today?', in 1783 (halfway between the publication of the WN and Smith's death) £1,500 and £1,800 were equivalent in 2002 purchasing power to £107,042 and £128,451, respectively.

4 Tribe records a price increase to £2.7s. for the eighth edition of 1796 and to £2.13s. for the eleventh (Playfair) edition of 1805 (Tribe 2002: 238, 243). Price hikes of this kind occurred throughout the industry at this time, largely as a result of the rising cost of paper.

5 I have excluded from this list David Hume, whose essays on political economy were frequently reprinted in various editions of his *Essays and Treatises on Several Subjects*.

Bibliography

Published sources

Amory, H. (1984) '"*De facto* copyright"? Fielding's *Works* in partnership, 1769–1821', *Eighteenth-Century Studies*, 17: 449–76.

Backhouse, R.E. (2002) *The Ordinary Business of Life: A History of Economics from the Ancient World to the Twenty-first Century*, Princeton and Oxford: Princeton University Press.

Carpenter, K.E. (2002) *The Dissemination of* The Wealth of Nations *in French and in France 1776–1843*, New York: Bibliographical Society of America.

Chisick, H. (2004) 'The Representation of Adam Smith and David Hume in the *Année Littéraire* and the *Journal Encyclopédique*', in *Scotland and France in the Enlightenment*, 240–63, D. Dawson and P. Morère (eds), Lewisburg, Pa.: Bucknell University Press, and London: Associated University Presses.

Craddock, P.B. (1989) *Edward Gibbon, Luminous Historian 1772–1794*, Baltimore and London: Johns Hopkins University Press.

Creech, W. (1793) *Letters, Addressed to Sir John Sinclair, Bart. Respecting the Mode of Living, Arts, Commerce, Literature, Manners, etc. of Edinburgh, in 1763, and since that Period*, Edinburgh. Originally published in 1783.

Darnton, R. (1995) *The Forbidden Best-Sellers of Pre-Revolutionary France*, New York and London: Norton.

ESTC (the online *English Short-Title Catalogue*).

Faccarello, G. and P. Steiner (2002) 'The diffusion of the work of Adam Smith in the French language: an outline history', in *A Critical Bibliography of Adam Smith*, 61–119, K. Tribe (ed.), London: Pickering & Chatto.

Fay, C.R. (1956) *Adam Smith and the Scotland of His Day*, Cambridge: Cambridge University Press.

Fleischacker, S. (2002) 'Adam Smith's reception among the American Founders, 1776–1790', *William and Mary Quarterly*, 3d ser., 59: 897–924.

Gibbon, E. (1966) *Memoirs of My Life*, G.A. Bonnard (ed.), London: Thomas Nelson and Sons.

Harlan, R. D. (1968) 'Some additional figures of distribution of eighteenth-century English books', *Papers of the Bibliographical Society of America*, 59: 160–71.

Hont, I. and M. Ignatieff (eds) (1983) *Wealth & Virtue: The Shaping of Political Economy in the Scottish Enlightenment*, Cambridge: Cambridge University Press.

'How much is that worth today?', at http://www.eh.net.

Kernan, A. (1987) *Printing Technology, Letters & Samuel Johnson*, Princeton: Princeton University Press.

Lai, C. (ed.) (2000) *Adam Smith across the Nations: Translations and Receptions of* The Wealth of Nations, Oxford: Oxford University Press.

Lernout, G. (1994) 'Reception Theory', in *The Johns Hopkins Guide to Literary Theory & Criticism*, 610–11, M. Groden and M. Kreiswirth (eds), Baltimore and London: Johns Hopkins University Press.

McDougall, W. (1997) 'Smugglers, reprinters, and hot pursuers: the Irish–Scottish book trade, and copyright prosecutions in the late eighteenth century', in *The Stationers' Company and the Book Trade, 1550–1990*, 21–46, R. Meyers and M. Harris (eds), Winchester: St Paul's Bibliographies, and New Castle, DE: Oak Knoll Press.

Mackenzie, H. (1989) *Literature and Literati: The Literary Correspondence and Notebooks of Henry Mackenzie, Volume 1/Letters 1766–1827*, H.W. Drescher (ed.), Frankfurt am Main: Peter Lang.

Mair, D. (ed.) (1990) *The Scottish Contribution to Modern Economic Thought*, Aberdeen: University of Aberdeen Press.

Mizuta, H. (ed.) (1999) *Adam Smith: Critical Responses*, 6 vols, London: Routledge.

Myers, R. (1985) *Records of the Worshipful Company of Stationers 1554–1920*, London: Chadwyck-Healey (microfilm).

O'Toole, F. (1997) *A Traitor's Kiss: The Life of Richard Brinsley Sheridan, 1751–1816*, New York: Farrar, Straus and Giroux.

Pollard, M. (2000) *A Dictionary of Members of the Dublin Book Trade 1550–1800*, London: The Bibliographical Society.

—— (1989) *Dublin's Trade in Books 1550–1800*, Oxford: Oxford University Press.

Rabinowitz, P.J. (1994) 'Reader-Response Theory and Criticism', in *The Johns Hopkins Guide to Literary Theory & Criticism*, 606–9, M. Groden and M. Kreiswirth (eds), Baltimore and London: Johns Hopkins University Press.

Rae, J. (1895) *Life of Adam Smith*, 1990 reprint, Bristol: Thoemmes Press.

Rashid, S. (1982) 'Adam Smith's rise to fame: a reexamination of the evidence', *The Eighteenth Century: Theory and Interpretation*, 23: 70–9.

—— (1992) 'Charles James Fox and *The Wealth of Nations*', *History of Political Economy*, 24: 493–7.

—— (1998) *The Myth of Adam Smith*, Cheltenham and Northampton, MA: Edward Elgar.

Rose, M. (1993) *Authors and Owners: The Invention of Copyright*, Cambridge, MA, and London: Harvard University Press.

Ross, I.S. (1995) *The Life of Adam Smith*, Oxford: Oxford University Press.

—— (ed.) (1998) *On the Wealth of Nations: Contemporary Responses to Adam Smith*, Bristol: Thoemmes Press.

Sakamoto, T. and H. Tanaka (eds) (2003) *The Rise of Political Economy in the Scottish Enlightenment*, London: Routledge.

Scarfe, N. (2001) *To the Highlands in 1786: The Inquisitive Journey of a Young French Aristocrat*, Woodbridge, Suffolk and Rochester, NY: Boydell Press.

Sher, R.B. (1998) 'Corporatism and consensus in the late eighteenth-century book trade: the Edinburgh Booksellers' Society in comparative perspective', *Book History*, 1: 32–93.

—— (1999) 'William Buchan's *Domestic Medicine*: laying book history open', in *The Human Face of the Book Trade: Print Culture and its Creators*, 45–64, P. Isaac and B. McKay (eds), Winchester: St Paul's Bibliographies, and New Castle, DE: Oak Knoll Press.

—— (2000) 'The book in the Scottish Enlightenment', in *The Culture of the Book in the Scottish Enlightenment: An Exhibition with Essays by Roger Emerson, Richard Sher, Stephen Brown, and Paul Wood*, P. Wood (ed.), Toronto: Thomas Fisher Rare Book Library.

—— (2002) 'Early editions of Adam Smith's books in Britain and Ireland, 1759–1804', in *A Critical Bibliography of Adam Smith*, 13–26, K. Tribe (ed.), London: Pickering & Chatto.

—— (forthcoming) *The Enlightenment and the Book: Scottish Authors and Publishers in Eighteenth-Century Britain, Ireland, and America*.

Sibbald, J. [1786] *A New Catalogue of the Edinburgh Circulating Library*, Edinburgh.

Smith, A. (1976) *An Inquiry into the Nature and Causes of the Wealth of Nations*, R.H. Campbell and A.S. Skinner (General eds), W.B. Todd (Textual ed.), Oxford: Oxford University Press.

—— (1987) *Correspondence of Adam Smith*, E.C. Mossner and I.S. Ross (eds), 2nd edn, Oxford: Oxford University Press.

Steuart, Sir J. (1805) *The Works, Political, Metaphysical, and Chronological, of the Late Sir James Steuart of Coltness, Bart. Now First Collected by General Sir James Steuart, Bart Hist Son, from His Father's Corrected Copies*, 6 vols, London: Cadell and Davies.

—— (1998) *An Inquiry into the Principles of Political Economy*, A.S. Skinner (ed.), with N. Kobayashi and H. Mizuta, 4 vols, London: Pickering & Chatto.

Teichgraeber, R.F., III (1987) ' "Less abused than I had reason to expect": the reception of *The Wealth of Nations* in Britain, 1776–90', *Historical Journal*, 30: 337–66.

—— (2000) 'Adam Smith and tradition: the *Wealth of Nations* before Malthus', in *Economy, Polity and Society: British Intellectual History 1750–1950*, 85–104, S. Collini, R. Whatmore, and B. Young (eds), Cambridge: Cambridge University Press.

Thomson, H.F. (1987) 'The Scottish Enlightenment and political economy', in *Pre-Classical Economic Thought: From the Greeks to the Scottish Enlightenment*, 221–55, S.T. Lowry (ed.), Boston, Dordrecht, and Lancaster: Kluwer Academic Publishers.

Tribe, K. (ed.) (2002) *A Critical Bibliography of Adam Smith*, London: Pickering & Chatto.

Willis, K. (1979) 'The role in Parliament of the economic ideas of Adam Smith, 1776–1800', *History of Political Economy*, 11: 505–44.

Unpublished materials

James Beattie Papers, Aberdeen University Library.

John Bell Letterbooks, 1764–71, Bodleian Library, Oxford, MS Eng. Letters, C20–21.

Bodleian Library, Oxford, Montagu d. 10, ff. 115–16: Dugald Stewart to William Preston, 16 March [1795].

William Creech Letterbooks, microfilm copy, National Archives of Scotland, RH4/26/3; quoted by permission of the Blair Oliphant of Ardblair family.

Longman Archive, University of Reading Library, MS 1393/26/2a–d.

National Archives of Scotland, RH9/17/195: William Creech to Thomas Cadell, Jr, 15 April 1802.

National Library of Scotland, MS 3,942, ff. 299–300: William Strahan to William Robertson, 6 December 1776.

National Library of Scotland, Acc 9546: Henry Mackenzie to Thomas Cadell, 2 August 1792.

National Library of Scotland, MS 23,157, no. 67: William Strahan to David Hume, 12 April 1776.

Strahan Ledgers, British Library, Add. MSS 48,800–48,918 (microfilm edition, 1990, 'The Strahan Archive from the British Library', 23 reels, Reading and Woodbridge, CT: Research Publications).

Adam Smith and disequilibrium economic theory

Takashi Negishi

I Introduction

A great classic often has many different aspects that permit many different and mutually inconsistent interpretations by later scholars. The *Wealth of Nations* (WN) of Adam Smith is a good example of such a classic. Smith's theory of natural prices has been interpreted and developed as an equilibrium theory by modern economic theorists.[1] We shall try, however, to interpret Smith's economic theory as disequilibrium theory. Of course, there already exist some disequilibrium approaches to Smith on the dynamic process of growth involving increasing returns to scale.[2] We shall rather be concerned, however, with a disequilibrium approach to the problems of markets, that is, international trade, competition and division of labour, and a disequilibrium interpretation of what economists now refer to as 'increasing returns to scale'. We shall start this disequilibrium analysis from a study of Smith's theory of international trade. Smith explained international trade by the existence of disequilibrium, that is, surplus, and was criticized by Ricardo from the point of view of the equilibrium theory.

To add a new interpretation to the already rich variety of interpretations of different aspects of the WN is certainly troublesome for those who wish to know what Smith really meant. But our purpose here is to examine the history of economics as a rich source from which we can obtain hints, suggestions, and encouragement to develop new economic theories. Thus we are asking Adam Smith to support our attempt to develop disequilibrium theories of economics against the modern equilibrium economic theory.

The plan of this article is as follows. We begin in Section II by explaining the difference between equilibrium theory and disequilibrium theory. Section III deals with Smith's theory of international trade. While the modern equilibrium theory assumes that the comparative advantages between trading countries are exogenously given from the differences in climate, technology, factor endowment and so on, Smith's theory can explain endogenously the comparative advantages between similar countries. We shall emphasize, however, that Smith's international

The Adam Smith Review, 1: 30–9 © 2004 The International Adam Smith Society, ISSN 1743–5285, ISBN 0–415–27863–5

trade theory can be interpreted only as a disequilibrium theory. Then, in the following Section IV, we shall argue that Smith's proposition on the division of labour and the extent of the market – which economists interpret as increasing returns to scale – can also be fully demonstrated only as a disequilibrium theory. Our aim is to argue that the division of labour is advanced by the existence of excess supply which large markets are more likely to generate. Finally, Section V provides a summary and conclusion.

II Equilibrium theory and disequilibrium theory

According to Schumpeter, modern economic theory has inherited its equilibrium theory from Book I, chapter 7, of Adam Smith's WN which analyses natural and market price:

> The rudimentary equilibrium theory of chapter 7, by far the best piece of economic theory turned out by A. Smith, in fact points toward Say and, through the latter's work, to Walras. The purely theoretical developments of the nineteenth century consist to a considerable degree in improvements upon it. Market price... is treated as fluctuating around a 'natural' price... which is the price that is sufficient and not more than sufficient to cover 'the whole value of the rent, wages, and profit, which must be paid in order to bring' to market that quantity of every commodity 'which will supply the effectual demand,' that is, the demand effective at that price.
>
> (Schumpeter 1954: 189)

> When the price of any commodity is neither more or nor less than what is sufficient to pay the rent of the land, the wages of the labour, and the profits of the stock employed in raising, preparing, and bringing it to market, according to their natural rates, the commodity is then sold for what may be called its natural price.
>
> (WN I.vii.4)

The natural price is the equilibrium price to which actual market prices are attracted. When the quantity of a commodity which is brought to market falls short of the effective demand, the market price will rise more or less above the natural price, at least one component part of the price (the rent, wages and profit) must rise above its natural rate, and more land, labour and stock are used in raising, preparing and bringing to market the commodity so that the quantity brought to market is sufficient to supply the effectual demand. This implies, then, that the market price falls to the natural price and each component part to its natural rate, respectively. Similarly, when the quantity brought to market exceeds the effectual demand, the market price sinks below the natural price and at least one component part falls below its respective natural rate, with the result that the quantities of labour, land and stock used are diminished, the quantity of the commodity is equalized to the effectual demand, and the natural price is regained with the natural rates of its component parts. In other words, the equilibrium price of a commodity is defined by the equality of the demand for it and supply of it in the market;[3] and it is reached through the adjustment of disequilibrium market price which rises if the demand is larger than the supply, and reduced if the supply is larger than the demand (WN I.vii.3–16).

Being based on the given natural rate of rent, wages and profits, the natural price of a commodity remains unchanged by changes in the market price through which it is established. In this sense, we may call Smith's theory of the natural price an equilibrium theory. It implies that disequilibrium soon disappears without any effects left on the equilibrium eventually established. As was pointed out by Schumpeter (1954:189), Walras' theory of equilibrium is the one of the most refined versions of such a theory (Walras 1954). Walras considered two different solutions in his theory of equilibrium, that is, the mathematical solution and the practical solution. The former solution is to confirm the equality of the number of unknowns (the equilibrium prices) with the number of equations (the conditions of supply and demand). The equilibrium is obtained without any consideration of the behaviour of markets in disequilibrium. The latter solution is the *tâtonnement*, which explains how the problems of equilibrium are solved practically in the markets by the mechanism of competition. Walras assumed that no actual exchange transactions take place at disequilibria where prices are being changed according to the law of supply and demand, so as to make the practical solution identical to the mathematical one (Negishi 1989: 253–4, 263–4). This ensures that the equilibrium outcome is independent of the disequilibrium path of adjustment.

If disequilibrium does not disappear soon and if its effects on the equilibrium eventually established are important, however, we have to give up the equilibrium theory and consider disequilibrium theory. In the latter, the equilibrium eventually established is not independent of the path in disequilibrium through which it is reached. Even though Smith's theory of the natural price can be considered as equilibrium theory, we can also find examples of disequilibrium theory in the WN.

III Smith's theory of international trade

Although Schumpeter mentioned only Say and Walras in the earlier passage, Ricardo and J.S. Mill also followed Smith's equilibrium theory in the development of the classical school of economics in England (see Negishi 1986 for the equilibrium theory of J.S. Mill). Thus, Ricardo even criticized Smith's theory of international trade from the point of view of Smith's equilibrium theory of natural and market price. The core of Smith's theory of international trade is based, however, not on the equilibrium analysis of natural and market price first presented in Book I, chapter 7, but on an analysis of the historical and natural progress of capital investment in different sectors of the economy in Book II.

> When the produce of any particular branch of industry exceeds what the demand of the country requires, the surplus must be sent abroad, and exchanged for something for which there is a demand at home. Without such exportation, a part of the productive labour of the country must cease, and the value of its annual produce diminish. The land and labour of Great Britain

> produce generally more corn, woollens and hard ware, than the demand of the home-market requires. The surplus part of them, therefore, must be sent abroad, and exchanged for something for which there is a demand at home. It is only by means of such exportation, that this surplus can acquire a value sufficient to compensate the labour and expence of producing it.
>
> (WN II.v.33)

> One would be led to think by the above passage, that Adam Smith concluded we were under some necessity of producing a surplus of corn, woollen goods, and hardware, and that the capital which produced them could not be otherwise employed. It is, however, always a matter of choice in what way a capital shall be employed, and therefore there can never, for any length of time, be a surplus of any commodity; for if there were, it would fall below its natural price, and capital would be removed to some more profitable employment. No writer has more satisfactorily and ably shewn than Dr. Smith, the tendency of capital to move from employments in which the goods produced do not repay by their price the whole expenses, including the ordinary profits, of producing and bringing them to market.
>
> (Ricardo 1951: 291, n.)

Clearly, Smith's theory is a disequilibrium theory, since he tried to explain the equilibrium of international trade from the existence of surplus, that is, excess supply, in the domestic markets that are out of equilibrium. He thus went beyond his equilibrium theory of the natural price by taking account of market disequilibria and framing an explanation of international trade on the existence of domestic disequilibria. Ricardo, on the other hand, stuck to Smith's theory of the natural price and assumed away the effects on the final equilibrium outcome of what happened during the disequilibrium process of adjustment, and so the classical theory of international trade developed by Ricardo (1951: 128–149) and J.S. Mill (1909: 574–606) was based on the equilibrium approach. Smith's disequilibrium theory of international trade is explained in more detail as follows:

> Between whatever places foreign trade is carried on, they all of them derive two distinct benefits from it. It carries out that surplus part of the produce of their land and labour for which there is no demand among them, and brings back in return for it something else for which there is a demand. It gives a value to their superfluities, by exchanging them for something else, which may satisfy a part of their wants, and increase their enjoyments. By means of it, the narrowness of the home market does not hinder the division of labour in any particular branch of art or manufacture from being carried to the highest perfection. By opening a more extensive market for whatever part of the produce of their labour may exceed the home consumption, it encourages them to improve its productive powers, and to argument its annual produce to the utmost, and thereby to increase the real revenue and wealth of the society.
>
> (WN IV.i.31)

Myint (1958) argued that there are two different and independent theories of international trade in the above passage, that is, the 'productivity theory' and the 'vent for surplus' theory. The former theory points out the possibility that, by widening the extent of the market, international trade improves the division of labour and raises the general level of productivity within the country, so that costs fall. The latter theory is considered by Myint as appropriate for analysing underdeveloped economies rather than advanced economies with well-developed markets.[4] The difficulty with Myint's explanation here as an account of Smith's intention is that Smith himself did not restrict the applicability of his theory in this way: 'In every period, indeed, of every society, the surplus part both of the rude and manufactured produce, or that for which there is no demand at home, must be sent abroad in order to be exchanged for something for which there is some demand at home' (WN III.i.7). Furthermore, the productivity theory has a difficulty as a complete theory since, as pointed out by Bloomfield (1975: 469), Smith did not insist on the converse proposition that increasing returns are a cause of trade, independent of the existence of a domestic surplus before trade.

A better interpretation would be to regard the productivity theory and the vent for surplus theory as two parts of Smith's single disequilibrium theory of international trade, rather than as separate independent theories.[5] Consider two countries very similar with respect to size, factor endowments, technology and demand patterns. The natural price of commodities would be similar in the two countries and there would be no international trade between them, given the existence of transportation costs. Even if it is assumed that industries are subject to increasing returns to scale, the equilibrium theory could not explain international trade between two such countries. No one can tell which of the two identical countries can enjoy the fruits of increasing returns through international trade. Even in advanced countries with well-developed and highly competitive markets, nay particularly in such countries, however, there often arises a disequilibrium, say, excess supply, in some domestic market. This is Smith's starting point of a surplus of some kinds of produce. The market price then falls below the natural price. In Smith's equilibrium theory of natural price, the supply will be decreased through the shift of factors of production out of such an industry. At the same time, the surplus of such a commodity beyond domestic demand can also be exported. But there is also the 'productivity' aspect of Smith's theory of international trade. When equilibrium is recovered, the natural price can be lower than before if there has been an improvement in the division of labour.[6] The final equilibrium outcome thus depends on what happens to productivity during the disequilibrium process of adjustment, since the equilibrium price achieved will be determined by changes in productivity introduced during the disequilibrium process of adjustment. The vent for surplus theory is, therefore, together with the productivity theory, an indispensable part of Smith's disequilibrium (or path-dependence) theory of international trade.[7] But how might productivity be improved during the disequilibrium process of adjustment? This question is considered in the following section.

IV The division of labour and the extent of the market

One of the best-known propositions in the WN is that the division of labour depends on the extent of the market, so that if the size of the market increases, the general level of productivity rises and costs fall. As seen in Section III, this gives the foundation to 'the productivity theory' of Smith's theory of international trade. Smith gave two different kinds of division of labour: one is concerned with the intra-firm subdivision of different operations to produce a given product, the extent of which is limited by the demand for output of a firm or a plant, and the other is concerned with an inter-firm division of labour or the specialization of firms in the same industry, the extent of which is limited by the demand for the industry as a whole.

If an increase in the demand for the industry not only induces the entry of new firms, but also expands the scale of production of each firm, then equilibrium theory shows that this causes changes in the intra-firm division of labour and the price of the product is reduced.[8] This is because 'the owner of the stock…necessarily endeavours, for his own advantage, to make such a proper division and distribution of employment, that they [the labourers] may be enabled to produce the greatest quantity of work possible…in a particular workhouse' (WN I.viii.57). Smith argued, however, that 'what takes place among the labourers in a particular workhouse, takes place, for the same reason, among those of a great society. The greater their number, the more they naturally divide themselves into different classes and subdivisions of employment'. If this implies the inter-firm division of labour in the same industry, it is difficult to explain it by the ordinary equilibrium theory. The reason is that there exists no one who endeavours to make such a proper division of labour among firms 'that they may be enabled to produce the greatest quantity of work possible' for the industry as a whole. In this case, the final equilibrium division of labour is not independent of divisions of labour made in disequilibrium situations of the adjustment process. Furthermore, as was studied in Negishi (2000), it is by no means clear how and why we can have increasing returns to scale from such divisions of labour.[9]

Most modern interpreters of Adam Smith refer to the following passage from the WN as a summary statement of Smith's theory that the division of labour is limited by the extent of the market (e.g. Hollander 1973: 212; Sylos-Labini 1976: 205–6; Richardson 1975: 353–4).

> The increase of demand, besides, though in the beginning it may sometimes raise the price of goods, never fails to lower it in the long run. It encourages production, and thereby increases the competition of the producers, who, in order to undersell one another, have recourse to new divisions of labour and new improvements of art, which might never otherwise have been thought of.
>
> (WN V.i.e.26: 748)

It is somewhat curious that this passage is not from Book I, chapter 3, of the WN, entitled 'That the division of labour is limited by the extent of the market', but from Book V, chapter 1, entitled 'Of the expences of the sovereign or commonwealth' where a problem of the East India Company is discussed.[10] It is very clear, however, that here what advances the division of labour directly, and hence pushes down prices, is not the increase of demand itself, but the resulting excess supply[11] through the increased competition which forces the suppliers to undersell each other. In this sense, it is not the increase of demand but the excess supply that can more directly advance the division of labour. If the enlarged size of a market, where the number of firms is larger, can reduce the equilibrium natural price, this is because the larger market is more competitive and is more likely to give rise to excess supply than a smaller market.[12] Since the final equilibrium outcome in Smith's analysis depends on what happens in disequilibrium when there is excess supply, Smith's analysis is a typical disequilibrium theory.

Why are larger markets more unstable[13] in that they are more likely to give rise to excess supply? In so far as the increase of demand induces the entry of new firms, the larger markets are more competitive in the sense that the number of firms is greater there.[14] So the question is, why is a greater number of firms in the market more likely to lead to excess supply? Perhaps, the modern theory of competition can answer the question as follows. Suppose for a moment that the cost of production is reduced. The equilibrium in an oligopoly market where the number of firms is small is likely to remain unchanged. This is because each firm does not increase its supply, taking seriously into consideration the reaction of other firms (see, e.g. Sweezy 1939). In a monopolistically competitive market where the number of firms is very large, however, the equilibrium is unstable in the sense that excess supply is very likely to appear, since each firm perceives its own demand curve (*dd*) as more elastic than the true demand curve (*DD*) and so expands its supply excessively for the given cost reduction.[15] Thus the larger the number of firms, the more likely it is that individual firms overestimate the elasticity of their own demand curve and so overestimate the returns from expanding production, whatever the original stimulus to do this. If all firms do this, however, there is excess supply and firms are then forced to find ways of cost-cutting in order to survive.

Although Smith was not referred to explicitly, it was Charles Babbage who developed the disequilibrium theory further and argued that 'one of the natural and almost inevitable consequence of competition is the production of a supply much larger than the demand requires' (Babbage 1835: 231) and that,

> The effect of gluts in producing improvement in machinery, or in methods of working…by the diminution of profit which the manufacturer suffers from the diminished price, his ingenuity will be additionally stimulated; that he will apply himself to discover other and cheaper sources for the supply of his raw materials…that he will endeavour to contrive improved machinery which shall manufacture it at a cheaper rate…or try to introduce new arrangements into his factory, which shall render the economy of it more perfect.
>
> (Babbage 1835: 233; see also Karayiannis 1998)

V Summary and conclusion

We have argued that Smith's theory of international trade may be reconstructed using both the vent for surplus theory and the productivity theory. The former is clearly a disequilibrium theory which explains the cause of international trade in excess supply, while the latter explains the effects of trade on an economy in the productivity gains arising from the divisions of labour which are made possible only in the large international markets. Why, then, is the division of labour limited by the extent of the market?

Referring to the argument of Smith in the WN (Book V, chapter 1), it is suggested that 'new divisions of labour' are introduced by producers who, facing excess supply in the market, must 'undersell one another'. It can be argued that larger markets with many competitors (e.g. monopolistically competitive markets with free entry) are more likely to produce such excess supplies than the small markets with a few competitors (e.g. oligopolistic markets).

If firms facing excess supplies in the market try to introduce 'new divisions of labour' in order to 'undersell one another', then we may shed new light on the relation between the two aspects of Smith's theory of international trade. It is the surplus theory (the existence of excess supply) which necessarily leads to the productivity theory ('increase in the real revenue and wealth of the society'). In other words, it is the existence of the initial surplus as such in a country, not the international trade induced, which leads it to 'improve its productive powers'.

Thus, the crux of Smith's disequilibrium economics is the market excess supply which causes individual producers to introduce 'new divisions of labour' so as to survive in the competition to 'undersell one another'.

Acknowledgements

For comments or other forms of help, the author is grateful to the Editor, referees and Professor Hiroji Nakamura. The usual caveat applies.

Notes

1 For Smith's theory of economic growth, see Kurz and Salvadori (2003), which emphasizes the classical traditions in the recent equilibrium theories of endogenous growth in the current mainstream economics.
2 See for such approaches, Arrow (2000) and Lavezzi (2003).
3 The natural rate of each component part of the price of a commodity, that is, the equilibrium price of a factor of production, is also determined by its demand and supply. See Negishi (1993).
4 Myint (1977) admitted that the vent for surplus theory cannot be applied to the highly advanced 'commercial nations' such as Holland and Hamburg even in eighteenth-century Europe. See Elmslie (1998) for a recent survey on vent for surplus.
5 Haberler (1959: 9) seems to suggest that the vent for surplus is part and parcel of the productivity theory.
6 One might ask whether the final equilibrium price can be higher if final exports were less than initial excess supply. Such seems unlikely, however, since increasing returns in Smith's theory is due to the division of labour which, once made, might not be lost.
7 An example of vent for surplus export in a developed country is the tendency of exports to increase in recessions, which has been observed in Japan since the end of the 1950s and called the export-drive effect of a recession. See Komiya (1990: 357).
8 On the comparative static analysis of a maximizing equilibrium, see Negishi (2000).

9 To explain rather than to assume increasing returns is very difficult, even for the case of equilibrium economics, in view of Robinson's (1933: 219) criticism against Pigou (1932: 338).

10 Smith criticized the East India Company which insisted that the increase of demand in the Indian market raised the price of Indian goods.

11 Even if the market is not perfectly competitive, excess supply will appear, since firms perceive subjective demand curves, like Chamberlin's *dd* curves, which are more elastic than the true objective ones. See note 15.

12 Vassilakis (1987) stated that Adam Smith, among others, formulated the proposition that the division of labour is limited by the stability of the market in the sense that a reduction in demand uncertainty is equivalent to an increase in market size and reduction in uncertainty will increase the degree of division of labour. We cannot agree with this statement in this otherwise highly instructive survey, since it is the demand uncertainty and the instability of the large competitive market which will increase the degree of division of labour.

13 The use of the term 'unstable' is not in the Walrasian sense. It is in the sense of Vassilakis (1987). See note 12.

14 'For Adam Smith, as well as for other classical economists, competition is characterized by free entry' (Sylos-Labini 1976: 200).

15 The firm's *dd* curve is perceived under the supposition that other firms' supply remains unchanged (Chamberlin 1948: 90–4). Roughly speaking, a demand curve is more elastic if the percentage increase in quantity demanded is larger for a given percentage reduction in price.

Bibliography

Arrow, K.J. (2000) 'Increasing returns: historiographic issues and path dependence', *European Journal of the History of Economic Thought*, 7: 171–80.

Babbage, C. (1832, 1835) *On the Economy of Machinery and Manufactures*, London: Charles Knight.

Bloomfield, A.I. (1975) 'Adam Smith's theory of international trade', in *Essays on Adam Smith* A.S. Skinner and T.Wilson (eds), Oxford: Oxford University Press.

Chamberlin, E.H. (1948) *The Theory of Monopolistic Competition*, Cambridge, MA: Harvard University Press.

Elmslie, B.T. (1998) 'Vent for surplus', in *The Elgar Companion to Classical Economics*, H.D. Kurz and N. Salvadori (eds) *L–Z*, Cheltenham: Edward Elgar.

Haberler, G. (1959) *International Trade and Economic Development*, Cairo: National Bank of Egypt.

Hollander, S. (1973) *The Economics of Adam Smith*, Toronto: University of Toronto Press.

Karayiannis, A.D. (1998) 'Supply-push and demand-pull factors of technological progress in the early decades of the 19th century (1800–1840)', *History of Economic Ideas*, 6: 45–68.

Komiya, R. (1990) *The Japanese Economy: Trade, Industry and Government*, Tokyo: University of Tokyo Press.

Kurz, H.D. and N. Salvadori (2003) 'Theories of economic growth: old and new', in *The Theory of Economic Growth, Classical Perspective*, H.D. Kurz and N. Salvadori (eds), Gloucester: Edward Elgar.

Lavezzi, A. (2003) 'Smith, Marshall and Young on division of labour and economic growth', *European Journal of the History of Economic Thought*, 10: 81–108.

Mill, J.S. (1909) [1848] *Principles of Political Economy*, London: Longmans, Green & Co.

Myint, H. (1958) 'The "classical theory" of international trade and the underdeveloped countries', *Economic Journal*, 68: 317–37.

—— (1977) 'Adam Smith's theory of international trade in the perspective of economic development', *Economica*, 44: 231–48.

Negishi, T. (1986) 'Thornton's criticism of equilibrium theory and Mill', *History of Political Economy*, 18: 567–77.

—— (1989) *History of Economic Theory*, Amsterdam: North-Holland.

—— (1993) 'A Smithian growth model and Malthus' optimum propensity to save', *European Journal of the History of Economic Thought*, 1: 115–27.

—— (2000) 'Adam Smith's division of labour and structural changes', *Structural Change and Economic Dynamics*, 11: 5–11.

Pigou, A.C. (1932) *The Economics of Welfare*, London: Macmillan.

Ricardo, D. (1951) [1817] *On the Principles of Political Economy and Taxation*, P. Sraffa, (ed.) Cambridge: Cambridge University Press.

Richardson, G.B. (1975) 'Adam Smith on competition and increasing returns', in *Essays on Adam Smith*, A.S. Skinner and T. Wilson (eds) London: Oxford University Press.

Robinson, J. (1933) *Economics of Imperfect Competition*, London: Macmillan.

Schumpeter, J.A. (1954) *History of Economic Analysis*, New York: Oxford University Press.

Smith, A. (1976) [1776] *An Inquiry into the Nature and Causes of the Wealth of Nations*, R.H. Campbell and A.S. Skinner, (eds) Oxford: Oxford University Press.

Sweezy, P.M. (1939) 'Demand under conditions of oligopoly', *Journal of Political Economy*, 47: 568–73.

Sylos-Labini, P. (1976) 'Competition: the product markets', in *The Market and the State*, T. Wilson and A.S. Skinner, (eds) Oxford: Oxford University Press.

Vassilakis, S. (1987) 'Increasing returns to scale', in *The New Palgrave*, 2, J. Eatwell, M. Milgate and P. Newman (eds), London: Macmillan.

Walras, L. (1954) *Elements of Pure Economics*, W. Jaffé (trans.), Homewood: Irwin.

'Great works upon the anvil' in 1785

Adam Smith's projected corpus of philosophy*

Ian Simpson Ross

Smith had a succinct theory of philosophy, which underpinned the two great works he left us, and two which he had in progress in 1785, but which he did not live to complete. His theory held that philosophy is rational inquiry, prompted originally by the sentiment of wonder (Smith 1980, *Essays on Philosophical Subjects* (EPS), 'Astronomy' III.3), then expressed through the 'systematical arrangement of different observations connected by a few common principles', and giving rise to aesthetic pleasure in contemplation of that arrangement (Smith 1976b, *Wealth of Nations* (WN) V.i.f.25). He believed it fell naturally into three great branches, and was so developed originally by the ancient Greek Stoics: Zeno of Citium (334–262) and Chrysippus (c. 280–206). The first was logic or the 'science of the principles of good and bad reasoning' (WN V.i.f.26), arising from metaphysics, which 'considered the general nature of Universals' (Smith 1980 EPS, 'Ancient Logics and Metaphysics' 1). The second branch was physics or natural philosophy, designated in general terms in the 'History of Astronomy' as the 'science of the connecting principles of nature' ('Astronomy' II.12), and thereafter more sceptically as 'that science which pretends to lay open the concealed connections that unite the various appearances of nature' (III.3). Making an important methodological point in the same text about the development of natural philosophy, Smith stated it was 'one of those arts which address themselves to the imagination' (II.12). 'By far the most important of all the branches of philosophy', if properly conducted, so Smith argued, was the third one, moral philosophy. 'Wherein consisted the happiness and perfection of a man, considered not only as an individual, but as the member of a family, of a state, and of the great society of mankind', was the object of its investigations (WN V.i.f.30).

Going along with the development of these three branches of philosophy itself, in the ancient classical period of the ascendancy of the Greeks and Romans, came the emergence from polytheism of a monotheism characterized as that 'pure and rational religion, free from every mixture of absurdity, imposture, or fanaticism, such as wise men in all ages wished to see established' (WN V.i.g.8). This religion was cultivated best by the Stoics (Smith 1980 EPS, 'Ancient Physics' 11).

The Adam Smith Review, 1: 40–59 © 2004 The International Adam Smith Society, ISSN 1743–5285, ISBN 0–415–27863–5

Smith's history of philosophy, as far as Western Europe is concerned, relates that in the times of Christian ascendancy, it was made subservient to theology, and divided into five branches taught in the universities:

1 logic of the schools' (scholastic Aristotelian logic);
2 'ontology' – a 'cobweb science' treating of qualities and attributes common to physics (bodies) and pneumatics (spirits), sometimes called 'metaphysics';
3 'pneumatology' – teaching comprehending the nature of the human soul and the deity;
4 moral philosophy debased into casuistry;
5 physics 'rendered short and superficial'.

But 'improvements' were introduced in 'modern times' in several of these branches, mostly outside of academia, but then taught with success in 'some of the poorer universities'. Smith has in mind those in Protestant Switzerland and Germany, the Netherlands, Sweden and Denmark, and Scotland, where there was competition between teachers who had to earn a living by keeping their instruction up to date (WN V.i.f.27–34, g.39).

Smith saw himself as fitting into this development, and contributing to it. His concept of a 'system' of philosophy, if we may call it that at this stage, consisted of three branches:

1 a *new rhetoric* of his own invention, in which he replaced the 'logic and metaphysics of the schools' by explaining and illustrating the powers of the mind, as revealed in our procedures of communication and composition;
2 a *new science* built on the doctrines of the intellectual revolution culminating in the work of Newton, though with sceptical reservations about its achievement, leaving open the way for further revolutions;
3 a *new moral philosophy*, comprehending ethics, jurisprudence and politics (including political economy), making advances from Greek thought in the area of moral, political and economic motivation, and drawing on the contributions of Grotius, Hobbes, Pufendorf, the Cambridge Platonists, Locke, Shaftesbury, Mandeville, Hutcheson, Butler, Hume and Rousseau, to all of whom Smith as a thinker responded and sought to complement if not replace.

Andrew Skinner (1996) is pre-eminent among recent commentators on Smith in accounting for Smith's systematic investigation of social science, and placing political economy within this field.

Enter now Charles Griswold, whose bold and original work, *Adam Smith and the Virtues of the Enlightenment* (1999), aims at giving Smith his due as an all-round moral philosopher in these latter days, when only his political economy seems to receive attention. Moreover, this is bestowed on a misunderstood version:

> [Smith] is seen solely as an economist, to the exclusion of his work in ethics, moral philosophy, jurisprudence, rhetoric, and belles letters, as well as political,

> economic, and intellectual history. Even worse, he is seen as an economist of a particular ideological bent. In short, he tends now to be known as an advocate of a crude laissez-faire capitalism and, to add insult to injury, of a capitalism inseparable from imperialism and colonialism.
>
> (Griswold 1999: 9)

In the run up to the publication of this book, Griswold corresponded with this writer about the part of his book (Griswold 1999: 29–39, 256–8) devoted to the highly controversial subject of Smith completing a 'system' of philosophy, apparently contemplated at the outset of his publishing career. Focusing on what Smith recorded about his plans, Griswold notes it was to be a corpus of writings intended to range beyond *The Theory of Moral Sentiments* (1976a [1759] TMS) and WN (1976b [1776] WN). It would fulfill a promise that Smith first made at the conclusion of TMS in 1759, that he would provide a 'system of natural jurisprudence' as part of an 'account of the general principles of law and government, and of the different revolutions which they had undergone in the different ages and periods of society; not only in what concerns justice, but in what concerns police, revenue and arms, and whatever else is the object of law' (TMS VII.iv.37).

When he reiterated this promise in the Advertisement to the sixth edition of TMS [1790], Smith stated that he had 'partly' fulfilled his promise in WN, 'at least so far as concerns police, revenue, and arms', but the 'long projected theory of jurisprudence' remained to be completed. He acknowledged that his 'very advanced age' – he was sixty-six – left him with 'little expectation' of being able to complete this work 'to his own satisfaction', yet as he had not altogether given up the design, he still wished to continue under the obligation of doing what he could, and he left the concluding paragraph of TMS to stand as he wrote it in 1759, when he 'entertained no doubt of being able to execute every thing which it announced' (TMS Advertisement 2).

Moreover, the corpus would include the connecting, supplementing and integrating of the pieces included in the posthumous volume, EPS [1795]. Smith's literary executors who edited EPS – the medical scientist Joseph Black, discoverer of the principle of latent heat, and James Hutton, proponent of the uniformitarian theory of the earth which underpins modern geology – described Smith's project in this second instance as aiming at providing a 'connected history of the liberal sciences and elegant arts' (Smith 1980, EPS 32).

The questions Griswold put to me concerned biographical and bibliographical facts about Smith and his writings, also about what Smith meant by 'philosophy' and the divisions into which 'philosophy' falls, and has fallen, historically speaking. Basically, I responded by sketching out the 'system' ascribed to Smith at the beginning of this essay. When I read Griswold's book fairly soon after its publication, I was much intrigued by the evidence and arguments he offered for concluding that the project of Smith's corpus was 'incompletable in principle' (Griswold 1999: 30).

In response, I will review here facts about Smith's life and writings available to Griswold and myself, though not all of them adduced in his book, and perhaps bring them into a perspective that he does not share. My intention is to argue that Smith's holistic project was realizable, that in fact he and others close to him left us with a great deal of evidence about his procedures and intentions, and that it merits urgent re-examination.

My reasoning is that Smith's advocacy of a free-market philosophy and economic growth through high wages and nation to nation trade has won global support. Neglect of his moral teaching, however, chiefly his contention that the 'establishment of perfect justice, of perfect liberty, and of perfect equality is the very simple secret which most effectively secures the highest degree of prosperity' for all contributors to the economy (WN IV.ix.17), has left modern commercial society seriously compromised. To be sure, on one side, he has been severely criticized for his culpability in severing the relationship between morals and economics (Lux 1990), though this allegation does not stand up to careful examination (Ross 1995: 418–20). On the other side, there has been a recent attempt to give a triumphalist account of Smith's 'narrowing of political economy' in WN, with the writer seemingly content to acknowledge that in the aftermath religion and politics wither before economics (Minowitz 1993).

Nevertheless, in the face of the systemic problems threatening to overwhelm national societies from within, also the danger of attacks from international terrorists committed to destroy our societies from outside, we desperately need a theory of natural jurisprudence to bind together profit and justice in our continuing era of commerce, and we need a philosophical history to remind us, as a constellation of civil societies, where we came from and what we are. Smith's projected works can be seen addressing these needs, at least in part. We also need this kind of project to bring home to us that success with a market economy is not an inevitable outcome of global recruitment of rational economic actors, but is related to a range of political, moral, and perhaps religious commitments of those who engage in it (Dutt and Jameson 2001), though not necessarily commitment to the nationalism which Liah Greenfeld (2002) has recently argued is the dominant factor (Gray 2002).

Further, we need to see where the emotional, creative and imaginative, also spiritual components of our nature, all fit together, to make us the kind of creatures we are as human beings, sharing the earth with basic cell, microbe, insect, plant and animal life, and responsible for actions and reactions affecting our own and other species, as well as the water, soil, rocks, minerals and atmosphere that together make up our fragile planet. Perhaps our responsibilities in these directions are best summed up in the natural law tradition of the preservation and conservation of our species and our habitat (Stankiewicz 1997). Of course, I am not suggesting that all answers to the problems of the human predicament are to be found in the writings or proposed writings of Adam Smith, as Indian wise men are reputed to argue that answers to the most abstruse questions of modern physics lie hidden in the Vedas. My submission is that Smith's ideas, amply and critically considered, about human nature at the individual and social levels, as our race has evolved into the commercial stage, are sufficiently suggestive and far-seeing, also disturbing, to be worthy of careful examination and evaluation, through offering some guidance to the choices that face us, particularly the economic ones, if humanity and our fragile planet are to survive in any form that we can recognize into further centuries.

Griswold argues that Smith could not have completed the plan he had projected for works ancillary to TMS and WN, that would have given us a philosophical history of jurisprudence attached to an emotion-based theory of the subject, as well as a comprehensive philosophy and history of humanity's expressive forms and scientific disciplines. As a starting point, Griswold features two papers of the 1980s that offer what I will call sceptical views of Smith's project (1999: 30–1, n. 48).

The first is by Donald Winch, a subtle historian of economic thought, recently retired from the University of Sussex, long noted for his perceptive and balanced investigation of Smith's ideas, particularly those found in WN (Winch 1994, 1996, 2000), but also in TMS and the other published writings, as well as those adumbrated in the 'vaster dream' which Walter Bagehot ascribed to the Scottish philosopher's 'comprehensive and diffused ambition' (1968, vol. iii: 86, 'Adam Smith as a Person'). Addressing part of the 'vaster dream', namely, the 'account of the general principles of law and government', Griswold endorses a candid admission by Winch:

> although we now have two sets of students' notes on the lectures on jurisprudence, there is a great deal of disagreement about the nature of the missing element and whether Smith simply failed to complete it or found himself incapable of doing so for reasons that have nothing to do with the Grim Reaper.
>
> (Winch 1983: 255)

Winch's scepticism here is more apparent than real, however, as he had already surveyed cogently how we might view Smith's 'missing politics' (Winch 1978: ch. 8).

Moreover, Winch also acknowledged, within a sentence of his Grim Reaper allusion, that Smith's jurisprudence lectures had not been fully explored to yield an understanding of his views on the science of jurisprudence, and on the science of politics – the 'science of a statesman or legislator' of which the political economy of WN is 'merely a branch' (Winch 1985: 255). To be sure, the distinguished philosopher and historian of ideas, Knud Haakonssen, has provided us with remarkably convincing accounts of Smith's jurisprudence and politics, as well as those of Smith's good friend and intellectual ally, David Hume, in *The Science of a Legislator* (1981; see also 1982).

The second paper is by the Italian moral philosopher Sergio Cremaschi, who since 1981 has published a series of highly stimulating criticisms of classical economists in relation to epistemological and ethical issues, addressing frequently the work of Adam Smith, but also other Scottish Enlighteners as he charmingly calls them. Griswold is particularly impressed by Cremaschi's argument (1989) that there is a deep *aporia* in Smith's epistemology and politics, that is, an instance of cognitive perplexity arising from assent to propositions plausible in the singular but mutually contradictory. According to Cremaschi, this stalemate made it impossible for Smith to complete the works he projected in these fields, leaving him with no choice but to deal satisfactorily only with the decentralized social order of the market. In confronting epistemology, so this critic puts the matter, Smith finds himself checked by the contrary pulls of an 'essentialist ideal of knowledge' and a 'pragmatic approach' to the history of science. In Smith's politics, so Cremaschi reasons, there is an attempt to find a basis in natural law, which is conceptualized, however, as 'non-absolute and changeable'. Griswold would probably be the first to admit that Cremaschi's thinking has moved on from his 1989 standpoint about Smith's *aporia*, in particular through absorbing Haakonssen's recent work on natural law traditions (Haakonssen 1996). This has led Cremaschi to fresh conclusions about the contemporary debate over the place of ethics within economics (Cremaschi 2000). I also think it can be claimed that Cremaschi's work challenges us to consider the place of economics within the field of morals: the science of ends and ethical means for obtaining them.

Griswold presents his own discussion of Smith's *aporia* at the end of Chapter 6 devoted to Justice (Griswold 1999: 256–8). Stimulated, apparently, by recent discussions with Haakonssen, who is his colleague in the Philosophy Department at Boston University, Griswold focuses on Smith's promise of 1759, already mentioned, that he would publish a 'system' of natural jurisprudence, comprehending an 'account of the general principles of law and government, and of the different revolutions they have undergone in the different ages and periods of society' (TMS VII.iv.37). Griswold takes these 'principles' to be the same as the 'general principles which are always the same', which ought to govern the deliberations of a legislator and are part of his science, as opposed to the 'skill of that insidious and crafty animal, vulgarly called a statesman or politician, whose councils are directed by the momentary fluctuations of affairs' (WN IV.ii.39). It seems that Griswold is puzzled by this formulation of 'principles' that are always the same, and yet undergo revolutions, thus of Smith's apparent resort to history for the elucidation of changeless 'normative principles'. He writes: 'how can history yield normative principles that are always the same?' In the same vein, he asks how could Smith 'illustrate' the 'principles which lead and direct philosophical enquiries' (a phrase from the title of the piece in EPS devoted to the 'History of Astronomy'), unless these principles were already known to him. Griswold's chief argument, of course, is that the first principles Smith alludes to must necessarily be ahistorical, so herein lies the ultimate check to his vast philosophic dream of a system of systems, because what can bridge the temporal and contingent world of history in which laws and governments change radically, and that ideal world of unchanging principles of justice?

At this point, we have to ask if Griswold's Platonic formulations are not leading him astray in contemplating Smith's enterprise? Should we not look more closely at what our Scottish Enlightener said he wanted to do, and what he achieved in the form of theory and philosophic history that point to what he planned? As well, should we not look over Smith's shoulder at the 'early modern natural jurists', Grotius, Pufendorf and Locke (Carmichael 2002: ix), whose tenets were the staple of his philosophic education, besides those of his contemporaries, Francis Hutcheson and, especially, David Hume, rather than Plato, to identify his philosophic commitments, practice, and teaching? Precisely here are to be found the considerations about natural law relevant to our day of awesome knowledge of, and power over, nature, as well as urgency of ethical choice over what we know and what we can do as individuals and societies to humanity, also to the environment of the planet we all share, dare we say to the universe of which we are seemingly so rebellious, inventive, appetitive and willful inhabitants? In this connexion, we can reflect on a challenging point made by Istvan Hont and Michael Ignatieff in their wide-ranging examination of the issue of 'needs and justice' in WN:

> [WN] was centrally concerned with the issue of justice, with finding a market mechanism capable of reconciling inequality of property with adequate provision for those excluded. Smith was simply transposing into the language of markets an ancient jurisprudential discourse, carried into modernity by Grotius, Pufendorf, and Locke, about how to ensure that private individuation of God's domain would not deny the propertyless the means of satisfying their needs... Smith's arguments were designed to show how an economy of abundance could be created in which this ancient jurisprudential antinomy between the needs of the poor and the rights of the rich could be transcended altogether.
>
> (Hont and Ignatieff 1983: 2)

In addition, we might consider how Smith's concept of combining theory and philosophical history has struck others and fertilized their thought. For example, there is Darwin's theory of natural selection coupled with his natural history of species. Griswold mentions Darwin among the 'admirers' of Smith (1999: 8, n.15), but, much more than an 'admirer', Darwin was a close student of Smith's thought as he found it presented in the *Principles of Political Economy* (2nd edn, 1830), by the post-Ricardian, classical economist, J.R. McCulloch (Schweber 1980: 268). Darwin recorded reading in May 1840 two central passages based on WN in McCulloch's textbook:

> Every individual is constantly exerting himself to find out the most advantageous methods of employing his capital and labour. It is true, that it is in his own advantage, and not that of society, which he has in view; but a society being nothing more than a collection of individuals, it is plain that each, in steadily pursuing his own aggrandizement, is following that precise line of conduct which is most for the public advantage.
>
> (McCulloch 1830: 149; cf. WN IV.ii.9)

> The true line of policy is to leave individuals to pursue their own interests in their own way, and never to lose sight of the maxim *pas trop gouverner*. It is by the spontaneous and unconstrained... effort of individuals to improve their conditions... and by them only, that nations become rich and powerful.
>
> (McCulloch 1830: 537; cf. WN II.ii.31, IV.ix.51)

In his capstone work, *The Structure of Evolutionary Theory*, the Harvard paleontologist and biologist, Stephen Jay Gould, argued that Darwin transferred Smith's principles applicable to the transactions of the marketplace to the biological universe, with its scene of 'natural selection', where individual organisms engage in the 'struggle for existence', a phrase Darwin borrowed from Malthus (Gould 2002: 122–3). Gould had a true insight about the appeal for Darwin of the structure of Smith's version of the economic theory of spontaneous order and the law of unintended outcomes (Barry 1982/2002; Hamowy 1987), as well, indeed, of Smith's theorizing in general. Moreover, Gould himself adopts Smith's methodological approach, coupling theory-building, consisting of the articulation of first principles or 'laws', which Gould denominates 'key postulates and assumptions' or 'essences', with accounts of the unfolding of the operation of these elements in 'histories' (Gould 2002: 6–12).

From Darwin's appropriation of Smith's economic theory for understanding evolution in nature through natural selection, as Gould presents it, I turn back now to Dugald Stewart, Smith's younger friend and first biographer, who tells us that the 'study of human nature in all its branches, more particularly of the political history of mankind', endlessly excited Smith's 'curiosity and ambition', provided scope for his 'genius', and satisfied his 'ruling passion', which was to contribute to the 'happiness and improvement of society' (Stewart 1980, 'Account' I.8). Here is the key to the vaulting ambition behind Smith's philosophy project.

Studying at Glasgow University in the late 1730s, Smith was obviously given a solid grounding in the mathematics and physics of Isaac Newton's scientific system, expounded in the *Principia Mathematica* (1962, revsd. Cajori [1st edn. 1686, 3rd 1726, trans. Motte 1729]). Its unique success in explaining physical phenomena gave tremendous confidence to the age for the building of systems of many kinds. In addition, the teaching of Hutcheson at Glasgow seems to have aroused Smith's interest in developing a moral philosophy embodying an analysis and synthesis of transactive human nature, comparable to the physical world system of Newton. While Hutcheson failed to produce a satisfactory 'system of moral philosophy' along this line, a greater philosopher, namely, Hume, was very likely inspired by Newton's injunction to enlarge the bounds of moral philosophy through adopting the scientific method he endorsed (*Opticks* 1952 [4th edn. 1730]: 405), and may have published his *Treatise of Human Nature* (2000 [1739–40]) in response to Newton's challenge, just as Smith was ending his stay at Glasgow.

According to J.R. McCulloch, in a biographical sketch (2000 [1838/1853]: iii.9) supplementing Dugald Stewart's 'Account of the Life and Writings of Adam Smith' (Stewart 1980 [1794]), Smith surreptitiously read Hume's *Treatise* when a student at Oxford in the early 1740s. Its subtitle revealed it was an 'attempt to introduce the experimental method of reasoning into moral subjects'. To be sure, Paul Russell has pointed out that Hume's 'experimental method' applied to 'moral subjects' is also that of Hobbes in his work, *The Elements of Law*, composed in 1640 and published ten years later (Russell 1985). Perhaps, then, owing something to Hobbes as well as Newton, the Advertisement and Introduction to Books I and II of the *Treatise* indicated they dealt with the understanding (epistemology) and passions (moral psychology), also that other parts would follow, assigned to morals (Book III), politics (including history and political economy) and criticism (aesthetics). The whole formed a comprehensive 'science of man', which its author may well have hoped would demonstrate a 'system' of the moral world equivalent to that framed so successfully by Newton as the 'system of the [natural] world' in the *Principia Mathematica*, Book III. The Balliol dons who detected Smith reading Hume's *Treatise* probably confiscated it as a dangerously sceptical work, but the young scholar seems to have read far enough into it on this, or a subsequent occasion, to be inspired to construct his own 'science of man' adopting the procedure adopted by Hume, or so he believed, of accounting for moral as for natural things through observation and experiment.

Completing his scholarly apprenticeship by self-directed study at home in Kirkcaldy from 1746 to 1748, very likely disappointed that he had not been chosen to be Hutcheson's successor as professor of moral philosophy at Glasgow, Smith was invited to give freelance courses of lectures to postgraduate students in Edinburgh. In the event, he devoted the three seminal years of 1748–51 to delivering 'systems' of rhetoric, philosophic and scientific discovery, and civil law or jurisprudence, involving attention to theory and history in each of these fields (Ross 1995: chapters 6, 7). In the Rhetoric Lectures, Smith states summarily that Hobbes had undertaken, like Shaftesbury, to 'overturn the Old Systems of Religion and Philosophy', but unlike Shaftesbury he had not attempted to 'erect a new one' (Smith 1983, LRBL i.142–8). Accordingly, it can be argued that Newton was Smith's inspiration as a system-builder, and his Edinburgh lecturing years saw him begin the vast project of what has been called 'moral Newtonianism', discussed later, that would yield a comprehensive 'science of man', to which we may believe Hume's *Treatise* had pointed the way for him.

The evidence for what Smith taught in his Edinburgh *Lectures on Rhetoric and Belles Lettres* course lies in the student report of lectures he subsequently gave at Glasgow in 1762–3, but which there is reason to believe he did not substantially change from the earlier Edinburgh version (Smith 1983, LRBL). One central part of the course is a theory of communication expressed through distinguishing between major types of discourse: descriptive and narrative in history; poetical; and didactic or scientific. Smith's emphasis is not on command of figures of speech, the stock in trade of the old rhetorics, but on awareness by the speaker (or writer) of the *sentiment* he feels and wishes to communicate by *sympathy* (my italics) to his audience (LRBL i.v.56). Sympathy is given a key role in the moral psychology Hume developed in the *Treatise*: 'no quality of human nature is more remarkable, both in itself and in its consequences, than that propensity we have to sympathize with others, and to receive by communication their inclinations and sentiments, however different from, or even contrary to our own' (Hume 2000: 206). It is a shrewd move by Smith to bring this emotive mechanism into an account of rhetoric, doubtless a step towards the transactive moral sentiments theory he was to develop in due course as a teacher of ethics, and then publish as TMS.

Smith's work on rhetoric, traditionally the art of persuasion, also connects with a fundamental part of Smith's theory of economics, for at the outset of WN he notes that division of labour is the unintended consequence of the human propensity to 'truck, barter, and exchange one thing for another' (WN I.iii.1,2), which he traced in the *Lectures on Jurisprudence* to 'that principle to persuade which so much prevails in human nature' (Smith 1978, LJB 221, LJA vi.56).

The Rhetoric Lectures are also notable for including Smith's first example of 'philosophical history', in this case deployed to account for the 'origin and progress' of language. Dugald Stewart commented that something similar is to be found in all of Smith's seemingly diverse writings, 'moral, political, or literary', involving a simple but effective procedure: 'in examining the history of mankind, as well as in examining the phenomena of the natural world, when we cannot trace the process by which an event has been produced, it is often of importance to be able to show how it may have been produced by natural causes' ('Account' II.44–8).

Smith argues that features such as word classes, grammatical inflection and parts of speech, emerged gradually and unintentionally over a long period of time, through processes such as comparison, abstraction and 'love of analogy', always limited by the shortcomings of the human memory. Smith offers his own version of socio-linguistics, suggesting that under the pressure to communicate, speakers of different languages that developed from jargons, when they mingled together through migration or invasion, accepted changes that produce simplification. Compound (or as we would say now analytic) languages such as modern English, from which complex inflection systems had been dropped, evolved from original (or synthetic) languages such as Old English. Smith here, as we find elsewhere in his writings, turns to a machine analogy to explain 'progress', suggesting that original languages have the complexity and cumbersomeness of primitive machines, but both become simpler, with fewer and more connected parts, that serve more functions, through slight, practical adaptations in use over time. Theorizing about the deep past of languages, Smith links his account of language typology, which still has relevance today, to revolutions in cognition and society (LRBL i.17–i.v.34). Similar conceptual themes and procedures are to be found in his 'philosophical histories' of science or, at least astronomy and ancient physics, morals, also economics and, pace Griswold, there seems no reason in principle why he could not have extended the series to law and government.

Concerning the building of a 'system', which is another name for theorizing, Smith dealt with this issue in Lecture 24 of the Glasgow series on rhetoric, which we are presuming was close to the Edinburgh series. Focusing on didactic composition, he suggests the aim of this type is to secure assent to a philosophical proposition, or to 'Deliver a System of any Science, for example, Naturall Philosophy' (LRBL iii.130). In the latter connexion, he contrasts the method he associates with Aristotle and the one he calls Newtonian. The first, so Smith says, consists of taking up the various branches of a science in the order in which they happen to present themselves to us, and commonly assigning to every phenomenon a new principle. He finds the Newtonian method undoubtedly the 'most Philosophical,... vastly more ingenious, and for that reason more engaging than the other', for it consists of laying down 'certain principles known or proved in the beginning, from whence we account for the severall Phenomena, connecting all together by the same Chain'. Smith continues, 'it gives us a pleasure to see the phenomena which we reckoned the most unaccountable all deduced from some principle (commonly a well-known one) and all united in one chain' (LRBL ii.133–4).

We have noted how he accounted for the development of language by attributing it to the operation of the well-known principle of abstraction. In the course on the 'history of philosophy', the second of those he taught in Edinburgh, also repeated later at Glasgow, he turned to the 'principles that lead and direct philosophical [or scientific] enquiries: illustrated by the history of astronomy' (EPS 31). Griswold asks, how could Smith 'illustrate' these principles unless he already knew them? (Griswold 1999: 257, n. 34) Smith's procedure seems to have been the one outlined by Hume in the *Treatise*, taking the approach of introspective observation and thought experiments (Hume 2000: 4–5). Smith gives the following account of theorizing in his 'History of Astronomy'. He argues this activity arises from the interplay of our emotions of wonder, surprise and admiration, also the creative role of imagination in bestowing order on the succession of our ideas. We observe in nature, according to Smith, objects of our attention that seem 'solitary and incoherent with all that go before them' ('Astronomy' II.12). Our wonder and surprise at this state of affairs excite the imagination: 'to find out something which may fill up the gap, which like a bridge, may so far at least unite those seemingly distant objects, as to render the passage of thought between them smooth, and natural, and easy' (II.8).

Thus a theory is an 'imaginary machine invented to connect together in the fancy those different movements and effects which are in reality performed' ('Astronomy' IV.19), and it is created to meet a psychological need: the pain of the awareness of incoherence is eased when the imagination can glide by means of a hypothetical system from one object to another. Smith provides the example of Descartes introducing the theory of 'invisible effluvia' communicating motion, to calm the tumult of the imagination faced with the lodestone (magnet) drawing iron after it (II.8). The discussion does not stop here, however, for such hypotheses are open to the criticism of being 'vague' or 'indeterminate', and inquiry into them has to deal with the fact that they become too complicated and fail to restore the mind to tranquility by removing wonder (Ross 2002).

Smith used this approach to examine successive theories of astronomy from that of the Pythagoreans and Eudoxus, the 'friend and auditor' of Plato, asserting the heavens displayed the movement of concentric spheres, down to that of Newton, comprehending a heliocentric universe which observes the laws of celestial mechanics. Resolutely, Smith rejects probability and verifiability, also, we may add, capacity to predict, as criteria of theories, and holds to his psychological and aesthetic viewpoint. To be sure, he has a further requirement, namely, the parsimony of explanatory principles, introduced when he describes the fading of the Ptolemaic theory of astronomy. Though at the last 'insensibly… drawn in' to describe the Newtonian theory as the 'discovery of an immense chain of the most important and sublime truths, all closely connected together, by one capital fact', namely, the action of gravity, which we experience daily, he draws back from this claim, and identifies Newton's theory like the others he has discussed, in the fashion of someone instructed by the sceptical Hume, as 'mere inventions of the imagination' ('Astronomy' IV.76). Smith's claim, therefore, is that theories are to be judged on the basis of their power to soothe the imagination, achieve coherence and enhance our response to the objects they cover. He considers this is the clue that guides us through the 'labyrinths of philosophical history' (II.12).

Smith's third freelance course at Edinburgh was devoted to a 'philosophical history' of civil law or, more broadly, natural jurisprudence, 'that science which enquires into the general principles which ought to be the foundation of the laws of all nations' (LJB 1). The evidence we have suggests it covered the emergence and transformation of the institutions of 'civil society', such as political as well as military leadership, also property, magistracy, and law and government, as humanity passed through four stages of socio-economic organization: hunting and fishing, herding, farming and commerce. The value of economic liberty for assuring the 'progress' of civil society seems to have been a major theme in this course. Smith urged that little more was needed to bring a state from 'barbarism' to 'opulence', but 'peace, easy taxes, and a tolerable administration of justice'. As well, in this Edinburgh course he denounced interventionist governments as 'unnatural' and forced to become 'oppressive and tyrannical' (Stewart, 'Account' IV.25). Thus, Smith foreshadowed here the free-enterprise model of the market economy in WN, also that book's allotment of the role of providing limited public goods to the state, for example, enforcing a justice system, funded from modest revenue collection. Moreover, he also foreshadowed the book which he stated in TMS would cover the 'general principles of law and government', and the 'different revolutions they have undergone in the different ages and periods of society' from the stage of 'barbarism' (hunting and fishing) to that of 'opulence' (commerce and industry).

At this stage, we might well ask what existed in 1751, in writing, of Smith's expression of that 'vaster dream' of a Newton-Hume inspired 'science of man'? Regarding the contents of the Edinburgh course on natural jurisprudence outlined earlier in relation to leading doctrines in WN, Dugald Stewart reports he had access to a paper, quoted from WN, drawn up by Smith in 1755 summarizing these very doctrines. Smith added to this paper an endorsement to the effect that his opinions therein had been the subject of lectures given in Edinburgh in 1750–1, also of lectures he gave in Glasgow when he took over part of the moral philosophy teaching programme in the autumn of 1751 (Stewart, 'Account' IV.25). The professor of that subject, Thomas Craigie, had taken sick leave, and Smith wrote to a colleague on 3 September 1751 that he accepted the suggestion that 'Natural Jurisprudence and Politics are the parts of [Craigie's] lectures, which it would be most agreeable for me to take upon me to teach' (*Corr*. No. 9). We can assume that Smith had lectures on these subjects written out by an amanuensis in Edinburgh available for his new duties.

He came to Glasgow in 1751, of course, as professor of logic, and one of his first students there, John Millar, later professor of civil law at Glasgow

(1761–1801), who also heard Smith's rhetoric lectures in Edinburgh, reported that Smith gave a very brief account of Aristotelian logic to gratify curiosity about an outmoded method of reasoning, and then devoted the rest of his time to the 'delivery of a system of rhetoric and belles letters', as the best possible foundation course for 'explaining and illustrating the powers of the human mind' (Stewart, 'Account' I.16). This suggests that Smith recycled his Edinburgh rhetoric lectures available in written form for his Glasgow logic course.

As for his Edinburgh 'history of philosophy' course, or history of philosophical and scientific enquiry, the pieces in EPS on the 'History of Astronomy', 'History of the Ancient Physics' and the 'History of Ancient Logics and Metaphysics' (Smith 1980), are surely connected with it, and with the 'private' courses Smith taught in Glasgow ancillary to the main moral philosophy series. Thus, Smith had in hand material for theories and philosophical histories both of the 'liberal sciences and elegant arts', and of natural jurisprudence and 'revolutions in law and government'.

Within a year of coming to Glasgow, Smith was elected professor of moral philosophy and assumed responsibility for the full course, which Millar described as made up of four parts (Stewart, 'Account' I.16–20). In the first, 'Natural Theology', Smith traced the argument for God's existence and attributes from design, and is likely to have described the emergence from polytheism of philosophic theism, as discussed earlier. The relevant lectures, in my opinion, would have been a basis for Smith's 'natural history of religion' forming one of the branches of his projected history of philosophy (*Corr*. No. 248). I also believe that Smith's contemplation of the system of the universe was a spiritual experience for him, associated with the 'pure and rational religion' he professed, in a fashion similar to that of his good friend Hume: 'The idea of an Infinite Mind, the Author of the Universe seems at first Sight to require a Worship absolutely pure, simple, unadorned: without Rites, Institutions, Ceremonies; even without Temples, Priest, or verbal Prayer & Supplications' (quoted in Mossner 1980: 307).

In the second part of his course, Smith presented his system of Ethics, which gave rise to TMS. Millar does not mention this, but Smith's history of systems of moral philosophy (TMS VII.ii.1–VII.iii.3.17) must have formed part of the original lectures, as well as the 'theory' of the moral sentiments delineating the origins of the virtues of justice, benevolence, propriety and prudence. The chief component of Smith's own system of morals is the role of sympathy in human transactions, through which we naturally judge the conduct and character of others and then ourselves. One of Smith's students and, later, a reader of TMS, James Wodrow, discerned here an example of 'moral Newtonianism'. He did not use this term, which seems to have been invented by the French intellectual historian, Élie Halévy (1955), but Wodrow did say '[TMS is] is founded on Sympathy, a very ingenious attempt to account for the principal phaenomina in the moral world from this one general principle, like that of Gravity in the natural world' (Ross 1995: xxi, 56–7). Another component of the system is the concept of the impartial spectator we fashion within ourselves, introduced to account for our normative judgments of our own motives and actions, through imagining how others would see and evaluate us. Smith left us some indication of how the impartial spectator might be thought to operate through pressure of a 'sense of justice', in matters within the purview of criminal and civil law, through humbling the 'arrogance of self-love' and toning down the drive for violent revenge for injury (TMS II.ii.2.1–4, 3.6–11; III.4.12; LJA ii.90–93, LJA v.17–19). His 'system' also offered a defence of claims to an acquired right (LJA i.36); prescriptive right to property (LJA i.77); and enforcement of contract (LJA ii.43–5). Vivienne Brown provides both a helpful account of the dialogic nature of the impartial spectator's role in our lives as we struggle to be just, and sharply focused criticisms of this feature in Smith's theory of justice (1994: 74–5, 112–20).

Justice was treated by Smith in the third part of his course, according to Millar, as a 'branch of morality… which, being susceptible of precise and accurate rules, is for that reason capable of a full and particular explanation' (Stewart I.18). Smith himself discusses his theoretical framework in a fragment of a lecture on Justice from his Ethics series, explaining he had in mind an analogy with the 'Theory of moral Sentiments':

> the Rules by which it is most suitable to the natural principles of Justice, or to the Analogy of those Sentiments upon which our Sense of it is founded that such decisions should be regulated, [constitute] what is called Natural Jurisprudence, or the Theory of the general principles of Law.
>
> (TMS 389: see Raphael's commentary 397)

This passage seems to reflect the Glasgow tradition of the teaching of natural jurisprudence, originating in Gershom Carmichael's commentary (2002 [1724]) on the seminal treatise by Pufendorf, *On the Duty of Man and Citizen according to the Laws of Nature* (1991 [1673, 1682]), which was valued as a textbook by Smith's teacher, Hutcheson.

In TMS, Smith discusses the virtue of justice and how its rules are accurate in the highest degree, and may be compared to the rules of grammar, which are precise and indispensible (TMS III.6.10; Haakonssen 1981: 86–7). This 'rule' character of law is an important constructive principle for Smith (Brühlmeier 1988: chapter III), and he clearly anticipated modern emphasis of this point, for example, in the work of H.L.A. Hart (1961). Smith notes that casuists, to be sure, have attempted to lay down these precise rules but without complete success. He suggests, however, that the rules of civil and criminal codes of individual states originate in the determinate principles of natural justice flowing from our natural sentiments. Thus raw rage and resentment over injury prompt us to seek revenge, but with human sociability comes a sense of justice that prompts us to conform to limits of punishment or damages for injuries, and a division of labour that entrusts decisions about appropriate retribution to magistrates, and meting it out to enforcers, in short, the creation of civil and criminal justice systems.

As for the historical side of the part on Justice, Millar provides this account:

> [Smith] followed the plan that seems to be suggested by Montesquieu [*De l'Esprit des lois*, 1748]; endeavouring to trace the gradual progress of

> jurisprudence, both public and private, from the rudest to the most refined ages, and to point out the effects of those arts which contribute to subsistence, and to the accumulation of property, in producing correspondent improvements or alterations in law and government.
>
> (Stewart, 'Account' I.19)

Millar goes on to note that Smith did not live to publish his projected book on justice, but neither he nor Stewart speculates in the vein of Cremaschi about a 'deep aporia' in Smith's thinking that blocked this project.

The fourth and last part of Smith's moral philosophy course covered Politics, which Millar describes as dealing with 'regulations founded not upon the principle of justice, but that of expediency, and which are calculated to increase the riches, the power, and the prosperity of a State', subject matter afterwards forming the substance of WN (Stewart, 'Account' I.18–20). Referring to the distinction Millar draws between 'regulations' founded on justice and those founded on 'expediency', Stewart called attention to passages in Bacon's *Exemplum Tractatus de Fontibus Juris*, Aphorisms 5 and 6, also *De Augmentis Scientiarum*, lib. viii. cap. iii (*Works* 1968/1857–74, i.71–2, xi.2). Here Bacon argues that the ultimate object of legislators is to promote the happiness of citizens, to be achieved through enjoying plenty under good government. In this interest, legislators must be prepared to investigate both the 'principles of natural justice', and those of 'political expediency' related to wealth and resources, so that the codes of laws of their societies can be corrected and improved (Stewart, 'Account' IV.7, n.5). Millar did not mean by the distinction he drew between the principles of 'expediency' and those of justice that political economy should be carved away from any connexion with justice, and Smith did not intend that this surgery should be performed on WN. As for correcting and improving codes of laws, or consolidating the laws of laws, Smith seems to have identified the political side of this in the form of constitution-building, to which he gave special attention in the sixth edition of TMS, perhaps with the preliminary constitutional debates of the French revolution in mind (TMS VII.ii.2.8, 11–12, 18; Ross 1995: 385–94).

Regarding the organization of WN, it can be noted that the first two books are mainly theoretical, modelling the processes of a freely-competitive and self-regulating market economy, while the last three books have a historical slant in evaluating alternatives in the form of the existing Mercantile system and the one recommended by the Physiocrats. Smith's call for economic freedom is unequivocal, but so also is his insistence on the requirement of a framework of justice:

> All systems either of preference or restraint, therefore, being thus completely taken away, the obvious and simple system of natural liberty establishes itself of its own accord. Every man, as long as he does not violate the laws of justice, is left perfectly free to pursue his own interest in his own way, and to bring both his industry and capital into competition with those of any other man, or order of men.
>
> (WN IV.ix.51)

Though Smith joked in October 1780 that he was his publisher's only customer for the second edition of WN, and had even forgotten he had written the book (*Corr.* Nos. 206, 207), the second half of his life was much taken up with publishing and revising the books which brought him fame: TMS [editions: 1, 1759; 2, 1761; 3, 1767; 4, 1774; 5, 1781, all 1 vol. 8vo; then 6, 1790, in 2 vols. 8vo, very much expanded]; and WN [editions: 1, 1776, 2 vols. 4to; 2, 1778 ditto; 3, 1784, in 3 vols. 8vo much expanded; 4, 1786 in 3 vols. 8vo; and 5, 1789 ditto]. While the authorized print runs of TMS were substantial, with approximately 7,750 copies available up to 1801, WN became a 'runaway bestseller', with at least 18,000 authorized copies (1,250 in 4to and 16,750 in 8vos) printed by 1802 (Sher 2002, 2004). Unauthorized editions of Smith's books were also printed in Dublin and America.

To be sure, Smith had other ventures in mind. He wrote to a Danish friend in October 1780 that following his return to Scotland after the publication of WN in 1776, he employed himself in writing a book on the Imitative Arts, but he was made a Commissioner of Customs in 1778, and his dutiful attendance at the Custom-house cut into time for new composition. Also, he revealed to the duc de La Rochefoucauld in a letter dated 1 November 1785 that he had two other projects in hand:

> I have likewise two other great works upon the anvil; the one is a sort of Philosophical History of all the different branches of Literature, of Philosophy, Poetry and Eloquence; the other is a sort of theory and History of law and Government. The materials of both are in a great measure collected, and some Part of both is put into tolerable good order.
>
> (*Corr.* No. 248)

Then he continued: 'But the indolence of old age, tho' I struggle violently against it, I feel coming fast upon me, and whether I shall ever be able to finish either is extremely uncertain' (*Corr.* No. 248). As I have described, John Millar heard a course of lectures that essentially covered the ground Smith sketched out for the second project, especially in respect of the historical part, and he reported that Smith hinted to him he intended to write a treatise on the Greek and Roman republics, which would certainly bring in the theme of 'revolutions' in law and government. The nature of the theoretical part of the project, in my opinion, is sufficiently outlined in the conclusion of TMS and the fragment of a lecture on justice, though we must also reckon with the addition of a fully developed concept of the impartial spectator melded with a theory of the sense of justice. A hint of how this would be worked out is to be found in TMS II.ii.2, 'Of the sense of Justice, of Remorse, and of the consciousness of Merit'. In his recent book, *Concepts of Justice* (2001), D.D. Raphael provides us with a trenchant review of Smith's contributions to theories of this subject, in particular noting his allegiance to the doctrine of 'natural equity', and acute criticism of the utilitarian model.

As for the philosophical history of the arts and sciences, the models for this would be the Languages essay and the 'History of Astronomy'. We might think of it as being somewhat like Vico's *New Science* (see Leon Pompa's edition and translation of Vico's *Selected Writings*, 1982). Smith would probably have linked lyric poetry to the hunting and fishing stage; epic to pastoralism; drama to farming; and prose, including fiction, history and philosophy (including science), also rhetoric, to commerce. A sketch something along this line is attempted in his twenty-third Rhetoric Lecture:

> Thus it is that Poetry is cultivated in the most Rude and barbarous nations, often to a considerable perfection, whereas they make no attempts towards the improvement of Prose. Tis the Introduction of Commerce[,] or at least of opulence which is commonly the attendant of Commerce[,] which first brings on the improvement of Prose.
>
> (LRBL ii.114–6)

WN's account of ancient and modern philosophy would have been worked into this book; in addition, a place would have been found for the already-mentioned 'natural history of religion' from the lost Natural Theology lectures; and also available was the history of historians in the Rhetoric Lectures. An embryonic history of moral philosophy was accessible in TMS, perhaps to be supplemented by the 'System of morality' provided by the satirists Lucian and Swift (LRBL i.125). As well, a mimetic aesthetic theory covering poetry, drama and the sister arts was adumbrated in EPS.

Smith ordered his executors, Black and Hutton, to burn the manuscripts of his incomplete great works (Stewart, 'Account' V.8), to our great loss, because he was a perfectionist about composition, not because he had experienced cognitive perplexity in his thinking. There is not a shred of biographical evidence for this claim.

Why does this matter? Well, in my opinion, Griswold's notion of Smith as a failed Platonist, and Cremaschi's, that he was silenced by an aporia or cognitive perplexity, undercut a submission that he speaks to the world predicament of affluent Westerners enjoying relative health and luxury, while there are many desperately poor and hungry people, subject to chronic sickness. William Rees and Mathis Wackernagel have estimated we would need 3.2 Planet Earths (1996: 12–15), if globally all were to enjoy the living standards of average North Americans.

Let us accept that we are all on the long, evolutionary march of bettering our condition, trucking, bartering and exchanging by the wayside to satisfy our wants, which is what a truly philosophical history of humanity would remind us. Let us not forget, however, the first sentence in TMS, reminding us our happiness is bound up with that of others, and Smith's injunctions in WN that prudence, circumspection and frugality should guide our use of resources. Also, let us strive to see ourselves as others see us, to allow sympathy with the feelings of others to cool us down from tendencies to indulge in intolerant, or otherwise oppressively self-interested behaviour, and to allow our natural sense of justice, connecting with our awareness of the force of natural law, to prevail in mediating between our own desires and our responsibilities to others, as Smith's moral theory seems to have indicated. I agree with Charles Griswold that Smith was not the apostle of selfishness and profit that some caricatures of his message in WN make him out to be. My contention is that awareness of the range of his writings and aspirations best scotches this travesty. Old age defeated his attempts to give us a better working understanding of justice and justice systems, also of the sciences and arts that are the glories of humanity everywhere. Smith's spirit, however, lives on to inspire us to do our share to create a more humane and a more just world.

Note

* A version of this paper was read at a Liberty Fund colloquium held in Indianapolis on 23 September 2002, and the ensuing discussion prompted further thought and changes.

Bibliography

Bacon, F. (1857–74/1968 reprint) *Works*, 14 vols. J. Spedding, R.L. Ellis and D.D. Heath (eds), New York: Garland.

Bagehot, W. (1968) *Collected Works*, 10 vols. N. St John-Stevas (ed.), London: The Economist.

Barry, N. (1982/2002) 'The tradition of spontaneous order', *Literature of Liberty*, V, No. 2, Summer 1982: 7–58, republished 2002 in the Library of Economics and Liberty on the Internet, with a Readers' Forum, at http//:www.econlib.org/library/Essays/LtrlLbrty/bryTSOtoc.html.

Brown, V. (1994) *Adam Smith's Discourse: Canonicity, Commerce and Conscience*, London/New York: Routledge.

Brühlmeier, D. (1988) *Die Rechts- und Staatslehre von Adam Smith und die Interessentheorie der Verfassung*. Berlin: Dunker & Humblot.

Carmichael, G. (2002) *Natural Rights on the Threshold of the Scottish Enlightenment: The Writings of Gershom Carmichael*, J. Moore and M. Silverthorne (eds), Michael Silverthorne (trans.), Indianapolis: Liberty Fund.

Cremaschi, S.V. (1989) 'Adam Smith, sceptical Newtonianism, disenchanted republicanism, and the birth of social science', in *Knowledge and Politics: Case Studies on the Relationship between Epistemology and Political Philosophy*, M. Dascal and O. Gruengard (eds) Boulder, Colorado: Westview Press.

—— (2000) 'Two views of the law of nature and the shaping of economic science', *Quaderni Storici*, 10 (in Italian).

Darwin, C. (1859) *On the Origin of Species by Means of Natural Selection*, London: Murray.

Dutt, A.K. and Jameson, K.P. (eds) (2001) *Crossing the Mainstream: Ethical and Methodological Issues in Economics*, University of Notre Dame Press.

Gould, S.J. (2002) *The Structure of Evolutionary Theory*, Harvard University Press.

Gray, J. (2002) Review of L. Greenfeld, *The Spirit of Capitalism: Nationalism and Economic Growth*, TLS 6 June: 9–10.

Greenfeld, L. (2002) *The Spirit of Capitalism: Nationalism and Economic Growth*, Cambridge, MA: Harvard University Press.

Griswold, C.L., Jr (1999) *Adam Smith and the Virtues of Enlightenment*, Cambridge: Cambridge University Press.

Haakonssen, K. (1981) *The Science of a Legislator: The Natural Jurisprudence of David Hume & Adam Smith*, Cambridge: Cambridge University Press.

Haakonssen, K. (1982) 'What might properly be called natural jurisprudence?' in *The Origins and Nature of the Scottish Enlightenment*, R.H. Campbell and A.S. Skinner (eds) Edinburgh: John Donald.

—— (1996) *Natural Law and Moral Philosophy: From Grotius to the Scottish Enlightenment*, Cambridge: Cambridge University Press.

Halévy, É. (1955) *The Growth of Philosophical Radicalism*, Mary Morris (trans.), Boston: Beacon Press.

Hamoway, R. (1987) The Scottish enlightenment and the theory of spontaneous order, *Journal of the History of Philosophy Monographs*: Southern Illinois University Press.

Hart, H.L.A. (1961) *The Concept of Law*, Oxford: Oxford University Press.

Hont, I. and Ignatieff, M. (eds) (1983) *Wealth and Virtue: The Shaping of Political Economy in the Scottish Enlightenment*, Cambridge: Cambridge University Press.

Hont, I. and Ignatieff, M. (1983) 'Needs and justice in the *Wealth of Nations*: an introductory essay', in *Wealth and Virtue: The Shaping of Political Economy in the Scottish Enlightenment*, Hont and Ignatieff (eds).

Hume, D. (2000) *A Treatise of Human Nature*, D. F. Norton and M. J. Norton (eds), Oxford: Oxford University Press.

Lunati, M.T. (1997) *Ethical Issues in Economics*, London/New York: Routledge.

Lux, K. (1990) *Adam Smith's Mistake: How a Moral Philosopher Invented Economics and Ended Morality*, Boston/London: Shambhala.

McCulloch, J.R. (1830) *The Principles of Political Economy*, 2nd edn. Edinburgh: Tait; London: Longmans.

—— (2000) [1838/1853] 'Sketch of the Life of Dr Smith', in *Adam Smith: Critical Responses*, H. Mizuta (ed), London/New York: Routledge: iii.8–22.

Minowitz, P. (1993) *Profits, Priests and Princes: Adam Smith's Emancipation of Economics from Politics and Religion*, Stanford University Press.

Montesquieu, C. L. de Secondat, baron de (1949) [1748] *The Spirit of the Laws*, Thomas Nugent (trans.), 1750; Franz Neumann (ed. and intro.) New York: Hafner.

Mossner, E.C. (1980) The *Life of David Hume*, 2nd edn., Oxford: Oxford University Press.

Newton, Sir I. (1962) *Mathematical Principles of Natural Philosophy and His System of the World*, A. Motte (trans.), 1729; F. Cajori (revised), 2 vols., University of California Press.

—— (1952) *Opticks, or A Treatise of the Reflections, Refractions, Inflections & Colours of Light*, based on the 4th edn. 1730, preface by I.B. Cohen, New York: Dover.

Pufendorf, S. (1991) *On the Duty of Man and Citizen According to Natural Law*, J. Tully (ed.), M. Silverthorne (trans.), Cambridge: Cambridge University Press.

Raphael, D.D. (2001) *Concepts of Justice*, Oxford: Clarendon Press.

Rees, W. and Wackernagel, M. (1996) *Our Ecological Footprint: Reducing Human Impact*, New York: Wiley.

Ridley, M. (1996) *The Origins of Virtue*, London: Viking.

Ross, I. S. (1995) *The Life of Adam Smith*, Oxford: Oxford University Press.

—— (2002) 'Adam Smith's theorizing and criticism', in *Talking Forward, Talking Back*, R. Ahrens and K. Cope (eds) New York: AMS Press.

Russell, P. (1985) 'Hume's *Treatise* and Hobbes's the *Elements of Law*', *Journal of the History of Ideas*, 46: 51–63.

Schweber, S.S. (1980) 'Darwin and the political economists: divergence of character', *Journal of the History of Biology*, 13: 195–289.

Sher, R.B. (2002) 'Early editions of Adam Smith's books in Britain and Ireland, 1759–1804', in *A Critical Bibliography of Adam Smith*, K. Tribe (general ed.) and H. Mizuta (advisory ed.), London: Pickering & Chatto.

—— (2004) 'New light on the publication and reception of the *Wealth of Nations*', *The Adam Smith Review*, 1: 3–29.

Skinner, A.S. (1996) *A System of Social Science: Papers Relating to Adam Smith*, 2nd edn. Oxford: Oxford University Press.

Smith, A. (1976a) *The Theory of Moral Sentiments*, D.D. Raphael and A.L. Macfie, (eds), Oxford: Oxford University Press.

—— (1976b) *An Inquiry into the Nature and Causes of the Wealth of Nations*, R.H. Campbell and A.S. Skinner, (General eds) W.B. Todd, (Textual ed.) Oxford: Oxford University Press.

—— (1978) *Lectures on Jurisprudence*, R.L. Meek, D.D. Raphael and P.G. Stein, (eds) Oxford: Oxford University Press.

—— (1980) *Essays on Philosophical Subjects*, W.P.D. Wightman, J.C. Bryce and I.S. Ross (eds.); D.D. Raphael and A.S. Skinner (General eds.), Oxford: Oxford University Press.

—— (1983) *Lectures on Rhetoric and Belles Lettres*, J.C. Bryce (ed.), also includes 'Languages': *Considerations Concerning the First Formation of Languages* [1761], Oxford: Oxford University Press.

—— (1987) *Correspondence of Adam Smith*, E.C. Mossner and I.S. Ross, (eds) 2nd edn, Oxford: Oxford University Press.

Stankiewicz, W.J. (1997) 'Ecology and natural law', in *Holding One's Time in Thought: The Political Philosophy of W.J. Stankiewicz*, B. Czaykowski and S.V. LaSelva (eds) Vancouver: Ronsdale Press.

Stewart, D. (1980) [1794] 'Account of the Life and Writings of Adam Smith, LL.D.', in *Essays on Philosophical Subjects*, A. Smith, (ed.) Oxford: Oxford University Press.

Vico, G. (1982) *Selected Writings*, L. Pompa trans. and (ed.), Cambridge: Cambridge University Press.

Winch, D. (1978) *Adam Smith's Politics: An Essay in Historiographic Revision*, Cambridge: Cambridge University Press.

—— (1983) 'Adam Smith's "enduring particular result": a political and cosmopolitan perspective', in *Wealth and Virtue: The Shaping of Political Economy in the Scottish Enlightenment*, Hont and Ignatieff (eds).

—— (1994) 'Nationalism and cosmopolitanism in the early histories of political economy', in *Political Economy and National Realities*, N. Albertone and A. Masoero (eds) Studi della Fondazione Luigi Einaudi, Turin: Olschki.

—— (1996) *Riches and Poverty: An Intellectual History of Political Economy in Britain*, Cambridge: Cambridge University Press.

—— (2000) 'A very amusing book about old times', in *Contributions to the History of Economic Thought: Essays in Honour of R.D.C. Black*, A.E. Murphy and R. Prendergast (eds) London/New York: Routledge.

A very cautious, or a very polite, Dr Smith?

Hedging in the *Wealth of Nations*

Willie Henderson

I

Adam Smith opens Book one, chapter one, of the *Wealth of Nations* (WN) with the following statement:

> The greatest improvement in the productive powers of labour, and the greater part of the skill, dexterity, and judgment with which it is any where directed, or applied, seem to have been the effects of the division of labour.
>
> (Smith 1976, WN I.i.1)

This is a striking opening sentence for it goes straight to the heart of Smith's treatise on the nature of economic growth. But it is a hedged statement. Smith does not claim in this sentence that all the improvement in productive powers of labour arise from the division of labour; and a similar modification is made with respect to the application of 'skill, dexterity and judgment'. Nor does Smith claim that the increases in the productive powers of labour are the consequences of the division of labour, only that they 'seem' to be.

Smith's sentence avoids the use of the unmodified verb 'to be'. The 'seem' is easily missed, and indeed there are, no doubt, some experienced readers who have missed it. Thus for example, although Groenewegen quotes the phrase in his investigation of Smith's notion of the division of labour, he makes no reference to the hedged nature of Smith's claim (Groenewegen 2002: 389).[1] Smith repeats the use of 'seems' later in the chapter: 'The separation of different trades and employments from one another, seems to have taken place, in consequence of this advantage' (WN I.i.4). Repetition of the verb suggests that this use of 'to seem' is not an accidental feature of the writing, but the result of authorial choice.

Another hedging word – 'perhaps' – also appears early in the opening chapter, in the context of the famous example of the pin factory, as well as (later) in a discussion of the price and quality of corn. It may be the case that 'everyone knows' that Smith is a highly hedged writer (though such an unhedged generalization

The Adam Smith Review, 1: 60–81 © 2004 The International Adam Smith Society, ISSN 1743–5285, ISBN 0-415-27863-5 could easily be shown to be rash). Even if it were to be the case, and that this is an obvious aspect of Smith's style, such a view cannot be used to suggest that the problem of investigating Smith's hedging is trivial. Far from it: if the phenomenon is so striking this in itself suggests a need for analysis. That some have noticed is not in doubt. Rothschild, without presenting much by way of evidence or of context with respect to making a judgment, contrasts Smith with Condorcet, a writer of considerable robustness, and says: 'Smith was, by contrast, extraordinary cautious and circumspect. The writings he published during his lifetime are replete with qualifications ("it seems", "frequently", "no doubt"); Dugald Stewart speaks of "those qualified conclusions that we admire in his writings"' (Rothschild 2001: 221).[2]

Smith goes on to demonstrate, in detail, the significance, through a number of examples, of his opening knowledge claim. He is also prepared, in other contexts, to use the unmodified verb 'to be' in making claims. Why then does he hedge this opening claim? There could be many reasons – including modesty. With respect to this particular proposition, it is clear that Smith sets out to support the proposition in the rest of the chapter. Is Smith suggesting that the proposition is yet to be proved? Smith is starting a book-length project, does not wish to claim certainty (in line with, say, David Hume's notion concerning the weakness of systems in which significant ideas are 'taken upon trust') for a proposition *a priori*, but nevertheless has to start somewhere (Hume 1978 [1739], THN Intro. xiii).[3] The pattern of a proposition (set out in each of the opening paragraphs of the first three chapters) followed by supporting evidence, is in keeping with Smith's view of an appropriate structure for didactic writing – didactic writing being 'best in all matters of science' – as set out in the *Lectures on Rhetoric and Belles Lettres* (Smith 1983, LRBL i.83; ii.126, 133).[4] A hedged statement avoids the implication of certainty before the matter has been supported by evidence.[5] Or it could be that Smith is aware of the exceptional weight he is putting on his claim as part of his theory of economic growth. Other influences on the growth of output, such as better nutrition, are possible, but such influences are covered by 'the greatest improvement'. We are not likely to have direct access to Smith's motives, in this respect, other than what is inscribed in the text.

Answering this question would contribute but a footnote in the study of Smith's work. Though, if Schumpeter is correct in his judgment that 'nobody, either before or after A. Smith, ever thought of putting such a burden upon division of labour', it may well be that Smith had every reason to be cautious (Schumpeter 1954: 187). Schumpeter also makes the point, without exploring the details of the writing whereby the features are realized, that Smith 'led them [his readers] on gently' (Schumpeter 1954: 185). This notion is common in studies of Smith. Brown refers to Smith's 'elegant eighteenth-century prose' that 'carries his reader along' (Brown 1994: 10).

It is not too difficult to show that Smith hedges propositions elsewhere, even in the opening chapter.[6] Groenewegen refers to the first three chapters as 'the oldest part of the building', echoing Schumpeter, and, again, as, 'by far the most polished part of the whole' (Groenewegen 2002: 389; Schumpeter 1954: 187).

However, in the unpublished Early Draft (ED) of a part of the WN, a key reference to the division of labour is unhedged: 'The division of labour, by which each individual confines himself to a particular branch of business, can alone account for that superior opulence which takes place in civilized societies…'. (Smith 1978, ED 6). This suggests that Smith, when it came to the prospect of publication, paid attention to the hedging of propositions.

How does Smith establish knowledge claims in writing and if he hedges them, how and why does he do so? What part, if any, does hedging play in 'gently' leading on the (target) reader? Insight on hedging in modern academic texts will be used to initiate an examination of knowledge claims in a sample of Smith's writing. The paper defines and categorizes 'hedging' with respect to Smith's writing, and attempts to identify Smith's approach to his target reader through an examination of hedged passages. Motivations for hedging, based upon 'politeness' and eighteenth-century views about scientific reporting, will be suggested. Since the notion that Smith is a writer who uses hedging in a distinctive way is essentially a comparative one, reference will be made to hedging in the philosophical and economics writing of David Hume.

II What is 'hedging'?

By 'hedge' is intended 'any linguistic device by which a speaker avoids being compromised by a statement' that turns out not to be valid. This is at least the essence of the definition in the *Concise Oxford Dictionary of Linguistics*. The term seems to have been first introduced into applied linguistics by Lakoff, who intended it to describe 'words whose job it is to make things more or less fuzzy' (Lakoff 1972: 183). Lakoff's notion is that of vagueness, and degrees of vagueness, with a purpose. There have since been many studies of hedging in academic writing (Myers 1985, 1989; Bloor and Bloor 1993; Markkanen and Schröder 1997; Hyland 1998). These have been focused on modern academic discourses. The term itself has been criticized for it suggests, at least in general English, 'pejorative connotations of deviousness and self-interest'; and this is not, according to Bloor and Bloor, what the use of modifiers is usually about (Bloor and Bloor 1993: 155). The substantive issue is that of an author legitimately moderating a commitment to a textual proposition or claim.

Myers suggests that hedging is a strategy that may be used not only because of any lack of certainty with respect to the knowledge claim that is being made, though this is one use, but, in addition, in order to show a degree of respect to others in the discourse community (Myers 1985, 1989). 'Hedging' in this context becomes another authorial device for creating a community of interest between an author and the target or imagined reader. Making knowledge claims is, in Myers' approach, potentially threatening, as it threatens the knowledge contribution of others and imposes restrictions on what the research community can subsequently do.

Smith was not, strictly speaking, writing for an established research community. This does not mean that Smith was exempted from social interactions with peers or with actual readers through his writing. As an act of communication, writing is socially situated and subject to authorial assumptions and expectations about the imagined or target reader (Coulthard 1994: 4). The notion of a target reader helps the analyst understand the assumptions that an author makes concerning, for example, what is taken as given (already known and understood) and what is new. In this approach, according to Coulthard, actual readers are understood to be working towards becoming the target reader. It could be argued that interpretations of the WN helped, over time, to create just such a specialist research community. Smith has to start somewhere and so assumptions about (target) readership and reader behaviour are therefore built into his writing. According to modern views, when hedging strategies are adopted this is so because writers are following 'rational strategies for dealing with the social interactions' involved in publishing (Myers 1989: 3). How this works out for actual readers cannot be determined by a textual study.

The point about rational strategies in writing is one that can be explored. Rommel, for example, has shown with respect to metastylistic comments, that Smith's narrative strategies are 'deliberately adapted to the form, content and implied reader' (Rommel 1997). According to Rommel, by drawing attention to aspects of his style, Smith is demonstrating his trustworthiness as narrator.[7] It is likely that Smith's hedging is also socially adapted to purpose.

In addition, although the term 'hedging' is a recent one, awareness of the phenomenon as an aspect of scientific writing is not. The nature of scientific writing is one that was extensively discussed from the late seventeenth century onwards within the developing institutional context of the Royal Society. Robert Boyle is credited with creating 'a rhetoric which laid the foundations for scientific communication' (Hyland 1998: 19). Boyle and other members of the Royal Society were clear that some thought had to be given to the reporting of scientific evidence. The issue of 'veracity' and 'verification' were issues current in the late seventeenth century (Cope 1990: 5). Even if participants in the discussion misunderstood, as Brown suggests, the role of metaphor in thought and language, a significant concern was the accurate communication of scientific results through written language, rather than directly through participant observation and demonstration (Brown 1994). Boyle was well aware of his resort, when writing, to words and phrases such as 'it seems', 'perhaps' and 'it is not improbable', and he argued for the need to distinguish between facts and interpretations (Shapin 1984: 495). A context for the development of scientific writing in which talk of certainty was restricted only to 'matters of fact' already existed (Shapin 1984: 496). The language, conventions and attitudes required for the reliable communication of science were not self-evident. Even now, it takes undergraduates time to learn the conventions. Boyle, according to Shapin, tried to become a 'reliable purveyor of experimental testimony and to offer conventions by means of which others could do likewise' (Shapin 1984: 493).[8] Being a 'reliable narrator' is relevant to thinking about Smith's writing strategy in the WN.

Smith may have absorbed the literary aspects of the developing scientific culture.[9] His stress on the significance of rhetoric may have also influenced his understanding of theory as a process of 'successive approximation' (Endres 1992: 231). Although Smith was not writing an experimental report, he is likely to have been aware that he himself was writing a didactic text. It is useful to keep in mind Endres' understanding that 'it is not immediately obvious to the reader what predominant discursive mode Smith had in mind' (Endres 1992: 223). The text is not wholly or merely a didactic text – Smith uses historical narrative as well as other forms of story. However, given what Smith says about such a text in the LRBL – that a didactic writer had a responsibility not to push interpretative claims further than the evidence would allow – then this and the consistency of use suggest a self-conscious strategy (LRBL i.150). In this context Rommel's notion that Smith sought to be a 'trustworthy narrator' takes on added significance, as it aligns Smith to the scientific rhetoric of the Royal Society.

The notion of being a 'trustworthy narrator' also links Smith's writing in the WN back to issues that he explores in LRBL, where issues of 'character', 'civility' and politeness are recurrent themes. The issues of 'civility' and 'politeness' are not simply concerns for Smith alone, they are part of eighteenth-century notions of sociability and manners. These notions informed an array of activities, including that of 'polite knowledge' (Klein 1994: 3–8). Politeness assumes sociability and the possibility of reconciling differences. According to Klein, it assumes intersubjectivity and exchange of 'opinions and feelings'. It also, as a technique, sets rules – such as the avoidance of 'excesses of assertiveness' in 'conversation' – 'governing the "how" of social relations' (Klein 1994: 4). An originating champion for 'civility' and 'politeness' was Shaftesbury, though the essays of Addison and Steel were also of significance.[10] Shaftesbury's aims were, according to Klein, political, concerned with securing the Revolutionary settlement and the 'dominance of gentlemen over English society and politics' (Klein 1994: 1).[11] Hume's contribution was that of making the systematic and objective discussion of political and economic life a subject fit for polite conversation (Phillipson 1988: 54). Smith, who may also have been concerned with making political economy fit for polite conversation, comments on English politeness and its integration into the political discourse of the House of Lords, where what is admitted (from outside) is expected to be 'a plain, just and exact account', in keeping with its own sense of political decorum (LRBL ii. 251). There is direct textual evidence, in the *Wealth of Nations*, of the significance of polite sentiments. Here is Smith on 'plans' for education: 'The good temper and moderation of contending factions seems to be the most essential circumstance in the publick morals of a free people' (WN V.i.f.40).

There is also reason for caution that comes from the nature of the evidence available to Smith. There are two key aspects to hedging, as established in today's literature, that may be relevant to Smith's work: politeness in discourse and the degree to which the writer is committed to a claim. The phenomenon of politeness in today's academic world is shorn of many of the social and cultural aspects of politeness in Smith's world. The word is the same but the social connotations and implications are different. Modern notions of politeness are reduced both in content and substance. The degree of commitment to a claim can be further divided, following Prince *et al.*, into 'approximators' (where claims made are approximate) and 'shields' (where the idea may be to deflect criticisms concerning over-generalization, for example, 'perhaps') (Prince *et al.* 1982). Established interpretations of Smith's theory of growth take Smith's commitment to it to be total, but such interpretations delete Smith's hedging.

English makes possible a range of 'hedging devices'. Myers establishes, for modern academic writing, a list of possibilities that include the use of modal verbs ('may', 'might'), the use of modifiers ('perhaps', 'probably'), the avoidance of the verb 'to be' (at least in an unmodified form) and the avoidance of factive verbs ('show', 'prove') (Myers 1989: 13; Dudley-Evans 1993: 136). Recent work by Hyland reviews how 'hedging' has been extended by further empirical studies to include the use of a number of other devices such as personal statements using modals, the use of a general rule, impersonal agency and direct apology (Hyland 1998: 45).

It has already been shown that Smith avoids the use of the unmodified verb 'to be' in the opening sentence. This is how he tells the reader that a common assumption about the division of labour is mistaken:

> It is commonly supposed to be carried furthest in some very trifling ones; not perhaps that it really is carried further in them than in others of more importance...
>
> (WN I.i.2)

The 'commonly supposed' suggests some other discourse, though it is not necessarily implied that a given reader shares this view. The phrase distances Smith from the proposition and anticipates a possible challenge. The episode, even if on a small-scale, is constructed dialogically within a 'response–counter-response pattern' as identified as a textual possibility by Brown (1995: 277) drawing upon Bakhtin: 'It is commonly supposed'/ 'not perhaps that it really is...' (WN I.i.2).[12] The challenge to this general view is modified by 'perhaps'. The full passage (including the skilful use of 'we' in the penultimate sentence) illustrates a carefully hedged strategy, based upon politeness or perhaps upon the, not unrelated, classical rhetorical notion of 'decorum' and even 'ethos'.[13] If contemporary readers shared this supposition (why write it if they did not?), then the text does not confront such readers directly. Smith, by using hedging, avoids challenging sensibilities unnecessarily. The dialogism is, in this case, gentle and is only formally revealed by close reading. As with many aspects of hedging, in this example another discourse is implied, either as an authentic discourse, presumed in this case, or as an imagined one.

Eighteenth-century conventions are different, with respect to outcomes, from modern conventions, but not radically so. The authorial contexts are, however, substantially different. It could be possible, nonetheless, to take all of the categories now used in hedging in academic writing and attempt to apply them to the WN. Here, a limited set of examples of hedged statements in Smith will be used to raise awareness of the issues involved in making such an analysis. The examples are drawn from the use of modals, the use of modifiers, the avoidance of the unmodified verb 'to be' and the avoidance of, or moderation of, factive verbs.[14]

III Hedging and the use of modifiers in the *Wealth of Nations*, Book one, chapter one

In this section only three modifiers are examined: the use of 'perhaps', the use of 'certainly' and the use of 'probably'. However, Smith uses a combination of elements in his approach to knowledge claims, and some of those combinations will be illustrated in the next section. Justification for the use of these terms is drawn from the WN, Book one, chapter one, where Smith uses 'perhaps' and 'certainly' in the context of the operation of the pin factory. Here are three examples:

> ...a workman not educated to this business (which the division of labour has rendered a distinct trade), nor acquainted with the use of the machinery employed in it (to the invention of which the same division of labour has probably given occasion), could scarce, perhaps, with his utmost industry, make one pin in a day, and certainly could not make twenty.
>
> (WN I.i.3)

And again:

> But if they had all wrought separately and independently, and without any of them having been educated to this peculiar business, they certainly could not each of them have made twenty, perhaps not one pin in a day...
>
> (WN I.i.3)

And at the end of the chapter:

> Compared, indeed, with the more extravagant luxury of the great, his accommodation must no doubt appear extremely simple and easy; and yet it may be true, perhaps, that the accommodation of an European prince does not always so much exceed that of an industrious and frugal peasant, as the accommodation of the latter exceeds that of many an African king, the absolute master of the lives and liberties of ten thousand naked savages.
>
> (WN I.i.11)

There are a number of interesting features in evidence in the first example. Take the claim that pin making is a distinct trade and that it has been made so by the division of labour. This is un-hedged, even though the role of the division of labour in creating new trades is hedged elsewhere in chapter one: 'The separation of the different trades and employments from one another, seems to have taken place, in consequence of this advantage' (WN I.i.4). These are similar claims but presented textually in different ways. Specialization of machinery is hedged: 'the invention of which the same division of labour has probably given occasion' (WN I.i.3).

The hedge here is 'probably'.[15] The main idea, which is that of an ineffective worker's performance, is nicely hedged: 'could scarce, perhaps, make one pin in a day, and certainly could not make twenty'. The hedging is double in that it involves both 'scarce' and 'perhaps'. 'Could' in this instance is probably not a hedge as it is the 'ability' meaning rather than the 'degree of certainty' meaning that is stressed. The whole seems to be, therefore a mixture of approximators and shield.

In the second example, the order of 'certainly' and 'perhaps' is reversed. Smith's knowledge is imprecise at this point, whereas with respect to other aspects of the case study he is backed by two sets of observations, those of others (evidenced by 'has been very often taken notice of...' I.i.3) and those of himself ('I have seen a small manufactory of this kind...' I.i.3). It may not be the imprecision that suggests the hedging but the degree of Smith's commitment to the knowledge. What has not been observed is the operation of the workforce 'separately and independently'. If observation is a source of knowledge, then that which cannot be directly observed may have to be carefully hedged. Conjectural propositions are, therefore, likely to be hedged.[16]

Does this hypothesis help with aspects of the other examples? There has been no observation of a pin maker making pins by himself. No authentic example is reported upon directly by Smith in his text (even if his targeted readers may be assumed to know about the *Encyclopédie* article and illustrative plate on pin manufacture, already, perhaps, indirectly referred to with 'very often taken notice of' (1.i.3; Editors' note p. 15, n. 3)). It is not unreasonable to present the trade textually as a separate trade, and to provide the division of labour as the source of the specialist activity. What about machinery? No argument has been presented about machinery and hence at this stage the knowledge claim is hedged. Smith, however, follows through with the hedging. Later in the chapter he states: 'that the invention of all those machines by which labour is so much facilitated and abridged, seems to have been originally owing to the division of labour' (WN I.i.8). He puts forward a reasoned case for the proposition but, again, it is a process over time that cannot be observed except in the present. However, hedging can imply the existence of a counter-argument, acknowledged indirectly by the hedge but not necessarily explicitly stated. The implied counter-argument here is likely to be that of specialist machinery as the product of individual genius (see Section IV).

The same would seem to be true for the passage on the accommodation of princes and peasants. It would be difficult in practice to observe all the elements required for the comparison and specify the basis for a correct judgment. It is an imaginative idea, the comparative elements are vague, and it is one that cannot be easily observed. Hedging assists with its plausibility.

IV Application to hedging elsewhere in the *Wealth of Nations*

The suggestion, from the analysis of Book one, chapter one, is that 'to seem' is used when a process cannot be directly observed or a fact cannot be directly verified or where some nod is required in the direction of other sources of knowledge.

It is also the case that hedging is often double and hedged phrases are often combined with 'perhaps'. Are these insights confirmed by other examples in Book one? Here are some further examples from Book one.

'Seems' and 'perhaps':[17]

> The difference between the most dissimilar characters, between a philosopher and a common street porter, for example, seems to arise not so much from nature, as from habit, custom and education. When they came into the world, and for the first six or eight years of their existence, they were, perhaps, very much alike, and neither their parents nor play-fellows could perceive any remarkable difference.
>
> (WN I.ii.4)

The first hedge is 'seems to arise' rather than 'arises' and is combined with another modifying phrase, 'not so much from'. The sentence could be rewritten so that the unmodified verb 'to be' is used rather than a modified 'arise'. The second hedge, modifying the verb 'to be', is 'perhaps'. But why is the idea hedged? Well, there is no possibility of any real observation (at this stage) and Smith is, in this respect, not in agreement with contemporary views on the nature of genius. This use of hedging would be in line with earlier uses. Even if the proposition, and its supporting argument (supplied in the second half of the paragraph), is plausible, some caution is likely to have been socially necessary to get the point accepted. This much can, by implication, be textually derived, for hedging often implies another discourse. Smith was writing against the prevailing notion of 'genius' and is therefore challenging views that 'took as the bases of social order the distribution of mental faculties and the accumulation of works of genius' (Tenger and Trolander 1994: 171). Such an insight helps explain the pattern of hedging with respect to knowledge claims made in discussing aspects of the division of labour. Smith next, however, throws caution to the wind (though there is a hedge in the use of 'scarce') and attacks the vanity of philosophers: 'till at last the vanity of the philosopher is willing to acknowledge scarce any resemblance' (WN I.ii.4).

A good contrast can be made, also in chapter two, with a related and un-hedged statement: 'By nature a philosopher is not in genius and disposition half so different from a street porter, as a mastiff is from a greyhound, or a greyhound from a spaniel, or this last from a shepherd's dog' (WN I.ii.5). The differences, once the initial and potentially challenging hedged proposition has been presented to the reader, can be quickly and directly observed and reflected upon, and Smith's conclusion reached.

'Seems' and 'perhaps' (again):

> The policy of Europe considers the labour of all mechanicks, artificers and manufacturers, as skilled labour; and that of all country labourers as common labour. It seems to suppose that of the former to be of a more nice and delicate nature than that of the latter. It is so perhaps in some cases; but in the greater part it is quite otherwise, as I shall endeavour to shew by and by.
>
> (WN I.x.b.8)

Two of the three sentences contain hedges. The hedges are 'seems', 'perhaps' and 'endeavour to shew'. In context, it would be hard for Smith to supply hard evidence, at this stage, of the 'policy of Europe'. 'Seems' is appropriate but Smith, next, wishes to challenge the supposition. The whole episode is one of small-scale dialogism with the putative interlocutor being personified as 'the policy of Europe'. 'Seem' and 'perhaps' belong to what is conceded to the interlocutor and the 'endeavour to shew' gently points to the challenge that Smith will mount. These small-scale examples of dialogism (see earlier paragraphs) may be more common in the WN than has been elsewhere supposed.

'Show' is an example of a 'factive' verb and modern analysis of hedging suggests that this will be hedged. Smith frequently uses 'show' in the main text of the WN but in the majority of instances, where he is making claims in the first-person singular for the impact of his own writing, he normally hedges by combination with 'endeavour'.[18] Smith is hedging in order not to claim, in advance, that his writing is effective and that therefore his argument is conclusive; the success of his argument, when it is made, is for others to judge. If this interpretation is correct, then motives for hedging would come from ideas, in formal discussions of rhetoric, such as 'ethos' or 'decorum' and, at a pinch, Boyle's related notion of 'modesty'.[19]

'Seems' and 'probably':

> Of all the countries on the coast of the Mediterranean sea, Egypt seems to have been the first in which either agriculture or manufactures were cultivated and improved to any considerable degree. Upper Egypt extends itself nowhere above a few miles from the Nile, and in Lower Egypt that great river breaks itself into many different canals, which, with the assistance of a little art, seem to have afforded a communication by water-carriage, not only between all the great towns, but between all the considerable villages, and even to many farm-houses in the country; nearly in the same manner as the Rhine and the Maese do in Holland at present. The extent and easiness of this inland navigation was probably one of the principal causes of the early improvement of Egypt.
>
> (WN I.iii.6)

In this example, the hedging ('seems', 'seem', 'probably') implies the possibility of another discourse: the 'best authenticated history' mentioned in Smith's preceding paragraph (WN I.iii.5). The evidence could in principle be disputed and evaluated elsewhere. The knowledge also relates to a process of historical development over time. It cannot be directly observed since it refers to an age long past. But, it is something that Smith and his readers could observe in the world of his time – for this is one of the purposes of the inclusion of references, by (hedged) analogy, to the Rhine and Maese. Notice how nicely the analogy is presented: 'nearly in the same manner as…'. Smith's precision is remarkable: 'nearly' also because these rivers gave rise to communities that engaged extensively in foreign trade. It can be assumed that he agrees with the proposition for he explores it in a related paragraph and reaches a related conclusion, also hedged: 'It is remarkable that neither the ancient Egyptians, nor the Indians, nor the Chinese encouraged foreign commerce, but seem all to have derived their great opulence from this inland navigation' (WN I.iii.7). He uses the verb 'to be' in the unhedged first part of the sentence but modifies it with 'probably' and so, to some extent, maintains his position whilst not encouraging any significant opposition. He is, modestly, not claiming expert knowledge in any direct sense – he is not an author of the 'best authenticated history' – but merely making a plausible argument. The tone is one of suggesting possibilities rather than of partisan advocacy. The passage follows his advice concerning exclamation in historical writing: the argument is entirely logical and unemotional (LRBL ii.38). The target reader's sensibilities are not disturbed. Dugald Stewart, an actual reader, wrote of Smith's 'judicious' synthesis and of his 'disinterested zeal for truth', features exemplified here (Stewart 1980: 320, 323). Few actual readers could then disagree with such a reasonable proposition, especially when made in support of a fact that can be observed in the modern world: the commercial advantages derived from location on 'the banks of navigable rivers'.

'Seems' when the knowledge is uncertain:

> The denominations of those coins seem originally to have expressed the weight or quantity of metal contained in them. In the time of Servius Tullius, who first coined money at Rome, the Roman As or Pondo contained a Roman pound of good copper... The Tower pound seems to have been something more than the Roman pound, and something less than the Troyes pound.
>
> (WN I.iv.10)

The examples are from the past. This may lead us to expect some hedging but, in addition, the knowledge is imprecise, even vague. Another discourse is implied; in this case, sources on knowledge of the values of ancient coinage. In the rest of the passage 'appears' is used as a hedge. So, unlike modern-day knowledge claims in some scientific contexts where the operating principle is 'social constructionist' – where the hedging originates in a relationship between the writer and the professional discourse community (Hyland 1998: 82) – Smith is acknowledging his target readers who share his own sensibilities and understanding (Servius Tullius is a given; that he 'first coined money' is new). Smith is also recognizing the uncertain and imprecise nature of the existing historical knowledge. Here 'seems' is working as an approximator (Bloor and Bloor 1993: 153).

'Perhaps' is complex. There are at least three different uses of 'perhaps' that can be identified in the WN – derived from an analysis of sixty passages (a non-random sample of the whole). These are:

(a) 'Perhaps' as a hedge for a potentially verifiable proposition;
(b) 'Perhaps' as a hedge in a hypothetical or conjectural situation;
(c) 'Perhaps' as a hedge to signal usuality or successive approximation.

Potentially verifiable propositions are normally about situations that are current but which have not yet been observed, by the author, for some reason. The conjectural context of hedging in Smith has been noticed in the early literature with respect to the contested concept of conjectural history (Stewart 1980: 293). What the present analysis has established for 'perhaps' is that hedging is associated both with counterfactual statements and other motives for hedging. The first two uses of 'perhaps', from the list provided, are illustrated in the passage that follows. Notice that there are other hedges such as 'seems', 'probably' and the use of hedged phrases including verbs. This pattern of multiple hedging in an argument is not untypical of Smith's writing in the WN and is certainly not confined to Book one. The category of 'usuality' or 'approximation' is used in contexts that do not require accurate reporting. In the following passage there is only once sentence that does not contain a hedge – 'It had not got to this height in any part of Scotland before the union'. No evidence is supplied here for the claim that is being made. It is simply reported as a matter of fact:

> There are, perhaps [hedge/verifiable], some parts of Europe in which the price of cattle has not yet got to this height. It had not got to this height in any part of Scotland before the union. Had the Scotch cattle been always confined to the market of Scotland, in a country in which the quantity of land, which can be applied to no other purpose but the feeding of cattle, is so great in proportion to what can be applied to other purposes, it is scarce possible, perhaps [hedge/conjectural], that their price could ever have risen so high as to render it profitable to cultivate land for the sake of feeding them. In England, the price of cattle, it has already been observed, seems, in the neighbourhood of London, to have got to this height about the beginning of the last century; but it was much later probably before it got to it through the greater part of the remoter counties; in some of which, perhaps [hedge/verifiable], it may scarce yet have got to it. Of all the different substances, however, which compose this second sort of rude produce, cattle is, perhaps [hedge/verifiable], that of which the price, in the progress of improvement, first rises to this height.
>
> (WN I.xi.l.2)

The first hedge is used for a proposition that could in principle be verified, but which has not been observed by the author for whatever reason. The second conjectural proposition is a complex one and is not capable of verification by observation. It is a theoretical notion and has the status of a counterfactual. Notice that, in the second example, the full hedged phrase is: 'scarce possible, perhaps…could…'. This is a very elaborate set of hedges. Both are examples of hedging as 'shield'. There are many other hedges in the passage, including other complex patterns.

This next example contains both 'perhaps' as 'usuality' and 'perhaps' as 'conjecture':

> Taking the whole kingdom at an average, nineteen houses in twenty, or rather perhaps [hedge: usuality/approximation] ninety-nine in a hundred, are not

> insured from fire. Sea risk is more alarming to the greater part of people, and the proportion of ships insured to those not insured is much greater. Many sail, however, at all seasons, and even in time of war, without any insurance. This may sometimes perhaps [hedge/conjectural] be done without any imprudence.
> (WN I.x.b.28)

The approximation is not likely to be challenged since it would be reinforced by readers' experience of the insurance of houses. The second sentence also contains the verb 'to be' and asserts an unhedged matter of fact.[20] The whole passage is about risk and estimations of risk (the 'presumptuous contempt of the risk') and not about details of the insurance market (assumed to be known to target readers) and hence the approximation is acceptable. Notice, in the first example, 'perhaps' is placed before additional information in a series of approximations. This upward progression of hedge exemplifications is encountered elsewhere: 'It [public admiration] makes a considerable part of that reward in the profession of physick; a still greater perhaps in that of law; in poetry and philosophy it makes almost the whole' (WN I.x.b.24).

This wider survey confirms the use of 'perhaps' in the earlier examples. The general pattern is also confirmed. Simple, directly observable statements tend not be hedged. Knowledge that could be observed in principle, but has not been so in fact, tends to be hedged. Conjectural statements, including predictions, tend to be hedged.[21] Indeed, Smith's characteristic method of linking many stages in a chain of argument (the 'Newtonian method', according to LRBL) itself suggests the need for multiple hedges (LRBL ii.133). Hedging is also implied by the realization of the didactic method in writing. Propositions are hedged before they are analysed and supported by evidence. Details of Smith's argumentation are suggested by characteristic arguments. Personal claims for what the writing has accomplished or will accomplish are, with few exceptions, also normally hedged.

V Hedging in Hume's writing

It may be useful, for comparative purposes, briefly to consider hedging in David Hume's writing. Smith and Hume were friends and the opening chapters of the WN, Chapter two in particular, attest to Hume's influence on Smith. Hume's relationship with the target reader is complex. In his philosophical writing, Hume is setting out difficult and socially unacceptable propositions about what can be known. His philosophical writing is shot through with irony, or rather multiple ironies, to which an unwary reader can easily fall victim (Price 1992/1965: 370). Smith's situational irony is gentle when compared to the variety of Humean ironic strategies, though it would be a mistake to underestimate the role of irony in Smith's writing. If we can extrapolate from what Smith said about style in his LRBL, he would have accounted for some of the differences between his writing and Hume's writing in terms of 'character' (itself a reflection of the notion of 'ethos').

In the analysis of the WN mentioned earlier, emphasis was placed on verbs and modifiers, and little attention was paid to personal statements (except with respect to Smith's claims about the success of his own writing), impersonal agency and personal apology – all of which can also be used as hedges. Given the different relationship with the target reader, when Hume hedges, the patterns and intensity of hedging are not likely to be the same as in Smith's writing.

A survey of Hume's essays classified by Rotwein as economics writing, suggests that 'perhaps' is used hardly at all. This does not mean that Hume does not hedge, for phrases such as 'no doubt' or even 'in my opinion' (strictly speaking this is direct 'authorial comment') are used, in context, as modifiers. Where 'perhaps' is used, the context is simple and no different from simple uses in Smith:

> But we may observe, that, at a time when they [arts and sciences] rose to greatest perfection among one people, they were perhaps totally unknown to all the neighbouring nations; and though they universally decayed in one age, yet in a succeeding generation they again revived, and diffused themselves over the world.
>
> (Hume, 'On the Populousness of Ancient Nations'; Rotwein 1955: 109)

A similar simplicity is found in 'Of the Balance of Trade': 'Our tax on plate is, perhaps, in this view, somewhat impolitic' (Hume; Rotwein 1955: 69).

The overall function of 'perhaps' is similar, at the level of the sentence, to those found in Smith. 'Perhaps' as a hedge for a potentially verifiable proposition, as a hedge for a conjectural proposition and even as a signal of successive approximation can all be evidenced from the essays, as can the use of 'perhaps' as a form of politeness. But Hume is a different writer from Smith. Here is Hume's evaluation of '*abstruse* thinkers':

> They suggest hints, at least, and start difficulties, which they want, perhaps, skill to pursue; but which may produce fine discoveries, when handled by men who have a more just way of thinking.
>
> (Hume, 'Of Commerce'; Rotwein 1955: 3)

The proposition, that such thinkers are not capable of pursuing a topic systematically, is modified by the use of the hedge 'perhaps'; politeness is in play. However, later on in the opening moves in the same essay, Hume says of his own writing:

> I thought this introduction necessary before the following discourses on *commerce*, *money*, *interest*, *balance of trade*, &c. where, perhaps, there will occur some principles which are uncommon, and which may seem too refined and subtile for such vulgar subjects.
>
> (Hume, 'Of Commerce'; Rotwein 1955: 5)

Hume is writing in anticipation of the fact that just such principles, in his own mind, will be presented. He is hedging (the 'perhaps' is supported by the 'may seem') in order to keep the reader reading on in a sympathetic way. But in the next sentence, there is a robust challenge: 'If false, let them be rejected'. There is, when read in the wider context of the developing text, just a hint that he will be both abstruse and just. This potentially undercuts the initial 'perhaps' as Hume hedges his own potentially 'abstruse' contribution whilst maintaining his reputation as a 'just' reasoner.

In the *Enquiry concerning Human Understanding* (ECHU), the use of 'perhaps' is spread evenly throughout the work with only one instance recorded of 'perhaps' being used more than once in a paragraph. The uses are not implied as part of a chain of reasoning (Hume 1975, ECHU V.i.43). There are no uses that match the serial and complex use of 'perhaps' and other forms of hedging that were illustrated (Section IV) for Smith's writing. Of the cases investigated from ECHU, a significant minority were accompanied by 'may' (in thirteen of the thirty-four examples). Although there were no examples of 'perhaps' being repeated in a series of hedged statements used in the construction of an argument, Hume's simple use of 'perhaps' does not mean that the relationship with the intended reader is straightforward. Consider the following two examples, found in close proximity in the ECHU:

> Can I do better than propose the difficulty to the public, even though, perhaps, I have small hopes of obtaining a solution?
>
> (ECHU IV.ii.32)

> I must also confess that, though all the learned, for several ages, should have employed themselves in a fruitless search upon any subject, it may still, perhaps, be rash to conclude positively that the subject must, therefore, pass all human comprehension.
>
> (ECHU IV.ii.33)

Both uses of 'perhaps' are conjectural and modify the relationship with the reader. In the first example, the question is itself a kind of hedge, an apology for inconveniencing the reader. It is also ironic, for this inconveniencing the reader is exactly what Hume intends to do. And does it not also carry a hint that Hume will, in fact, propose a solution? In the second example, Hume is on the face of it, avoiding the charge of arrogance but, once again, Hume's 'shot-gun irony' is in play (Price 1992/1965: 39). Both are examples of 'perhaps' being used in the context of a question or a personal statement (direct authorial comment) being used as a hedge. Such uses are likely to be found frequently in Hume's writing.

This survey of Hume's ECHU does not reveal 'perhaps' and other modifiers being used as hedges in the same serial way as in the WN. There is no evidence either in the *Enquiry* or in the economics essays of whole paragraphs being made up of a variety of (mainly) hedged sentences, with the repeated use of 'perhaps' in a chain of reasoning, as exemplified in selected passages from the WN. Hume, in distinguishing between 'particular' and 'general' subjects, makes it clear that a chain of reasoning supported by principles is significant for 'general' subjects

(Hume, 'Of Commerce'; Rotwein 1955: 3). Both Smith and Hume are interested in making such connections but differ in the ways that such arguments are realized in argumentation as exemplified by the use of 'perhaps'. However, Hume also hedges, although the predominant use is likely to be based on personal statements, apologies and questions, all potentially negated by irony. Hume's politeness may be no politeness at all.

VI Discussion

Hedging of knowledge claims is a significant phenomenon in the WN, as it is likely to be for any serious discourse but, even so, there is a sense in which Smith may be a distinctively hedged writer. The comparison made with Hume's writing is merely indicative, with respect to modifiers, rather than definitive. In the textual relationship between author and reader, hedges serve a purpose. What is that purpose in the WN? The answer is complex. Smith is writing a 'didactick discourse' and, ideally, such a discourse would 'persuade us only so far as the strength of the arguments is convincing...' (LRBL i.149). Of course, the WN exhibits a variety of traits, including story telling, but the primary aims are to explain and instruct. Cope categorizes Smith as 'a professional explainer' (Cope 1990: 168). The notion of a didactic text could imply, following through Smith's own terms, caution in stating the initial proposition and some form of authorial evaluation concerning the merits of an argument. Hedging – rather than formally and overtly stating possible weaknesses in the chain of reasoning, as direct authorial comment – is one way that this can be achieved since hedging often implies other possibilities, other arguments.

Because the observation of the details of hedging, and how it works, relies on close reading, the quantity, quality and nature of Smith's hedging can be overlooked, or read as 'obvious' and not worthy of reflection. This may well be a result of Smith's rhetorical strategy; if the (actual) reader is 'led on gently' then Smith has created a text that serves its didactic purpose without drawing attention to itself as writing, at least in this respect. It is polite discourse, in the sense identified by Klein, and culturally informed by notions of agreeable conversation (Klein 1994: 3–8). If readers do not notice the hedged nature of significant claims, a community of interest and an agreement to read on quietly has been maintained. Awareness of hedging changes the experience of reading Smith, however, as a sense of robustness gives way to some caution or at the very least some curiosity.

Given all this hedging, is Smith's 'controlling voice' still in control (Brown 1994: 191)? The instance of double and even triple hedging that have been presented here, including the phenomenon of 'negated hedging', carried by 'perhaps'...'certainly not', suggests that any analytical reading concerned with evaluating Smith's ways of arguing ought to take hedging, and its varying intensity, into account. Are we justified in 'reading out' Smith's hedges? Smith's writing in the WN may work on two levels, rather than one. Too much awareness of Smith's hedging can serve to undercut the argument or at the very least to promote further reflection upon it. How actual readers negotiated hedged statements cannot be derived from a textual study.

It is important to locate the interest in hedging in the relationships revealed through text, with Smith's target readers and even with Smith's sense of self. Smith chooses to hedge some knowledge statements and not others. He is able to use the unmodified verb 'to be' in making knowledge claims about aspects of the world that can be simply and directly observed, and capable of independent verification by the target reader, though even here there may well be other forms of hedging that have not been explored in this article.[22] Smith is more likely to hedge claims that cannot be directly observed (statements about the past, or about processes in the present, or about process that are still being worked out), either because they rely on theoretical knowledge or because the facts are not likely to be readily ascertained or because he is dealing essentially with counterfactuals. If he is concerned with making the experience of observation of the economic world available to his readers, as Brown suggests, then, hedging where such observations cannot be made is a rational strategy, closely related to the objectives of the writing overall. A didactic text aims to alter the target reader's understanding. Smith's hedges, by not alienating the reader, increase his chances of rhetorical success. In this respect, Smith is exhibiting through hedging, as suggested by Rommel for metasylistic statements, evidence of his reliability as a scientific narrator with respect to knowledge claims (Rommel 1997). On these counts, Smith's use of hedging is compatible with Boyle's views on the reporting of scientific observations (reliability and 'verifiability') and the distinction between 'fact' and 'interpretation'.

Some of Smith's hedging is about lack of precise knowledge. His arguments, as in the case of the output of an unskilled worker trying to undertake every aspect of pin making by himself, or in the measurement of the value of former monetary units, can only be imprecise. Sometimes hedging is about modifying claims for which he would not be seen, and would not necessarily wish to be seen, as an authority. We may suppose, from evidence elsewhere in the text, that claims about river navigation in ancient Egypt are claims that Smith believes; but they are nonetheless hedged either because he is not an authority and does not wish to be seen as one, or because the process can no longer be observed even if it can be linked to a modern one. Hedging also implies the existence of other texts and discourses, and hence hedges can be associated with an implicit dialogism.

The case for observation of some of the conventions suggested by classical rhetoric, decorum and ethos, added to by eighteenth-century notions of civility and politeness, perhaps mixed with Boyle's notion of modesty and Smith's sense of character in LRBL, also suggest that motivations are more complex than a simple comparison with today's writing may imply. Smith usually hedges when, using the first-person singular and fictive verbs such as 'show', he makes claims about the standing and impact of his own work as author. Decorum and ethos may be the operating influence as far as such claims are concerned. Of course, caution and politeness can work in the same direction in the sense that both maintain a sense of reasonableness.

There is more, therefore, to hedging – and to leading readers along gently – than simple questions of style. There are cultural as well as logical and evidential aspects, some found explicitly or implicitly in Smith's LRBL. The textual realization of hedging and the associated motives in Smith and other samples of eighteenth-century economic and philosophical writing, are not likely to be identical to those established by Myers, Hyland, Bloor and Bloor, and others, for modern academic writing. Cultural practice and personal preferences are relevant as well as the nature of the evidence available in the eighteenth century to back knowledge claims. However, as with other aspects of Smith's economics writing, the motives and purposes are likely to share some family resemblance with hedging in (say) modern-day introductory economics textbooks. The distinction between 'actual' readers and 'target' readers is also a useful distinction to make, and further work is required if we are to develop a fuller understanding of Smith's economic and philosophical writing, as writing.

Acknowledgements

I am grateful to Roger Backhouse, Vivienne Brown, Martin Hewings, Susan Hunston, Alison Johnson, Ann Lewis and Warren Samuels, for comments on an earlier draft. I am grateful to Sunganthi Jones for advice on making an analysis of hedging and to Ramesh Krishnamurthy for technical assistance. Thanks must also go to two anonymous reviewers for this journal for their insightful comments.

Notes

1 West notices one aspect of the hedging (if this is the correct interpretation of italicization of 'greatest' and 'greater') but does not notice the 'seems'. He does not otherwise draw any attention to the hedging (West 1964: 24). Rosenberg notices Smith's hedging with respect to his view of slaves: 'Slaves…are very seldom inventive; and all the most important improvements, either in machinery, or in the arrangement and distribution of work which facilitate and abridge labour, have been the discoveries of freemen' (WN IV.ix.47; Rosenberg 1965: 131). Rosenberg also notices a link between hedging and conjectural history (Rosenberg 1965: 133). Rosenberg does not explore the issue of hedging more widely.

2 Stewart states that Smith's conversational style differed from his writing style. The full passage is: 'But, in the society of his friends, he had no disposition to form those qualified conclusions that we admire in his writings; and he generally contented himself with a bold and masterly sketch of the object, from the first point of view in which his temper, or his fancy, presented it' (Stewart 1980: 331). This extra-textual evidence suggests that Smith was a reflective writer.

3 A similar instance can be drawn from Hume's 'Of the Jealousy of Trade'. This opens with the following sentence: 'Having endeavoured to remove one species of ill-founded jealousy, which is so prevalent among commercial nations, it may not be amiss to mention another, which seems equally groundless' (Hume; Rotwein 1955: 78). Hume suggests that it 'seems' groundless to look upon trading neighbours as necessarily rivals, but uses the rest of the essay to show that it is, in fact, groundless.

4 This pattern is found for chapters as a whole, see for example chapters one, two and three in Book one where the pattern is very clear (though there are other textual patterns within each). It can also be found within paragraphs where a hedged proposition, developed as part of a wider argument, is stated and then justified by evidence.

5 In Book one, chapter two, the opening sentence assumes that the case has already been argued: 'This division of labour, from which so many advantages are derived…' (WN I.ii.1). This is an example of the link between didactic writing and hedging.

6 Details of Smith's writing, for example, the use of the phrase 'if one may say so' and closely related varieties of it, have been explored by Rommel who reaches the conclusion that Smith is concerned with building a sense of 'trustworthy narrator' (Rommel 1997). Rommel does not investigate knowledge claims but, rather, Smith's use of vivid images.

7 Smith's authorial comments can be provocative and far from polite (see Brown 1994: 192–3).

8 Boyle also recommended a 'naked way of writing' that avoided being trapped by preconceived ideas founded on other texts (Shapin 1984: 496–7). The experiment was more important than references to other systematic texts. Could such views have influenced Smith, given the scarcity of citations in the WN?

9 A collected edition of Boyle's *Works*, edited by T. Birch, was published in London in 1772 (Shapin 1984: 511).

10 Stewart refers to Smith's interest in 'polite literature both of ancient and modern times' (Stewart 1980: 305).

11 Smith found Shaftesbury to be a shallow thinker (LRBL i.136,140). Smith is scathing about Shaftesbury's style: 'Polite dignity is the character he aimed at, and as this seems to be best supported by a grand and pompous diction that was the Stile he made choice of' (LRBL i.146).

12 Such small-scale examples of dialogism are likely to be found in other places in the WN.

13 The concept of decorum is one explored in Cicero's *Orator*, a work that Smith refers to in his LRBL. According to Jasinski, decorum is difficult to define but it can carry the idea of appropriateness to subject matter, audience and occasion (Jasinski 2001: 147). Ethos is another concept that seems simple but can become complex. It is a notion 'used by Aristotle to refer to the ways in which the perceived attributes of a speaker, manifest in discourse, are persuasive' (Jasinski 2001: 229). Thus Rommel's view of Smith's stance can be integrated with both notions. Smith's use of 'we' suggests that he, too, modestly shares in the potential failure to understand the significance of the observation. The 'we', in the passage cited, creates a community between himself and the reader and does not then put the reader at a disadvantage. There are other ways of creating such a community. For a detailed analysis of passages in WN and TMS containing 'I' and 'we' see Brown (Brown 1994: 28–45). Smith accepts in LRBL that Cicero's 'character' is able to 'shine out…thro all his writings', so although 'ethos' does not seem to be directly mentioned by Smith in the passage on Cicero, the author's 'spirit and mind' shines through (LRBL ii.2334; Brown 1994: 10).

14 A factive verb commits a speaker to the truth of a proposition contained in a subordinate clause. Some verbs are factive ('show', 'know') and others not ('think').

15 When the statement is repeated later in the chapter 'probably' is replaced by 'seems': 'I shall only observe, therefore, that the invention of all those machines by which labour is so much facilitated and abridged, seems to have been originally owing to the division of labour' (WN I.i.8). The recurrence of hedging increases the sense of cautious claims.

16 The link between conjectural history and 'hedged' language use (though the term is not used nor the point made generically) is made by Dugald Stewart: 'In examining the history of mankind, as well as in examining the phenomena of the material world, when we cannot trace the process by which an event *has been* produced, it is often of importance to be able to show how it *may have been* produced by natural causes' (Stewart 1980: 293; original emphasis).

17 There is another hedged sentence at the start of chapter two: 'Whether this propensity be one of those original principles in human nature, of which no further account can be given; or whether, as seems more probable, it be the necessary consequence of the faculties of reason and speech, it belongs not to our present subject to enquire' (WN I.ii.2).

18 Here is a sustained example from the introduction to Book two:

> In the following book I have endeavoured to explain the nature of stock, the effects of its accumulation into capitals of different kinds, and the effects of the different employments of those capitals. This book is divided into five chapters. In the first chapter, I have endeavoured to show what are the different parts or branches into which the stock, either of an individual, or of a great society, naturally divides itself. In the second, I have endeavoured to explain the nature and operation of money considered as a particular branch of the general stock of the society. The stock which is accumulated into a capital, may either be employed by the person to whom it belongs, or it may be lent to some other person. In the third and fourth chapters, I have endeavoured to examine the manner in which it operates in both these situations. The fifth and last chapter treats of the different effects which the different employments of capital immediately produce upon the quantity both of national industry, and of the annual produce of land and labour.
> (WN II.Intro.6)

Factive verbs are here modified by the use of 'endeavoured'. Smith modifies 'explain' and 'examine' similarly. There are few counter-examples but there are some, for example, 'This rate is naturally regulated, as I shall show hereafter, partly by the general circumstances…' (WN I.vii.1).

19 In LRBL Smith sets out his delight in Addison as a writer who exhibits 'modesty', a trait that leads Addison to express his sentiments 'in the least assuming manner' (LRBL i.126–8).

20 Smith hedges the following statement: 'Live cattle are, perhaps, the only commodity of which the transportation is more expensive by sea than by land' (WN IV.ii.17). This is followed by an analysis and justification, including a reflection on the importation by sea of Irish cattle. The hedge itself, if readers notice it, invites investigation of other exceptions such as horses, geese and other livestock. There is a potential here for the hedge to undercut the main point. The hedged proposition is then explored and so provides a paragraph-level example of textual organization following didactic rules established by Smith in LRBL.

21 A good example of a conjecture hedged as prediction is found in Smith's discussion of the 'freest importation of foreign goods': 'The silk, perhaps, is the manufacture which would suffer the most by this freedom of trade, and after it the linen, though the latter much less than the former' (WN IV.ii.41).

22 Thus, for example, the chapter on Colonies is relatively unhedged as it is descriptive and factual, though there are exceptions: 'Plenty of good land, and liberty to manage their own affairs their own way, seem to be the two great causes of the prosperity of all new colonies' (WN IV.vii.b.16). This example is consistent with the use of hedging of knowledge claims elsewhere in the work.

Bibliography

Bloor, M. and Bloor, T. (1993) 'How economists modify propositions', in *Economics and Language*, W. Henderson, T. Dudley-Evans and R.E. Backhouse (eds), London: Routledge.

Brown, V. (1994) *Adam Smith's Discourse: Canonicity, Commerce and Conscience*, London: Routledge.

—— (1995) 'The moral self and ethical dialogism: three genres', *Philosophy and Rhetoric*, 28: 276–99.

Coulthard, M. (1994) 'On analysing and evaluating written text', in *Advances in Written Text Analysis*, M. Coulthard (ed.), London: Routledge.

Cope, K.L. (1990) *Criteria of Certainty: Truth and Judgment in the English Enlightenment*, Lexington, KY: University of Kentucky Press.

Dudley-Evans, T. (1993) 'The debate over Milton Friedman's theoretical framework: an applied linguist's view', in *Economics and Language*, W. Henderson, T. Dudley-Evans and R.E. Backhouse (eds), London: Routledge.

Endres, A.M. (1992) 'Adam Smith's treatment of historical evidence as illustrated from the theory of investment priorities', *Journal of European Economic History*, 21: 217–49.

Groenewegen, P. (2002) 'Adam Smith and the division of labour', in *Eighteenth-century Economics: Turgot, Beccaria and Smith and their Contemporaries*, London: Routledge.

Hume, D. (1978) [1739–40] *A Teatise of Human Nature*, 2nd edn, L.A. Selby-Bigge (ed.), Oxford: Clarendon Press.

—— (1975) [1748, 1751] *Enquiries concerning Human Understanding and concerning the Principles of Morals*, textual revisions by P.H. Nidditch, 3rd edn, L.A. Selby-Bigge (ed.), Oxford: Clarendon Press.

Hyland, K. (1998) *Hedging in Scientific Research Articles*, Amsterdam/Philadelphia: John Benjamins Publishing Company.

Jasinski, J. (2001) *Source Book on Rhetoric: Key Concepts in Contemporary Rhetorical Studies*, Thousand Oaks: Sage.

Klein, L.E. (1994) *Shaftsbury and the Culture of Politeness, Moral Discourse and Cultural Politics in Early Eighteenth-century England*, Cambridge: Cambridge University Press.

Lakoff, G. (1972) 'Hedges: a study in meaning criteria and the logic of fuzzy concepts', *Chicago Linguistics Society Papers*, 8: 183–228.

Markkanen, R. and Schröder, H. (eds) (1997) *Hedging and Discourse: Approaches to the Analysis of a Pragmatic Phenomenon in Academic Texts*, Berlin: de Gruyter.

Myers, G. (1985) 'Texts as knowledge claims: the social construction of two biology articles', *Social Studies of Science*, 15: 593–630.

—— (1989) 'The pragmatics of politeness in scientific articles', *Applied Linguistics*, 10: 1–35.

Phillipson, N. (1988) *Hume*, London: Weidenfeld & Nicolson.

Price, J. V. (1992) *The Ironic Hume*, Bristol: Thoemmes Press; reprint of 1965 edition, Austin, TA: University of Texas Press.

Prince, E.F., Frader, J. and Bosk, C. (1982) 'On hedging in physician–physician discourse' in *Linguistics and the Professions*, R.J. di Pietro (ed.), Hillsdale, NJ: Ablex.

Rommel, T. (1997) 'A reliable narrator? Adam Smith may say so.' Available HTTP: <http://www.cs.queensu.ca/achallc97/papers/p032.html> (accessed 2 July 2002).

Rosenberg, N. (1965) 'Adam Smith on the division of labour: two views or one?', *Economica*, 32: 127–39.

Rotwein, E. (ed.) (1955) *David Hume: Writings on Economics*, Madison, WI: University of Wisconsin Press.

Rothschild, E. (2001) *Economic Sentiments: Adam Smith, Condorcet and the Enlightenment*, Cambridge, MA: Harvard University Press.

Schumpeter, J. A. (1954) *History of Economic Analysis*, London: Allen & Unwin.

Shapin, S. (1984) 'Pump and circumstance Robert Boyle's literary technology', *Social Studies of Science*, 14: 481–520.

Smith, A. (1976) *An Inquiry into the Nature and Causes of the Wealth of Nations*, R.H. Campbell and A.S. Skinner (eds), Oxford: Oxford University Press; reprinted, Liberty Press (1981).

—— (1978) *Lectures on Jurisprudence*, R.L. Meek, D.D. Raphael and P.G. Stein (eds), Oxford: Oxford University Press; reprinted, Liberty Press (1982).

—— (1983) *Lectures on Rhetoric and Belles Lettres*, J.C. Bryce (ed.), Oxford: Oxford University Press; reprinted, Liberty Press (1985).

Stewart, D. (1980) [1794] 'Account of the life and writings of Adam Smith, LL.D.' in *A. Smith's Essays on Philosophical Subjects*, W.P.D. Wightman and J.C. Bryce (eds), Oxford: Clarendon Press; reprinted, Liberty Press (1982).

Tenger, Z. and Trolander, P. (1994) 'Genius versus capital: eighteenth-century theories of genius and Adam Smith's *Wealth of Nations*', *Modern Language Quarterly*, 55: 169–89.

West, E.G. (1964) 'Adam Smith's two views of the division of labour', *Economica*, 31: 23–32.

Translation of Ernst Tugendhat's Lecture on Adam Smith's Moral Philosophy

Introductory remarks on the context of Tugendhat's Lecture on Adam Smith

Christel Fricke

After a long period of silence on Adam Smith's moral philosophy, Ernst Tugendhat is the first German philosopher to pay attention to it in recent years, arguing for its plausibility and merits by contrasting it with Hume (1998, 2000) and Kant (1997, 1998) and by relating it to Aristotle (1984), all of whose moral philosophies are omnipresent in ongoing debates. Since the publication of Tugendhat's *Vorlesungen über Ethik* (*Lectures on Ethics* (1993)), which has been very well received and is widely read in Germany, there is also in Germany a developing interest in Adam Smith as a moral philosopher.

Ernst Tugendhat's 'Universalistically approved intersubjective attitudes: Adam Smith' is the fifteenth lecture in his *Vorlesungen über Ethik*. This volume comprises eighteen lectures based on the last lecture course Ernst Tugendhat taught at the Freie Universität Berlin, during the Winter-semester 1991/1992. In Lectures 1–5 Tugendhat presents what he then considered the most plausible notion of the morally good[1] and defends its claim to universal validity: morally good is what can or could be accepted as good by everybody. On this point, the contractarian (Hobbes 1985, Locke 1990, Rousseau 1988) and the Kantian philosophical traditions agree. But they disagree on the justification of the corresponding moral norms, not only with respect to the procedures of justification but also with respect to the kind of justification needed.

Tugendhat rejects any attempt at justification that has been proposed within the framework of these traditions. He also rejects Rawls' *Theory of Justice* (1971), discussing in detail Kant's moral philosophy in the *Groundwork of the Metaphysics of Morals* (1998) (Lectures 6 and 7) and its modern versions, the ethics of discourse by Karl Otto Apel, and Jürgen Habermas (1984) (Lecture 8). That we are obliged to endorse morality as a value cannot be deduced from our natural egoism or from our faculty of reason; nor can we simply rely on an analysis of our moral intuitions in order to justify this obligation. Whether we conceive of ourselves as

The Adam Smith Review, 1: 85–104 © 2004 The International Adam Smith Society, ISSN 1743–5285, ISBN 0-415-27863-5 moral persons or not is neither a question of reasons nor one of obligation. Tugendhat proposes instead to ask for motives we might have to conceive of ourselves as moral persons, as members of a moral community.

He defends an Enlightenment understanding of moral philosophy, focussing on the individual person and his or her moral responsibility. Not only does he reject Schopenhauer's (1977, 1999) ethics of sympathy (Lecture 9); he also rejects different versions of what he calls 'the ethical counter-Enlightenment', discussing Hegel's *Philosophy of Right* (1991) and referring briefly to theories of the so-called Ritter-school (Joachim Ritter, Odo Marquard and Hermann Lübbe). After that, he discusses Alasdair MacIntyre's *After Virtue* (1985) (Lecture 10) and the notion of moral virtue (Lecture 11).

Tugendhat holds (as does Bernard Williams (1985) to whom he briefly refers) that when we ask for good motives for endorsing the idea of being a good member of a community, we are not concerned with moral goodness but with goodness in a broader, ethical sense that concerns our well-being or happiness. In Tugendhat's defence of convincing motives for being a morally good person, the notion of a 'moral attitude' plays a crucial part. Moral motivation arises from a moral attitude that Tugendhat describes as a moral sense, where this 'moral sense' is understood in terms of an attitude manifest both on the level of judgment and on the level of feeling. He introduces and develops the notion of a moral attitude with reference to Aristotle's notion of virtue in the *Nicomachean Ethics* (1984) (Lectures 12 and 13), and to Hegel's notion of respect ('*Anerkennung*') as developed in his *Philosophy of Right* (1991) and Erich Fromm's attempt at bridging the gap between a desire for happiness and a moral character in his *Escape from Freedom* (1941) and *Man for Himself* (1947) (Lecture 14).

Lecture 15 deals with Adam Smith's moral philosophy and is published here in English translation for the first time. As Tugendhat reads *The Theory of Moral Sentiments*, it contains a theory of moral virtues that corresponds to the contractarian and Kantian idea of universalizable moral rules.

The remaining lectures complete the discussion by dealing again with the problem of moral motivation (Lecture 16) and discussing human rights (Lecture 17) and justice (Lecture 18).

Acknowledgement

Acknowledgement is gratefully made to Suhrkamp Verlag for permission to translate the fifteenth lecture in Ernst Tugendhat (1993 u.ö.) *Vorlesungen über Ethik*, Frankfurt: Suhrkamp, pp. 282–309.

Note

1 Meanwhile, Ernst Tugendhat has revised his views on moral philosophy. For his most recent position see Tugendhat (1997, 2001).

Bibliography

Aristotle, (1984) *Nicomachean Ethics*, in *The Complete Works of Aristotle: The Revised Oxford Translation*, J. Barnes (ed.), vol. 2, Princeton, NJ: Princeton University Press.
Fromm, E. (1941) *Escape from Freedom*, New York, Toronto: Rinehart.
—— (1947) *Man for Himself: An Inquiry into the Psychology of Ethics*, New York, Toronto: Rinehart.
Habermas, J. (1984) [1981] *The Theory of Communicative Action*, vol. I, T. McCarthy (trans.), Boston: Beacon Press.
Hegel, G.W.F. (1991) [1820] *Elements of the Philosophy of Right*, A.W. Wood (ed.), H.B. Nisbet (trans.), Cambridge: Cambridge University Press.
Hobbes, T. (1985) [1651] *Leviathan*, C.B. Macpherson (ed.), London: Penguin.
Hume, D. (1998) [1751] *An Inquiry concerning the Principles of Morals*, T.L. Beauchamp (ed.), Oxford: Oxford University Press.
—— (2000) [1739–40] *A Treatise of Human Nature*, D.F. Norton and M.J. Norton (eds), Oxford: Oxford University Press.
Kant, I. (1997) [1788] *Critique of Practical Reason*, Mary Gregor (trans. and ed.), Cambridge: Cambridge University Press.
—— (1998) [1785] *Groundwork of the Metaphysics of Morals*, Mary Gregor (trans. and ed.), with an introduction by Christine M. Korsgaard, Cambridge: Cambridge University Press.
Locke, J. (1990) [1690] *Two Treatises on Government*, introd. by W.S. Carpenter, London: Everyman's Library.
MacIntyre, A. (1985) *After Virtue*, London: Duckworth.
Rawls, J. (1971) *A Theory of Justice*, Cambridge, MA: Harvard University Press; revised edition 1999.
Rousseau, J-J. (1988) [1762] *On the Social Contract*, D.A. Cress (trans. and ed.), Indianapolis: Hackett.
Schopenhauer, A. (1977) [1841] *Die beiden Grundprobleme der Ethik*, in *Werke in zehn Bänden*, A. Hübscher (ed.), vol. VI, Zürich: Diogenes Verlag.
—— (1999) [1840] *Prize Essay on the Freedom of the Will*, G. Zöller (ed.), E.F.J. Payne (trans.), Cambridge: Cambridge University Press.
Tugendhat, E. (1993 u.ö.) *Vorlesungen über Ethik*, Frankfurt: Suhrkamp.
—— (1997) *Dialog in Laeticia*, Frankfurt: Suhrkamp.
—— (2001) 'Wie sollen wir Moral verstehen?', in *Aufsätze 1992–2000*, Frankfurt: Suhrkamp, pp. 163–84.
Williams, B. (1985) *Ethics and the Limits of Philosophy*, London: Fontana Press/Collins.

Universalistically approved intersubjective attitudes: Adam Smith

Ernst Tugendhat (Translator: Bernard Schriebl)

Two lectures back I tried to clarify that Aristotle's theory of virtues has two aspects: we can understand the virtues (or some of them) as those dispositions that serve for well-being, or we can understand the virtues (or some of them) as the dispositions that are being morally approved. In the last lecture I interpreted Erich Fromm as a modern author who deals with virtues in the first sense, and in the present lecture I shall deal with an author who has given a new interpretation of the virtues in the second sense: Adam Smith in *The Theory of Moral Sentiments* (1759).[1]

I shall be concerned with the question whether for a universalistic morality there exist any moral virtues above and beyond the well-known set of Kantian rules or contractual rules, rules reducible to actions or rules for actions; that is, whether a universalistic morality requires a set of *attitudes*. This constitutes a new terrain, one that has been prepared only vaguely by the interpretation I gave of Aristotle's social (intersubjective) virtues.[2] This too was concerned with the balance between self-control and relatedness, and therefore the conceptual closeness of these virtues to the virtues of happiness. However, if sentiments of this sort should have a normative place in a universalistic morality, they would have to be desired from the perspective of all (or: of anyone). We are of course not concerned here with a philosophical construct, and Adam Smith himself believes that the virtues pointed out by him are in fact generally recognized in everyday life (I.i.3.8). The reasons that they haven't been seen in the utilitarianism of Smith's predecessor David Hume and in Kantianism would then conversely be the consequence of a philosophical short-sightedness. I will say something about presumable grounds for this short-sightedness later.

From a systematic point of view, Adam Smith constructed his book in a less than satisfactory manner. In accordance with his somewhat curious empiricist assumptions, according to which moral consciousness does not proceed primarily from rules, therefore neither from principles, but inductively from concrete emotional experiences (III.4.8), the book proceeds from the fact of sympathy, whose normative implications are shown only gradually.

Smith does not attend to his predecessor David Hume until Part VI of his work, which functions as an appendix. Here, we have a panorama of virtues, which – as it does throughout in Hume – relates to usefulness: the virtue of *prudence* is the character needed by the individual in order to be directed towards his own happiness.[3] Justice and benevolence are dispositions directed at the happiness of others.

These virtues *can*, says Smith (VI. Concl.1), be explained, as Hume thinks, through our egoistic passions on the one hand, and through our altruistic passions on the other. However, no one would be able to develop these virtues in a steady manner who did not let himself also be determined by the consideration of others' feelings in such a way that the impartial spectator is authoritative for him. After all, there exists the further basic virtue of self-command, whose development can be brought under the point of view of prudence – but only in a manner that represses excessive emotions rather than transforming them. Transformation of excessive emotion is possible only through the sentiment of propriety, whose criterion is the possibility that other people impartially participate in it (VI. Concl.3–7).

In the first two parts of Smith's work, however, we find another construct, in which the propriety determined by the impartial spectator – the foundational point of view for Smith – is considered as determining *the whole of virtue*. According to this point of view, the virtues are organized into two kinds (I.i.3.5–7, I.i.5, and II.i.Intro.). Of the first kind are the virtues of propriety in the narrower sense, and these concern the possibility of affective associations with others. Here we find the core of Smith's ethics: it refers entirely to a universalistically commanded relatedness of one's own affectivity to that of others, to an affective openness to others – that is, to their affects or to their affective capacity. The second kind of virtue relates to one's merit or demerit, the characteristics according to which one deserves reward or punishment. Only this second kind of virtue relates to justice and beneficence. Likewise, only the latter is considered by Hume and also by Kant; they are Kant's negative and positive duties. In Part II of his book Smith goes so far as to try to ground even these virtues in the virtue of propriety.

Let us begin however by examining the core of Smith's conception, which he introduces very hesitatingly in the opening of Part I. Smith begins with the empirical phenomenon of sympathy. We understand pity and compassion to be the fellow-feeling with the sorrow of others. Sympathy can also be understood in this narrow sense; it can also be understood, however, and should be understood, in a broader sense, in which it signifies fellow-feeling with all the affects of others (I.i.1.5). Of course, not all affects and feelings of others arouse sympathy. Feelings of bodily lust scarcely do so, and our initial reaction to negative social affects like anger and resentment tends to be negative as well. In general however, everyone, albeit to a greater or lesser degree, has an inclination to participate in the joy and sorrow of others.

So far, Adam Smith's starting point could appear to be similar to, if more comprehensive than, Arthur Schopenhauer's. In Smith, however, there occurs a series of steps that show that his concept is completely different than it might appear at first. Of course it is clear from the outset that sympathy with the other's pleasure could not – like compassion in Schopenhauer – be understood as a motive for something else (moral actions). Therefore, Smith's concept of sympathy also differs fundamentally from Hume's (VII.iii.3.17.)

The first step, which occurs in the second chapter of Section I, consists in Smith's pointing out that one's inclination to have fellow-feeling with others corresponds to a reciprocal wish on the part of those others, that people have fellow-feeling towards them: 'nothing pleases us more than to observe in other men a fellow-feeling with all the emotions of our own breast; nor are we ever so much shocked as by the appearance of the contrary' (I.i.2.1). This reciprocity in fellow-feeling and dependency on fellow-feeling appears in the first sections to be one that takes place particularly between friends.

> But if you have either no fellow-feeling for the misfortunes I have met with, or none that bears any proportion to the grief which distracts me; or if you have either no indignation at the injuries I have suffered, or none that bears any proportion to the resentment which transports me, we can no longer converse upon these subjects. We become intolerable to one another. I can neither support your company, nor you mine. You are confounded at my violence and passion, and I am enraged at your cold insensibility and want of feeling.
> (I.i.4.5)

Soon it becomes apparent, however, that Smith thinks of this reciprocity of the affective accord as in no way restricted to those who are close to one another. While we expect it to a greater degree amongst those who are already close (I.i.4.9), it also occurs between strangers. This may first appear as another, more or less strongly supported, empirical fact. But Smith now explicitly adds a normative aspect.

For from the outset, a person who feels sympathy judges the propriety of that affect (I.i.3–4). Smith gives an initial reason for this in chapter 1 (I.i.1.20): the sympathy-arousing factor is not, as it is in Schopenhauer, the other's affect (or its expression), but the situation causing that affect. For example, someone who suffers a painful physical affliction arouses our compassion even when he himself does not express any pain. Conversely, we are incapable of sympathizing with the affect of someone who complains excessively over a small misfortune. Similarly, we feel ashamed for someone if he acts in a shameful manner, even if he does not feel ashamed himself. This distinction between our fellow-feeling and the other's affect implies a judgment about the appropriateness of his affect relative to the affect-causing situation. What is the criterion for this judgment?

Again, Smith first provides an answer he later corrects. In chapter 3, he says that the only standard for judging the appropriateness or inappropriateness is whether another's situation is capable of arousing my sympathy, that is, whether I can imagine myself reacting likewise in a similar situation. The obvious objection is that it is possible for my affective reaction to a situation of this sort, that is, my capacity to sympathize, to be inadequate. One has then two alternatives: either we have the mere fact of an agreement between two persons, which would be something purely subjective (this is an alternative Smith never even contemplates), or one has to take into account the possibility that one's kind of reaction also appears inadequate from the perspective of a third or fourth person, and thus eventually from the perspective of *anyone* at all. This is how Smith arrives at his concept of the impartial spectator.

In order to understand Smith correctly, one must first consider that he speaks in this objective manner about the judgment of the appropriateness of the other's affect as if that were obviously the right way to speak. This emphasizes the fact that approval or disapproval of the other's affect depends on the outcome of this judgment. At first, this explicitly normative implication seems not to fit very well with the empirical introduction. In order to understand what Smith means by this impartial spectator, one needs to consider that he leads the reader from one, not further qualified, spectator, through several small modifications which are not presented as very significant, to, finally, the impartial spectator. It is important to note that at first he only talks about the spectator *simpliciter* (I.i.4.6). Even when Smith later talks about the impartial spectator, he never means a theoretical spectator, but always has in mind one who stands ready to sympathize with those directly affected. And from this arises an initial, and for Smith fundamental, factor in the difference between one person's affect and another's (the 'spectator's') sympathy: the person who himself suffers the affect (joy, pain, resentment, and so on) normally suffers it to a greater degree than the person who, by way of his imaginative capacity, and because he puts himself into the position of the other (I.i.4.8) and sympathizes with it as a 'reflected' affect (I.i.4.5–7).

If a reciprocally resonating condition comes about at all, it is a double-sided one. Both the person participating and the one primarily affected must have developed an *enabling general disposition* that makes an appropriate affective attunement possible. For Smith, both of the general dispositions required here are virtues. Moreover, he considers them to be the two basic virtues: sensitivity on the one side and self-command on the other (I.i.5.6). Smith brings them to a common denominator by stating:

> [a]nd hence it is, that to feel much for others and little for ourselves, that to restrain our selfish, and to indulge our benevolent affections, constitutes the perfection of human nature; and can alone produce among mankind that harmony of sentiments and passions in which consists their whole grace and propriety. As to love our neighbour as we love ourselves is the great law of Christianity, so it is the great precept of nature to love ourselves only as we love our neighbour, or what comes to the same thing, as our neighbour is capable of loving us.
>
> (I.i.5.5)

We saw earlier that in Part VI Smith confronts the self-control resulting from the motivation of propriety, that is, from the capacity for affective agreement, with the self-control developed only from a prudential point of view. The person aiming at propriety endeavours to 'flatten'... 'the sharpness of... [his affects'] natural tone' so that the spectator can participate in them (I.i.4.7); 'he is as constantly led to imagine in what manner he would be affected if he was only one of the spectators of his own situation' (I.i.4.8).

The locution 'one of the spectators' already has the implicit meaning that Smith later expresses with the word 'anyone'. At the first occurrence of the term 'impartial spectator' (I.i.5.4), 'impartial' seems to mean nothing more than 'not affected', and it seems that Smith is still speaking of a friend of the person principally concerned. But Smith then also talks of the 'indifferent spectator'. By this, however, he again just means a person other than the primarily affected one, not an insensitive person. Later Smith uses the term 'bystander': one who is present only coincidentally. As a general criterion, it is finally established that 'these, as well as all the other passions of human nature, seem proper and are approved of, when the heart of every (!)[4] impartial spectator entirely sympathizes with them, when every indifferent by-stander entirely enters into, and goes along with them' (II.i.2.2). Later, Smith says at one point that '[t]he conversation of a friend brings us to a better, that of a stranger to a still better temper' (III.3.38).

One criterion for the appropriate sensitivity named from the outset is that the sympathetic one 'must adopt the whole case of his companion with all its minutest incidents; and strive to render as perfect as possible, that imaginary change of situation upon which his sympathy is founded' (I.i.4.6). Smith goes on to take up this point in later parts of his book by talking of the 'impartial and well-informed spectator' (see e.g. VII.ii.1.49).

Of course, one expects a different degree of participation from a friend than from a stranger (I.i.4.9). However, from this, first, it follows that the person concerned will attempt to achieve a higher degree of self-control in front of a stranger (I.i.4.9). Second, it does not follow that a stranger is less capable of judging whether or not an affect is appropriate. People who are close will sympathize more intensely with one another. But whether it is appropriate to sympathize, whether the other's affect should be approved or not, is decided from the perspective of any arbitrary spectator.

This last point can be elucidated with an affect that Smith rightly shows as especially problematic: anger and resentment (I.ii.3). Since this affect concerns a third person negatively, even a friend of one expressing the affect will at first react to it negatively and without sympathy. The often especially brash expression of anger appears initially inappropriate. I sympathize only to the degree to which I learn the reasons for (the situation that causes) my friend's emotional outburst: my indignation then corresponds to his resentment. For my friend it will be more important that I go along with his anger than with his other affects. It is in this situation that Smith says a lack of understanding becomes unbearable (I.i.4.5; see p. 90). On the other hand, as long as the friend who is not directly affected does not simply submit to the one who is, it is he who by nature sees the situation more objectively and sees it 'with the eyes of a third person' (III.3.3). Thus the situation may arise in which the friend does not consider himself capable of going along with the affect of the person expressing anger, much as he may wish to do so. In exceptional cases, the other may appear contemptible if he does not react with controlled anger towards what I consider insults (I.II.3.3).

A special case, one which Smith does not actually examine, is of course the one in which friends (but also those not so close to one another) harbour resentments against each other. As Smith points out, the person directly affected tends to react in an overly sensitive manner. The opponents thus not only harbour negative feelings towards each other, but also such that are especially difficult to reconcile, since each considers his own feelings worthy of approval. Because of their peculiar affects, each views a different aspect of the complex action as decisive. Putting oneself into the position of a judging third party appears to be particularly important here, in order to bring the supposedly disinterested spectator in one's own inner self into accord with that of the other (III.3.3).

Quarrelling, whether between people close to each other or people less close, almost always has this component of reciprocal resentment, which implicates the attitude of self-righteousness. This permits us to better appreciate the important role played by morality between people closely related with one another.[5] The closer people are to each other, the greater are the points of contact and the greater, therefore, the number of differing points of view involved in moral judgment. The status of moral differences between people close to each other is of course determinable only here, because now the topic of discussion is not the morality or the immorality of actions or omissions. Instead, we are concerned with the morality or immorality of affective reactions to the morality or immorality of actions, that is, the appropriateness of the judgments serving as the bases for these reactions. We are moving, as it were, on a second moral plane. This is valid not only for reciprocal resentment, but also for the possibility, mentioned by Smith, of associating with another's resentment against a third party. The modern reader, who, starting out from Kant or Hume, may tend to deny the justifiability of judging affects morally – something considered self-evident by Aristotle and taken up by Smith in a new way – has to ask himself whether avoiding such a judgment in the special case of moral affects is really thinkable. Since every moral affect implies a moral judgment, and it is possible for judgments claiming to be morally justified to be unjustified, the existence of moral judgments of moral reactions is not only an omnipresent everyday phenomenon, but a necessary consequence of moral judgments on the first level, namely that of actions. The moral affect – the resentment – is not a private matter. Rather, it affects the other often more severely than an appropriately reactive action, even if we set aside the fact that this affect is the starting point for further actions (retaliation, distancing, and so on). Whoever admits the existence of moral and immoral actions also has to admit the existence of moral and immoral reactive attitudes. Of course, one cannot consider either the moral affect or its judgment as an attitude. Affects in themselves are not yet attitudes even in Aristotle, although the firm dispositions of character are to be described as attitudes, as particular ways of conducting oneself towards one's own and others' affects (moral and non-moral). These are Smith's virtues of self-control and sensitivity (see p. 91).

Now we are in a position to consider Smith's ethics of propriety, presented only in review so far, in its systematic place. Smith explicitly makes a link with the Aristotelian tradition (I.ii.Intro.1–2). Only the affect that achieves a happy medium between excess and insensitivity is one in which others (Smith's 'disinterested spectators') are able to participate. Smith explains only at a late point (VII.ii.1.49) that none of the ethical systems that regarded propriety in its primary sense – a propriety of affects – as the source of approval, was able to provide a 'precise and distinct measure' for this propriety: 'That precise and distinct measure can be found nowhere but in the sympathetic feelings of the impartial and well-informed spectator' (VII.ii.1.49). It is therefore Adam Smith's claim that in the part of morality he wants to have recognized as central, and as going beyond the positive and negative duties of benevolence and justice, he has on the one hand taken up the Aristotelian tradition and on the other hand, with the help of his impartial spectator, provided for the first time a precise sense for the mean.

This confronts us with three questions: (1) Is this claim justified, that is, does appealing to the possibility of affective participation through the impartial spectator provide us with a criterion which gives talk about the mean a well-defined sense? (2) Is it sensible to say that the affects, if they are so judged, are judged morally, and is this judgment a universalistic one? Further, does this entail that universalistic morality, as presented on a Kantian basis, necessarily has to be expanded in this manner? And (3) How is the moral principle to be understood?

In answering the first question, we should note that the difference between the person principally concerned and the one capable of sympathy entails that the affect will be judged as lying somewhere between excess and lack. A person growing up alone would simply have the feelings he does. He would not have any cause to reflect on them (III.1.3). Even with aesthetic feelings, in which there is no person principally concerned, there is a difference between shared feelings and merely subjective ones (I.i.4.1–4). Someone has 'good judgment' if he judges as others do from different points of view and different experiential backgrounds. On the other hand, as with affects, one who is especially moved finds this 'harmony and correspondence [at once more difficult to preserve], and at the same time, vastly more important' (I.i.4.5). Here, two aspects supplement each other, and this provides the basis for talking about something as objective or right (proper): the difference of perspective, which we also have in aesthetics, *and* the difference between the person affected and those not directly affected. These two aspects concern the two moments that Smith connects in talking about the 'impartial': the primary unaffectedness ('indifference') of the spectators *and* the arbitrariness of the position ('any' spectator).

Of course, it is presupposed that the unaffected one will or should sympathize with the affected one. It is necessary to make a distinction here [between two aspects of the tendency towards sympathy] not explicitly made by Smith. The first aspect is the propriety of the two basic virtues, that is, the readiness to decrease or to increase one's own affects (in the case of the person principally concerned) or one's affective disposition (towards the other) in order to allow a mutual concord. As the earlier-cited paragraph concerning the perfection of human nature reveals (see p. 92), this is the basic value for Smith: affective openness towards others both from the perspective of the person principally concerned and from the perspective of the spectators. (What is missing is a consistent term for the two perspectives' affective openness; 'sympathy' is more appropriate for the perspective of the unaffected one, and one would have to understand the word as encompassing both dimensions.) The second aspect is that the affects themselves (they are always those of the person principally concerned) are judged as appropriate relative to the realization of this basic value.

The propriety of the basic virtues and the concept of the 'perfection of human nature' thus understood refer to the third question posed above. It does not require any further explanation to recognize that these dispositions are basic for the possibility of friendship. If one understands friendship in the Aristotelian sense as wanting to be together, in a way that implies a disposition to share joy and pain, then Smith's sympathetic affective concord belongs to the latter disposition. To what extent can Smith understand the 'perfection of human nature' universalistically? Are we to develop this disposition so that it relates to *all* others (even if, of course, in a weakened intensity)? We cannot expect a fully satisfying answer in Smith's explicit treatments of this central question. Smith wavers, as has become apparent already, between a conception oriented towards the description of our factual feelings and a normative conception: 'Nature', he says, implanted these feelings in us, and we can explain that they contribute to survival and harmony within society. The latter can be thought of on several levels (II.ii.3). A mere subsistence of society is possible based only on the 'mercenary exchange of good offices': this is a contractual society, constitutive also of a 'society among robbers and murderers'. Better, however, is a harmonious society that not only enforces justice, but in which the virtues of justice, benevolence and propriety rule (II.ii.3). Smith thus clearly distinguishes between a contractual subsistence society and a society that is good in being moral. Nowhere, however, does he explicitly draw a line between a moral society, along the lines of Humean (or Kantian) principles, and a yet better one, determined in addition by the principle of propriety.

It is easy to articulate now how Smith would distinguish his concept from the Kantian. Smith might respond to the Kantians and utilitarians:

> You see people in their relations with each other like knights enclosed in armour. Morality then consists only in that no knight may harm another (negative duties) and that each one should be concerned about the interests of the others (positive duties) – but that means only that everyone, when needed, should slip good offices through the slits in the others' armour. Is it not true, however, that in our actual everyday moral consciousness we expect more from one another? Do we not expect that we will open our visors and, instead of just slipping good offices to one another and protecting one another from harms, will *truly relate to*[6] one another? But what does truly relating to one another mean if not participating in one another's feelings?

One can explain this concept of affective communication by contrasting it with Jürgen Habermas' concept of communicative action. For Habermas, an action is communicative if it pursues its ends without ignoring the interests of others, that is, if it, in Kantian terms, treats others not merely as means but always as ends (so that they may agree to my action). 'Communication' is fundamental for communicative action in Habermas' sense. But this is only a reciprocal communication *about* the interests of others, whereas the communication Smith has in mind is one *with* those others. This is a communication that is only possible as affective with the affects of others. It is not interests that are being brought into agreement but affects. Rather than aiming at a balancing of interests, one aims at a harmony of affects.

According to Smith, and against Hume's orientation towards goods (and freedom is also a good), this is what we expect from one another in 'common life' in our moral consciousness (I.i.3.8). Moreover, this is not just a fact of moral consciousness. Rather, Smith's principle, the judgment of the impartial spectator, includes and explains *both* the virtues of negative and positive duties (those of justice and beneficence), on the one hand, *and* those of propriety, on the other. This can also be achieved with the formula of the Kantian categorical imperative: I shall act in accordance with what is willed from the perspective of anyone. What everyone wants from others is not only that he shall not be harmed, that others keep their promises to him and that others help him in the case of need. He also wants to be met with sensitivity and, on his own part, to present himself in such a (self-controlled) way that others can meet him with sensitivity. It is therefore the correctly understood Kantian principle itself that reaches beyond the duties of cooperation and includes the reciprocal affective receptiveness demanded by Smith.

Smith's two basic virtues of sensitivity and self-control are not dispositions for acting. Rather, they are virtues that are irreducibly attitudes, because they are understood as attitudes of intersubjective receptiveness. We may now say that these attitudes are demanded by the principle of the universalistic morality as set up by Kant; they are universalistic morally demanded attitudes. Does it follow from the distinction I drew earlier (see p. 95) that also affects are morally judged? Is this also a universalistic judgment? Moreover, does the inclusion of affects in moral judgments not lead to the extension of morality into the private sphere?

To begin with the last question, the extension of moral judgments into the private sphere is something essentially different from the extension of the penal law into the private sphere.[7] This is also Smith's view. Only actions are subject to penal law (II.ii.3.2); their motivations, however, are judged morally. Insofar as all affects – as Smith understands them – possess a social aspect, they are subject to moral judgments. We don't dictate to each other how we should act, except where the actions concern others. But we do dictate to each other how we should conduct ourselves towards our affects, that is, how we should develop the affects themselves, because these possess an at least potentially essential element of cooperation. From here Smith is able to build virtues like moderation (even though they do not refer to other persons, for which reason we had difficulties understanding their explanation in Aristotle) into his concept of propriety.[8] Moderation with respect to bodily desires (the only ones mentioned by Aristotle) but also with regard to affects like ambition, envy and so on, is not in itself a form of openness to others but is the condition for such openness. It does not seem necessary that the to be approved or disapproved affects resulting in this way be considered universally in the same manner. In a given society something may appear as moderation, while counting as excess or insensitivity in another. Factors of convention are relevant here, but they have to be understood as expressions of an intersubjective basic attitude, which itself is not conventional.[9]

I also have still to account, as Smith tries to do, for how the virtues of justice and benevolence can be built into Smith's conception of propriety. Smith explains in I.i.1.3 that complete moral judgment relates to two different aspects of acting: first, the motivation for an action (the corresponding virtue is propriety) and, second, the effect of the action. If the action is beneficial to others, one speaks of merit; if it is harmful, of demerit. Hume's error lies in having considered only this second aspect. Where Smith treats this aspect in Part II, he attempts to show that merit itself is based on propriety. The consideration is the following: resentment is the natural reaction if I am harmed, gratitude if I am benefited. Thus introduced, resentment and gratitude are pre-moral affects. Talk of a 'natural reaction' means that the connection is analogous with the one, for example, between jealousy and its object. Moreover, it is 'natural' in the same sense as repaying good with good and bad with bad. The former is called reward, the latter punishment. The affect of gratitude and the tendency to repay positively, and the affect of resentment and the tendency to repay negatively, are also connected analytically.[10] The impartial spectator judges these affects, like all other affects, in relation to the situation to which they are reactions. However, this implies in this case a compound feeling of sympathy.[11] The spectator has an 'indirect sympathy' with the affected person, because he projects himself simultaneously into the motivations of those who harmed or benefited that person. It is this double affective projection into the positions of both parties, that grounds the judgment about whether to approve of the gratitude or the resentment. Only if the agent *deserves* the affective reaction, whether gratitude or resentment, of the recipient, are those reactions to be approved, and he deserves them if he acts out of propriety or impropriety. If someone benefits, by contrast, through a benefactor's improper motivations – for example, if the benefactor is offering a bribe or acting from a 'foolish and profuse generosity' – then the gratitude is inappropriate and the benefactor does not deserve any reward (II.i.3.2). Similarly, if harm goes back to a just indignation, then reacting resentfully to that harm is improper.

Smith therefore bases the disapproval of unjust actions on sympathy with the resentment of the affected person, and the approval of useful actions on sympathy with the gratitude of the affected one. In II.i.5.7 Smith anticipates scepticism on the part of the reader regarding this interpretation of the disapproval of injustice (for Smith 'injustice' always means harm). In response to this reaction, he emphasizes the complete analogy between resentment and gratitude. But I question whether he is successful in eliminating this doubt. In other places in the book, Smith presents the negative duties (those of justice) as a foundation for morality (III.6.10). In his explanation of the resentment that should be approved, as a feeling which presupposes that the harm was not in turn based on a justified resentment, Smith seems really to presuppose that harm is to be disapproved of in and of itself regardless of motive. Instead of basing injustice on impropriety, it seems more natural to simply say that unjust actions are disapproved of by the impartial spectator. Smith probably does not do this because his 'spectator' is never understood purely theoretically: he is always primarily the sympathizing one, and only on this basis the one who judges (approvingly or disapprovingly). But then it seems to make sense to extend Smith's concept of the impartial spectator in a manner that connects it with the Kantian question: how would everyone will that I act? At the same time, the Kantian question itself would have to take up Smith's concept of the capacity for sympathy. The impartial spectator in Smith's sense would be the one who judges all affects and attitudes according to whether he can sympathize with them from the perspective of the uninvolved. In Kant's sense, the impartial spectator would at the same time be the one who judges all actions according to whether he could will them from the perspective of anyone.

Furthermore, gratitude and resentment would not be seen as analogous, because the negative duties and the positive duty of generosity and of help are not on the same level. In contrast with Smith's explanation, resentment would then have to be considered as an affect containing an immediate moral implication, because harming, *ceteris paribus*, is to be disapproved of from the beginning. Resentment would not win its moral dimension because of impartial sympathy; rather, it would demand impartial sympathy because it is the reaction to an injustice. Matters are different with gratitude. Gratitude is a reaction to a positive action that is free and to which one is not obligated. Smith's attempt to incorporate the diffuse positive duty to help into his theory of propriety could contribute to taking away the indeterminacy that this duty has in Kantian ethics. Smith winds up reincorporating the duty to help in the virtue of generosity, where it belonged in the Aristotelian tradition. In this way, the moral motivation to give is easier to understand. Joy, according to Smith, produces sympathy. If it is the effect of someone's action whose motive is approved of, it produces joy in the impartial spectator as 'redoubled sympathy' (I.ii.4.1).

By comparison, it is secondary how far Smith is successful in his attempt to base the positive and the negative duties in propriety, and whether that was important to Smith (compare the different characterization in Part VI, discussed earlier at p. 90).[12]

The decisive thing is that the morality of duties to act and to desist has been supplemented with the morality of propriety, which is a morality of attitudes concerned with the affects we should have for others. Let me add two aspects to what I have said so far about this supplementary part of morality – which is still to be understood as the morality of the categorical imperative. First, this part of morality is not to be subsumed under rules, for the earlier-mentioned reason.[13] Moreover, Smith's balanced discussion of the morality of rules in chapters 4 and 5 of Part III can be understood only if one keeps in mind that he is thinking especially of the virtues of attitudes. Second, this supplement is naturally a supplement of positive duties. The inclusion of affects and attitudes enables the area of positive duty, which in the morality of rules shrinks to the single indeterminate duty to help, to reclaim basic significance for the demands of cooperation.

In comparing this result in Adam Smith with the social virtues in Aristotle, it is best to set aside Smith's special idea of a possible reduction even of the negative and positive duties and to consider the virtues of propriety simply as supplementing the Kantian concept. It is better to consider Smith's ethics as supplementing the Kantian rather than the Humean concept: first, because of his recourse to the impartial spectator, which can be directly connected with the categorical imperative, and second, because Smith, in the fundamental significance he gives to sympathy, rejects Hume's orientation towards usefulness for *society* and emphasizes that all moral precepts relate to individuals (II.ii.3.10).

As regards content, one may now say that both of Smith's virtues of propriety – sensitivity and self-control – are close to Aristotle's social virtues, since they are also modes of balanced openness towards others. The important progress made by Smith consists not in the content of these modes, but in grounding them in a universalistic moral principle. This principle is identical with Kant's. While Fromm's advantage consisted in giving independent sense to talk about the mean, because the extremes received a sense of their own (although the result there was not moral virtues but virtues of happiness), in Smith talk about the mean remains as formal as in Aristotle. Smith's mean receives determination, however, by being connected back to the impartial spectator. To put it in a nutshell: the Aristotelian empty formula is replaced by the Kantian principle.

Once the Kantian principle is extended to intersubjective attitudes, however, we have a key to include additional virtues and vices, recognized in our daily consciousness, in the universalistic foundation. It makes sense to relate this question first to the remaining Aristotelian social virtues. With his orientation towards reciprocal affective sympathy and the resulting virtue of sensitivity, Adam Smith works out a kind of attitude towards others not present in Aristotle at all. With the exception of the virtue of moderation, which Aristotle relates solely to bodily desires, and whose social character is only pointed out by Smith, the inclusion of affects in virtue ethics remains largely undeveloped in Aristotle. On the other hand, we find virtues in Aristotle that are primarily related to actions rather than affects, yet those actions have to be understood as actions of behaving oneself towards others and so were likewise attitudes.[14] This comes out especially in giving and the giving of oneself,[15] in character traits like generosity and the social virtues. In Smith, virtues of this kind appear only peripherally, because they do not lend themselves to being understood by way of the interplay of affectivity. The answer to the question whether they are nevertheless to be recognized as moral virtues is, on the basis of the Kantian criterion, without a doubt in the affirmative: everyone would prefer others to encounter him with behaviour marked by generosity,[16] friendliness and kindness. We therefore demand this from one another universalistically.

We must not and cannot limit ourselves, however, to the Aristotelian virtues. In particular, I would like to mention two [additional] attitudes. The first relates to the second plane of morality, which I mentioned earlier (see p. 93). The second expresses the morally basic attitude underlying all individual moral actions.

What I mean by the second plane of morality are moral feelings (which themselves always imply moral judgments) insofar as they are expressed towards others. If I proffer my resentment or indignation to someone, there can be no doubt that this is a linguistic or otherwise symbolic action (often a facial expression suffices) that can hurt, and insofar as it does, it is subject to moral judgments. Adam Smith puts great emphasis on resentment as the affect that most requires temperance, from the perspective of the impartial spectator, not only when we express it in confrontation with the person against whom we have this affect, but generally. The implication of resentment is always that we consider ourselves morally damaged or disparaged; we feel insulted but consider ourselves to be right. We are therefore not only angry, but the feeling we have towards the other takes itself to be morally, and thus objectively, supported. Thus understood, resentment is always self-righteous and therefore tends towards inexhaustibility. I have already pointed out that in his discussion Smith does not single out the case, common in everyday life, of reciprocal resentment between friends, colleagues and all who have to cooperate. It is a natural necessity that we make our resentment understood to the person who caused it (only in this way can we intend to clear things up with him morally). Most of the time, however, the other interprets the situation of reciprocal behaviour differently and considers himself either not at all or only partially wrong; he therefore considers our reaction to him as injurious. For this reason, resentment, if it is not swallowed or repressed, results in counter-resentment. This is the common situation of reciprocal quarrels, which are almost always pursued under moral descriptions, and which should not be dismissed as superficial phenomena. In this arena there is without a doubt, a universalistic virtue: the readiness for reconciliation. This is an attitude to be approved of universalistically, since it is demanded from the impartial spectator's perspective. The impartial spectator demands not only, as is the case with simple resentment, a readiness to avoid a merely one-sided view of the situation for action – this is of course an essential component of the capacity for reconciliation – but also, given this readiness, a will to re-establish unanimity. To that will belongs the affective readiness, communicated so that the other can understand it, to explicitly withdraw from positions that have been taken and to overcome self-righteousness. This virtue has its opposing vices in irreconciliability on the one hand and in simply giving in on the other. It is worth noting that conciliatoriness is not merely a disposition but a communicative attitude that strives to be expressed.

The communicative attitude in which the basic moral disposition of universal respect is expressed can be grasped by way of its opposite: humiliation. There are actions whose effects are humiliating. They are not necessarily expressions of a humiliating attitude, however. Sometimes the person who commits such actions is not even aware of their humiliating character. On the other hand, one can treat someone in a particular way *in order* to express contempt. One's actions are then also symbols of humiliation. The following story, which took place in West Berlin a few years ago, illustrates this well. Someone applying for asylum asks an official in the public health department for a medical insurance record card for his leg, which needs an operation. The official refuses, arguing that the leg does not need to be healed, since the asylum seeker is not permitted to work anyway. The immoral *action* consists in the official's refusing the asylum seeker the help to which he is entitled. This may already be humiliating in, and of, itself, but the official explicitly expresses a humiliating *attitude* in making the asylum seeker understand that his value is a merely instrumental one, the one he would possess in the work process.[17]

The attitude of respect becomes more explicit in its revocation, because we usually confront our fellow man with a minimum display of respect. I have already pointed out that courtesy, and especially greetings, are to be understood as attesting respect.[18] One could want to push the meaning of greetings into the conventional realm, but everyone knows how important they are who has had the experience of another person ceasing to greet him. By ceasing to greet another, one lets the other know that he no longer exists for him as a person (a moral subject).

In class societies, in which there is a view that people belonging to different classes or castes possess different values, differentiated respect is expressed through the form of asymmetrical greeting and asymmetrical address. One has to recognize that symmetrical greeting is a precept, if not a very significant one, of a universalistic morality.

The word 'respect', like the word 'recognition', is not entirely unambiguous.[19] What is the object of recognition, what is the object of respect? Here, one can distinguish three realms. The most basic one is the one in which, if we have respect for someone, we recognize him as a legal personality. To this corresponds the fact that, if individuals are treated with differential respect in a traditional society, they take on a different 'value', that is, they are purported to have different rights. Most of the time, when we talk about self-respect, we also mean that people are aware of their rights, even if others do not respect them. Within universalistic morality, it is the precept of the communicative basic attitude to treat other individuals in a way that they will understand that they have the moral rights that everyone has.

We have seen that G.W.F. Hegel relates recognition to the freedom of the others.[20] Even in contemporary usage, it seems widespread to understand respect for a person as recognition of his autonomy. One *could* consider this, as Hegel does, as the recognition of a fact, but it is more natural to understand it from a moral perspective, as the recognition of the other's right to his freedom. Moreover, the latter is to be understood in the special sense that one regards oneself as bound by the duty to restrain oneself in order to afford freedom to the other. Seen in this way, respect for the other's freedom is an important *part* of respect for him as a subject of justice. Again, one may be able to say that one often understands talk about self-respect as a matter of being aware of one's autonomy and wanting others to recognize it. Insistence on independence is perhaps one of the earliest stirrings of morality in the small child (albeit a one-sided one) for which there seems to be no equivalent in other animals.

A third component in the understanding of respect appears to be that we respect a person's *value*. Naturally, respect for a person's moral value is implicated in respecting him as a subject of law, but this is not sufficient for anyone. Everyone possesses moral value. Above that, everyone wants to be recognized for his performances, that is, for his capacity to perform. The most important maxim of everyone who has to do with the upbringing and education of others (regardless of the level) is that he instills those he teaches with the confidence to use their abilities. Recognizing someone's moral value therefore always implies recognizing him in his self-value and, at least, in his need for self-value. This implication exists less directly than the last one, of autonomy. One must recognize here that this need for recognizing one's self-value is just as basic in human beings as the need to be loved. While the latter can be fulfilled only by a few, the former is directed towards all. Frequently, conflicts result for teachers between justice and truthfulness in judging value, on the one hand (and in the development of the corresponding truthfulness of the adolescent in relation to himself), and the precept of respecting the need for self-value, on the other.

The three aspects of the understanding of respect are therefore analytically connected. The importance of making respect understood in this threefold sense differs in different spheres of intersubjective contact. It is naturally central in relations of love and friendship, but it is also fundamental in asymmetrical relationships, as in the teacher-pupil relationship mentioned earlier or in the manner in which the 'civil servant' deals with his client. (In German, we don't have a good word for 'civil servant', because the '*Beamte*' (official or clerk) primarily relates to the '*Dienstherr*' (employer) and thus rather to the state than to the public.) The asymmetrical relationship in which the 'civil servant'[21] finds himself, like that of the teacher (and all relationships of power), tempts people into the misuse of that relationship. There is a natural tendency to disrespect, which may be motivated not only by lust for power but simply by indifference. One thinks for instance of an immigration department: in Germany, the official[22] is often seated behind an opaque glass window. Applications and their responses are pushed back and forth through a slit in the window (like the slit in the armour of the knights mentioned earlier (see p. 95). The authorities mean to protect the official even from the glance of his opposite number. Bureaucratic apparatuses are becoming larger everywhere in the world at the moment, and the crisis in the behaviour of bureaucracies is likewise universal. It is a challenge for one used to close relationships to be confronted with a stream of strangers, a situation for which the institution itself and his education leave the official unprepared and without assistance. One could imagine that it would be a great, but perhaps not so difficult task for the educators of 'civil servants' to demonstrate to them the satisfaction won from treating others – in whose service they are – in a manner characterized by respect. Perhaps modern ethics, which so one-sidedly emphasize actions and overlook the importance of interpersonal attitudes, bear part of the responsibility for the current mentality of the opaque window.

Explaining why the virtues of interpersonal attitudes are not considered in Kant, for example, although they result so naturally from the categorical imperative once one has become aware of them, would be a separate task, which I won't get into here. Making things more difficult is the fact that for a modern ethical system, based on a uniform, grounding principle, it must appear unacceptable that virtue ethics in the Aristotelian tradition takes the form of a mere list. It may have required Smith's unique and brilliant idea of connecting the principle of impartiality with that of affective concord – an idea whose significance has been forgotten – to make the virtues again accessible to the modern consciousness. As for why Kant overlooked interpersonal attitudes, the strong directedness of his conception of the moral towards the just may play a role, as well as his orientation towards the duties available to contractarianism.

As concerns contractarianism, one has to ask whether at least a part of the virtues of the intersubjective attitudes would not lend themselves to being based on contractarian grounds. This appears impossible where, as in the process of making respect for the other understood, there is more implied than is available in a quasi-morality (one could however imagine a contractual society of hypocrites). Virtues like the readiness for reconciliation, but also those of kindness, and so on, appear on the other hand to be required by contractarianism, *provided* that the affected person is interested in having others encounter him in a similar manner. It therefore depends on what needs we presuppose on the part of the contracting parties. From the newly-won perspective, is it not just as naïve to assume that only material needs are presupposed by the contractarian, as it is to assume that of one who starts from the concept of the good person defined by the categorical imperative?

To view the possibilities of contractarianism as generously as possible is of fundamental significance because the *motives* for taking on a genuinely moral attitude are so weak, as far as we have been able to determine, at any rate. In contractarianism, by contrast, there are no problems regarding motivation.

Acknowledgements

Translator's note: I would like to express my gratitude to Vivienne Brown and Sam Fleischacker for the opportunity of translating this text. Moreover, I am indebted to them for their criticism, and their many suggestions and comments on earlier drafts. I would also like to thank Christel Fricke for her comments and insights.

Notes

1 A. Smith (1976) [1759] *The Theory of Moral Sentiments*, D.D. Raphael and A.L. Macfie (eds), London and New York: Oxford University Press. Quotations are from this edition.
2 Trans.: see Lectures 11 and 12.
3 Trans.: D. Hume [1751] *An Inquiry concerning the Principles of Morals*. Sam Fleischacker points out that Tugendhat does not include Hume's *Treatise* in his bibliography. Most Smith scholars see implicit references to Hume in TMS before Part VI; see under 'Hume' in the index to the Raphael and Macfie edition of TMS.
4 Trans.: Tugendhat's insertion of parenthetical exclamation mark.
5 Trans.: see Lecture 14.
6 Trans.: The German uses '*eingehen*'.
7 Trans.: see Lecture 11.
8 Trans.: see Lecture 13.
9 Trans.: see Tugendhat's discussion of politeness in Lecture 13.
10 One could consider it as belonging to the definition of an affect that it not only has a propositional content, but that to it belongs a particular tendency for acting. Cf. A. Kenny (1967) *Action, Emotion, and Will*, London: Routledge and Keagan Paul.
11 Trans.: see TMS I.ii.5.2–4.
12 Cf. otherwise unambiguous passages like III.1.7.
13 Trans.: see Lectures 4 and 5 and the speech about the knights above on p. 95.
14 Trans.: see Lecture 13.
15 Trans.: the German uses '*Geben*' and '*Sich-Geben*'.
16 One cannot simply replace generosity with the precept that one ought to help one another. Admittedly, we are to think of both generosity and the precept that one ought to help one another in a nuanced way, depending on one's closeness to others (family, friends, neighbours). The precept that one ought to help one another relates to actions, whereas generosity is primarily an attitude. As such, the latter does not simply relate to others but at the same time to oneself. What is required is to have a balanced relation in the keeping house of one's own needs and those of others. The virtues of 'giving and taking' are not directly transferable to presenting oneself and permitting others to participate in one's resources of any sort, for example, that of time. For this reason, the one who is miserly with his money is normally also miserly with his time. Related

to the vice of miserliness is the vice of not being able to accept. Following Aristotle, generosity is the virtue of giving *and* receiving; and the ability to receive appropriately, which again lies between two extremes, is an attitude related to the ability to give appropriately, which naturally cannot be seen in an ethics concerned only with actions.

17 In reports about survival in concentration camps, torture centres and military labour camps one can read again and again that the humiliation of depersonalization constitutes the pinnacle of sadistic pleasure, worse than anything one is subjected to physically. In the terminology of the Judeo-Christian tradition, it is the defilement of the human countenance.

18 Trans.: see Lecture 13, p. 256f. Page numbers to lectures other than this translation refer to those of the German edition.

19 Trans.: see Lecture 14, p. 275f.

20 Trans.: see Lecture 14, p. 275.

21 Trans.: the German uses the English term here.

22 Trans.: the German uses '*Beamte*'.

Perspectives on recent developments in Adam Smith scholarship

Reading Adam Smith in the light of the classics

Gloria Vivenza

I

Adam Smith, it has been frequently observed, won great renown in the fairly new field of political economy; and this was enough to overshadow for more than a century the fame of his moral treatise, *The Theory of Moral Sentiments* (Smith 1976a, TMS), although it had been a success. Even the emergence of the 'Adam Smith Problem', which drew scholarly attention to TMS, had the purpose of examining how it was possible for the author of the *Wealth of Nations* (Smith 1976b, WN) to have written so different a book.

Obviously these conditions were not conducive to arouse scholarly interest in the influence of the classics on Smith's thought. Only in 1940, with W.R. Scott's *Greek Influence on Adam Smith* (about twenty pages), do we have a short essay completely devoted to the subject. This does not mean that Smith's good knowledge of the classics passed unobserved in some works or monographs about other aspects of his thought; and analogies were noticed in some of his arguments – as, for instance, the relation observed in 1922 by Bonar between Smith and Plato on the division of labour (Bonar 1922: 15, 155 ff.), although Bonar in fact underlines the main difference between the two.

The new interest in Smith as a philosopher called attention to some aspects of his thought derived from the classics; it is enough to glance through the pages of monographs such as those by J. Cropsey (1977), G. Morrow (1969) and T.D. Campbell (1971) to find important and also substantial references to this aspect of Smith's cultural heritage (Vivenza 2001a). Time brought to the fore also Smith's juvenile essays on natural philosophy, published posthumously in 1795 and then sunk in oblivion like the TMS. After that, valuable investigations and researches were devoted to illuminate Smith's thought as a whole: I refer to the well-known contributions of A.L. Macfie (1967), D.D. Raphael (1972, 1973, 1979) and A.S. Skinner (1972, 1974); and to the renowned bicentennial Glasgow Edition of Smith's *opera omnia*, where the different aspects of his culture, included the classics, are made conspicuous.

The Adam Smith Review, 1: 107–24 © 2004 The International Adam Smith Society, ISSN 1743–5285, ISBN 0–415–27863–5

The publication in 1976 of V. Foley's *The Social Physics of Adam Smith* may be considered a turning point because it was the first book entirely devoted to an interpretation of Smith's thought in the light of a classical philosophical theory, namely the atomism of Democritus. It was also, however, the first interpretation of Smith's thought through a scheme suggested by Havelock (1957) and Cole (1967) (*The liberal temper in Greek Politics*; *Democritus and the Sources of Greek Anthropology*) who had tried to reconstruct Democritus' political theory, of which almost nothing survives, in a highly conjectural way. I have already expressed doubts about Foley's hypothesis that Adam Smith also reconstructed Democritus' theory in the same way two centuries earlier, while keeping his enterprise concealed because he judged it dangerous (Vivenza 1982). Foley's interpretation would oblige us to read the whole of Smith's work as a sort of cryptogram. In 1984, N. Waszek's article 'Two concepts of morality' brought research to safer grounds. His analysis, although debatable on single topics, points out some important aspects of Stoic influence on Smith's moral philosophy. So the already recognized importance of a Stoic influence on Adam Smith was confirmed, in particular the writings of Cicero, Seneca, Epictetus and M. Aurelius (Waszek 1984: 601).

Meanwhile a very important change had taken place, beginning with the history of political thought, a change sometimes described as the 'linguistic turn' and involving also the traditional fields of social and intellectual history. It is obviously impossible to give here even a short summary of the issue, not only because of the enormous amount of literature, but also because each historical 'school' made its own contribution in different forms (cf. the recent articles of Guilhamou 2000, 2001).

Among the perspectives opened by the overflow of studies originated by the 'linguistic turn', two have relevance for the present essay: the 'civic humanism' and the 'natural law' paradigms. Both influenced the Scottish Enlightenment, and in consequence also Adam Smith, whose works reveal traces of them, according to many scholars. His moral and political thought has been interpreted as greatly influenced by the first, by the second, or by both paradigms.[1] The main purpose has been to study, discuss and clarify Smith's thought on *modern* topics, on which I cannot dwell; many valuable studies inspired by the 'paradigms' have been devoted to Adam Smith's political ideas; to the military problem so relevant for Scotland in those days; to the place of Smith's juridical perspective in relation to his moral, political and economic thought – all these being obviously connected with issues relating private and public morals. This may, to some extent, recall a special kind of *querelle des anciens et des modernes* if it is true, as many of these studies demonstrate, that it was the tension between the 'new' values of commercial society and the 'old' ones of civic virtue that stimulated the best minds of the Scottish Enlightenment and produced the amazing flourishing of their works.

II

It is to recent scholarly research about this aspect of the so-called Scottish Enlightenment that we owe new and fresh insights into Adam Smith's thought; but obviously this is not the place for dealing with this aspect of the literature (for valuable reviews of the main literature on these and other interpretations, see Brown (1997) and Tribe (1999)). What is of interest for my present purpose is that, from this point onwards, Adam Smith's classical heritage was taken into account because it was somehow implied in these paradigms, although perhaps the pervasive influence of the classics is not always fully recognized. For instance, E.J. Harpham, in his comment on D. Winch's (1978) authoritative support for the influence of civic humanism on Adam Smith, objects to Winch's interpretation of the famous paragraph of WN V.i.f.50[2] as a civic humanist motif, saying that Smith's sentence shows his belief that a modern labourer is unable to participate in politics (Harpham 1994: 289–90; cf. Winch 1988 for a complete reply). True, but nonetheless Smith does use a very classical and civic humanist argument, taken from Xenophon's *Oeconomicus* IV, 2–3, where the Greek author describes the 'illiberal' arts, which oblige the labourer to live an unhealthy life that renders him unfit both for social and for military activity. This was a *locus classicus* for ancient thought, and Smith knew it perfectly well.[3] Whether he consciously recalled it or not, the fact is that the 'mental mutilation' of the modern worker is expressed with exactly the same arguments of the ancient author.

Both paradigms use classical arguments but are engendered by the problems of modern Europe. Anyway, as regards their classical sources, 'civic humanism' is essentially Aristotelian, while the classical doctrine underlying the natural law paradigm is Stoic, mainly because the natural law treatises opposed Hobbesian theories on the basis of the Stoic principle of man's natural 'sociability' (cf. among others, Buckle 1991: 23–9, 69–77).

I think it important, however, to recall that the two paradigms have a fundamental assumption in common: the natural inequality of men, and this is of a Platonic–Aristotelian origin, not Stoic.[4] According to a recent interpretation, some representatives of the Scottish Enlightenment synthesized the two paradigms by means of a justification of inequality by natural law, derived from Heineccius and leading to a 'benevolent restraint on property and authority' recognizable in Francis Hutcheson's Christian Stoicism (Haakonssen 1996: 97) – from which, however, Smith parted by adopting a perspective centred on rights rather than duties, possibly derived from the German Romanist Cocceius (Haakonssen 1996: 86–7, 96–7, 129–48).[5]

I have expressed elsewhere doubts on the possibility that Stoicism was *really* compatible with Christianity (Vivenza 2001a: 209–10); but obviously this does not mean that a 'christianized Stoicism' did not exist: on the contrary, since the Middle Ages some similarities between the two doctrines were perceived, to such a point that a legend was created on the relationship of Seneca with St Paul (Colish 1992: 338–40). It must be recognized, however, that some classical themes could easily be adapted to Christian precepts: for instance, the desirability of wealth and power 'to benefit others'; or the Stoic principle of the cosmic order, so misleadingly similar to the Christian providence.

Although I am not able to ascertain whether Adam Smith's 'primacy of subjective rights' was derived from Cocceius,[6] I can agree that the idea of a 'benevolent restraint' was not in keeping with his thought, even if we admit that Smith would never have accepted riots or unlawful actions in order to remedy differences of wealth and power, despite the asserted equality of philosopher and porter at WN I.ii.5. But I think that he was not ready to accept a distributive-charitable perspective, according to which the only thing to do was to rely on the benevolent restraint of the owners of riches and power: after all, everyone had to forward his own interest to enable the invisible hand to work.[7]

The fact is that Stoicism gave powerful weapons to this perspective, too. It has been frequently noticed that the principle of forwarding one's own (legitimate) interest is grounded on Stoic self-preservation; which, however, is not so contrary as it may appear to the other, also Stoic, principle of the prevalence of the common over the individual good. I could see that, even prior to Adam Smith's invisible hand, it was asserted, in a treatise on natural law inspired by Stoicism, that the best means to forward the common good is by forwarding one's own.[8]

The scholarship dealing with these subjects is not always precise in identifying both the classical sources at the basis of the modern 'paradigms' and the related position of Adam Smith. I have frequently come across a 'Stoic-Ciceronian morals' (or 'virtue'), vague in its content, and used to explain the connection of civic values with 'those jurisprudential traditions which, increasingly centred upon the concept of sovereignty, regarded monarchy as the exemplary, because unitary, form of government' (Robertson 1983: 140; 1985: 12).[9] I would be cautious before attributing all this to Cicero: he lost his life because he rejected the idea of a monarchy, and fought with all his formidable dialectical weapons in order to save the constitution of the Roman Republic, where authority and power were divided among a limited number of *patres familias* endowed with equal rights. It was, therefore, a collective rule, that is, of the 'civic humanist' type, not a single source of authority,[10] whose supposed superiority is an effect of monotheistic religion, but which would have been labelled as tyrannical in the time of Cicero. The Stoics, on the contrary, could easily live together with monarchy; but, as noticed by P. Brunt (1975) in a masterly article, it was because they were indifferent to whatever form of government took place.

III

An interesting result of the comparative study of the two paradigms was a focus on virtues on the one hand, and rights on the other (probably derived from Pocock 1983: 248). On virtues I shall speak later; as regards rights, it is my opinion that the lengthy modern discussions on the relationship between duties, obligations and rights are derived after all from Cicero's *De Officiis*; and from the same source there is also derived the dichotomy between justice and the other virtues 'generally represented by beneficence' (Haakonssen 1982: 212), so evident in Smith. I must point out, however, that although Cicero declares a mainly Stoic source for his *De Officiis*, it was realized since the humanist-Renaissance commentaries that he had also Aristotle's moral writings, especially *Nicomachean Ethics*, at hand.

Apart from this, it is impossible to deny a strong presence of Stoic principles even in some key elements of Smith's thought; but it is not right to underrate his explicit rejection in TMS VII.ii.1.43. The most thoughtful interpreters, naturally, do not underrate it; but they have some problems in reconciling the 'Stoic' Smith with this resolute assertion which cannot be misunderstood. V. Brown, who devotes many pages of her *Adam Smith's Discourse* to the relation of Smith to Stoicism, attributes Smith's rejection of it to his impossibility to consider reason and nature one and the same thing, as the Stoics did (Brown 1994: 73–4).[11] With this book we are in the field of the philosophy of language, recently applied also to the language of economics (Henderson *et al.* 1993; useful summaries in Backhouse 1993: 3–17 and Lagueux 1999: 1–22); it is, after all, another kind of 'paradigm' which questions the univocal interpretation of the 'canon' of a science – in the present case, economic thought and its history. It also questions, within the single texts, the reading that aims to recover the 'authorial intention'.

In this case, too, I do not wish to tackle a complex subject which had the result of questioning the usual presuppositions of historians, and of pointing out the capacity of the discourse to shape the structure of ideas and behaviour. The most surprising result was perhaps the inclusion of economics among the 'humanities' (novel, rhetoric, conversation, georgic)[12] rather than among sciences.[13]

Many analyses of Smith's works, inspired more or less directly by this stream, tend towards a 'reconciled' interpretation of his thought, so to speak. It has been pointed out that social and moral life, in Smith's writings, is not formed by fixed schemes of behaviour, but by an unceasing game of adaptations, negotiations, reconsiderations, due to a network of different interrelations among men driven by the desire of being approved, esteemed, 'recognized'. This means that even in the field of economic behaviour a moral element is included, because the struggle for moral approbation shows that, at the basis of the bargain, there is not only self-interest, but also other-regarding sentiments like the pleasure of agreement (Young 2001: 101, 107). So the market is the modern substitute for ancient institutions, apt to promote social order and progress. This kind of interpretation ends by reconciling differences too harshly contrasted in the 'Adam Smith Problem', like self-interest versus benevolence: now it is maintained that, with this approach, public and private, individual and community, civic humanism and commercial society, are reconciled in Smith's thought.

At present not only TMS, but also the *Lectures on Rhetoric and Belles Lettres* (Smith 1983, LRBL), with their wealth of classical examples, are considered important for Smith's thought, even in the field of economics, as emblematic of his will to persuade by means of sentiment rather than of reason (cf. Kalyvas–Katznelson 2001: 562–3),[14] attributing to the rhetorical 'speech' an important role in shaping a mentality of cooperation, fundamental in a commercial society.

On the whole, I think that these critical trends (the analysis both of the contexts and of the linguistic strategies) have made a good contribution to our knowledge of Adam Smith's classical training. I would also call attention to the less frequent analysis of the relations between rhetoric (classic and modern) and juridical-moral language, by means of which only A. Giuliani (1997), at least in Italy, has ventured to analyze Smith's text.

IV

The interpretations that pay large attention to the classics in Smith's work frequently reach conclusions considered valid for all his writings, including WN; but it is obvious that the inquiry is usually made by means of examination, more or less accurate, of TMS and the *Essays on Philosophical Subjects* (Smith 1980, EPS). Sometimes it seems that there is some overlapping between epistemological and scientific issues on the one hand, and moral or social issues on the other. This may perhaps be caused by the key role of the imagination, which allows some sort of connection between the hypothetical and relative character of scientific theories, illustrated in the *History of Astronomy* (HA; in EPS), with the 'theatricality' attributed to TMS on the basis of its theatrical language. Some interpretations of Smith in a Stoic dress, for instance, are to some extent connected with the metaphor of the impartial spectator. It has led some authors to give too much weight, to my mind, to Smith's 'construction' of moral life as a stage with actors and spectators, or to extend the principle of 'spectatorship' to very different issues, such as the point of view of the Deity on the one hand, and the splitting or duality of the self on the other (e.g. Brown 1994: 55ff.; Griswold 1999: 104ff.; Heise 1995: 23). Imagination seems to have an almost demiurgical power in 'building' the world, external and internal.

Now it is true that many of these metaphors are well represented in ancient philosophy, not only Stoic (Brown 1994: 59–60; Griswold 1999: 66 n.50). But one should correct an unduly extensive application of these devices, which have been used for centuries in moral philosophy in order to illustrate some topics which are always the same: the relationship between self and others; the right 'balance' between virtue and excesses. Smith's spectator does not limit himself to watching; besides, I would say that this is not his most important task: he must evaluate and make a judgment.[15] And the circumstance that he must be 'well informed' seems to allude to the fact that only to look is not sufficient – or, as is said by an old adage, that appearances may deceive. Moreover, to apply divine spectatorship to Stoic philosophy (Heise 1995: 22), in the sense of considering the Stoic God as transcendent, is incorrect: this is a character of the Christian, not of the Stoic deity.

I shall not repeat what I have already said on the epistemological position of Smith, and on his 'principles which lead and direct philosophical enquiries', where an antirealistic aspect (of classical origin, by the way) is clearly recognized and corresponds to well known philosophical positions. I do not agree, however, that it can be applied also to moral philosophy.[16] This is the general interpretative frame, a little too elaborate perhaps, of C. Griswold's recent interpretation of Smith as sceptical, contrary to the prevailing Stoic trend. I would emphasize that I am speaking here of Scepticism applied to moral philosophy, not to epistemological questions or political positions, about which I would call attention to the work of S. Cremaschi (1984, 1989).[17]

Therefore, although I find interesting many of the recent interpretations which attribute to Smith an over-extensive classical perspective, I think it is better to be careful: certain of his positions are mistaken for Stoic (or Epicurean, or Sceptic) without being so.

V

Perhaps it is relevant to recall here the well known classical distinction between theoretical philosophy, and the philosophy of practice formed by ethics, politics and economics. I think it was still valid for Adam Smith, as demonstrated by the well-known passage of TMS VI.ii.3.6. The prevalence of the 'smallest active duty' leads naturally to the subject of virtue; in fact, many of the studies of Smith's classical culture give attention to his treatment of virtues. Four of them have been considered fundamental: prudence, justice, benevolence and self-command. Few authors (among them, Muller 1993: 98)[18] have given attention to a string of minor virtues (prudence, vigilance, circumspection, temperance, constancy, firmness, TMS VII.ii.3.15) about which Smith ventures a criticism of his beloved teacher Hutcheson, who did not explain the origin of their approbation.

The four mentioned virtues were examined by N. Waszek (1984), and after him other scholars gave their attention to them. Let us begin with the virtue of prudence, which aroused a special interest, being perhaps the most 'economic' of Smith's virtues. But some difficulties arose from not knowing its long history. It was created by Greek philosophy as the 'practical' companion of science; the main difference between the two being that the one was only theoretic, the other devoted to practice, or, to be more precise, an intellectual virtue directed to action (Sorabji 1980: 205–14). This special quality of prudence gave rise to a very complex issue, also because, once the contact of Christianity with classical philosophy had taken place, the first cardinal virtue was deemed to be *sapientia*, but it is frequently found also in the dress of its 'practical' version of *prudentia* (cf. Martin 1982: 52; Den Uyl 1991: 85).

I cannot give even a short summary of the subsequent history: prudence was identified with very different things, all connected with action directed by knowledge, that is knowledge of ends, and of the means to reach them. If the end was the good of the universe, or of the state, or the best way of administering something, we have the 'noble' kinds of prudence of the great statesman/administrator: *prudentia civilis, prudentia militaris, prudentia politica*, which were, however, joined, during the Renaissance and the Counter Reformation, by a 'jesuitical' prudence which was dissimulating and even false. If the end was the definition of one's own private interest, then we have the 'private' prudence which was directed towards the self: without being a vice, or a moral fault, it was the opposite of, say, unreflective generosity, altruism, self-denial and so on. This ambivalence is clearly recognizable in Adam Smith's text, with its inferior prudence of Epicurean origin, which is at the head of the minor virtues and which can arouse nothing more than a 'cold esteem'; and the superior prudence of the great man, at which Smith hints briefly, taking care, however, to be precise in defining it as Platonic-Aristotelian.

This distinction between Aristotelian and Epicurean prudence goes back to a difference already present in Greek thought, taken up again and developed by Italian humanism, and then spread all over Europe with a great range of different *prudentiae*, as mentioned earlier (Oestreich 1982: 90–117, 155–65; De Mattei 1951: 129 ff.; Viroli 1994: 25–8).

Adam Smith's prudence has been sometimes identified directly with self-interest (Heise 1991: 72, 1995: 23), or with the first cardinal virtue (wisdom) (Waszek 1984: 602–3; Fitzgibbons 1995: 105; cf. Vivenza 2001a: 196–7). Den Uyl (1991: 137) maintains that there is a tension between the 'two prudences' of Smith because, unlike Aristotle's ethics, which aimed at self-perfection, Smith's was directed towards social cooperation, and his inferior prudence was self-regarding while the superior was other-regarding.[19]

Recently, an attempt has been made to connect Smith's 'judgment' with Aristotle's *phronesis*. The usual connection of *phronesis* with modern prudence has been challenged since the time of the authoritative comment by Gauthier and Jolif (1959) on the *Nicomachean Ethics*, but nonetheless it is relevant and appropriate. S. Fleischacker says that 'in the eighteenth century "prudence" is the badly attenuated descendant of, and the common if misleading translation for, Aristotle's "practical wisdom"' (Fleischacker 1999: 135).[20] The translation, as is well known, goes back to Cicero and is not at all misleading; *phronesis/prudentia* is *sapientia* applied to action, and in the same place, Cicero also says that *cognitio contemplatioque naturae* is incomplete and void if it is not followed by action (*De Off.* I.153; also cf. I.19: *virtutis enim laus omnis in actione consistit*): Smith almost certainly had these passages in mind.

It has to be stressed, therefore, that the whole evolution of a concept should be considered: it may be true that Aristotle's *phronesis* was different from modern prudence; but a scholar living in the eighteenth century could not avoid having in mind the complete string of meanings, and there is an indisputable relation between Cicero's *prudentia* and the various applications of mind (knowledge *and* wisdom[21]) to the 'practical' or active sides of life, whether noble or mean.

VI

Justice is another of Smith's virtues on which scholarship has exercised much exegesis, especially in relation to the Aristotelian distinction between commutative (rectificatory) and distributive justice. This distinction also has a very long history, impossible to summarize here.

One of the first interpreters of Smith's political thought, D. Forbes, speaking about Grotius, noted that it is confusing to apply the term justice also to a concept of distribution (called *iustitia attributrix* by Grotius) (Forbes 1982: 188). As for Smith's justice, commentators have often stressed its negative character, to abstain from injury, a view that originated with Roman jurisprudence. But there is also, in modern thought, a positive aspect of justice (= to do good), which, to my mind, arose from its direct relationship to another virtue, beneficence, frequently connected, by Smith and by many others, with justice itself.[22] This connection is the source of all the modern reasoning about rights (perfect-imperfect; natural-acquired) and duties (positive and negative). The author who has contributed most to illuminate Smith's thought on these problems is K. Haakonssen (1982, 1990, 1996), whose interpretation rests on sound historical grounds. In fact, distributive justice, although called 'justice' since Aristotle's well-known definition, is not a juridical concept and eventually protects only imperfect rights, which are no rights at all, according to the already mentioned criticism of Forbes and others. It has been usual, however, to consider as 'distributive justice' beneficence and other virtues relating to the 'positive' aspect of justice, namely to do good. There were centuries of discussion about this, and I would not enter into related problems like the enforceability of *true* justice and the discretionary character of distributive justice. Smith, however, is very clear when he says that 'justice proper' is only the commutative, and that when it is said that the poor have a right in our charity, the word ('right') is used in a 'metaphoricall sense' (LJA i.15).

In recent years, a literature on Smith's 'distributive' concerns has grown up. It seems, however, that to connect distributive economic justice with the classical (Aristotelian) (*Nicomachean Ethics* 1130b30–1131b24) concept is incorrect. Distributive justice in the modern sense is 'the obligation of the community to the individual' (Verburg 2000: 23; cf. also Young 1997: 131); the discussion about its place in Smith's thought, starting from a well-known article of Hont and Ignatieff (1983), centred on the (imperfect) 'rights' of the poor over the property of the rich in case of extreme need. Was this a question of justice for Smith? Scholars do not agree about that; and have devoted valuable essays to elucidate Smith's attitude towards problems of social justice connected with the relief of poverty, or with a better distribution of wealth. It is debated whether Smith thought that the economic structure of a commercial society was able to produce sufficient welfare for all, or if he trusted in a moderate government intervention to correct the most extreme inequalities (e.g. Young 1997; Salter 1994, 1999; Witztum 1997). However interesting these problems are, they have nothing to do with Aristotle's distributive justice, and were born in the modern age.[23]

Although Smith's position has been interpreted in different ways, in this paper I concentrate on only one aspect, namely the classical roots of Smith's stance. The difference among the authors who maintain that Smith did *not* consider distributive economic problems as pertaining to justice (Haakonssen, Winch, Salter) and those who think the opposite (Young, Witztum) has relevance for my purpose only on the question whether or not they derive their argument from Aristotle. It is obvious that, if one wants to maintain that Smith included (re)distributive programmes in the field of justice, one must connect distributive justice with the rectificatory principle, that is, with commutative justice. Both Young and Witztum do that, by saying that commutative and distributive justice are united in Smith's thought (Young); or that there is only a difference of degree between the two forms of justice, which have the same origin (Witztum). The origin from Aristotle, however, is much more stressed in Young, who begins his analysis from the Aristotelian–Scholastic position. I do not think, however, that Aristotle's distributive justice can be considered a 'communal obligation', nor that 'distributive justice is a part of beneficence' (Young 1997: 133): quite the contrary, in fact, since it is beneficence which is a part of justice. The connection justice – beneficence, although present in Cicero, has been elaborated mainly by modern thinkers, who had to reconcile the inviolability of the property rights with the duty of charity and brotherhood towards the poor: a problem which did not exist in the classical world.

Another problem, relevant to the modern analysis of economic distribution, may be its 'borderline' character: although prompted by solidarity, which is a moral motif, distribution based on equity should be enforced by law. This dual character shows the ambiguity of giving the name of 'justice' both to a legal and to a moral concept.

The question of reconciling commutative and distributive justice does not arise in ancient Greek thought because Aristotle's account of 'corrective' justice (later called 'commutative') has little to do with his account of distributive justice (Raphael 2001: 50, 57). In modern thought, the difference was still perceived, but had partly been overwhelmed by the continued efforts, originated by Cicero's connection of justice with *beneficentia* (*De Off.* I, 20; cf. Vivenza 2001b: 210–22), to find a relationship between justice on the one hand, and appropriate moral behaviour, including distribution, on the other: an insoluble problem, in fact, which anyway transferred the couple justice – charity (the final transformation of beneficence) well into the nineteenth century. At this point, the paternalistic attitude of the ancien régime which deemed it *just* that distribution be unequal, accepted by all and relieved by charity, was replaced by the post-revolutionary attitude which felt as *unjust* the unequal distribution and thought that it had to be redressed. The consequence was that redistribution was no longer an option entrusted to personal goodwill, but became a charge of government. This attitude, however, was not yet prevailing in Smith's day.

So, I think that Adam Smith did not reconcile commutative with distributive justice more than Aristotle did; and that he carefully defined the difference between the two especially in TMS VII.ii.1.10 and LJA i.15, and in the manuscript fragment on justice published in TMS, 389–90. In any case, returning to Adam Smith's knowledge of the classics, I wish to stress that it was accurate and deep. It is true that he used their arguments to support his own views, combining different elements according to his purpose; but he is not in error about their meaning. I have limited my discussion on virtues to prudence and justice, but in both cases Smith's analysis shows more insight and accuracy than some modern authors in explaining the classical stance. I am tempted to conclude that it is difficult, if not impossible, in the case of the classics, to choose between historical and analytical comment: if the historical setting is lacking, the analytical exegesis is likely to go astray.

VII

Now I would say that the recent analyses on Adam Smith's classical culture may be divided in two main streams. One comes from 'readings' of his work, usually in its entirety,[24] by means of a particular interpretative key which, in the instances here considered, is grounded on a classical philosophy reworked by modern minds: so Smith passes through a double filter, so to speak. These readings give to Smith's thought a certain compactness, derived from the thesis on which they are grounded; so, for example, we have the Democritean Smith (Foley 1976), the partially (Brown 1994) or completely (Heise 1991, 1995) Stoic, the Sceptic (Griswold 1999).[25] This is not a problem, from my point of view – I would agree that Smith's thought encompasses all these, and other, components. The problem is that many of these authors do not limit themselves to reading what Smith wrote, they read also what he did not write, and by dint of 'implications', 'indirect reading' and so on, they work out a text of their own which has a tendency to prevail both over Adam Smith and over the classics. There is an inextricable mix between arguments which may be plausible, or consistent with what Smith said, and arguments indispensable to support their own thesis, but forced when applied to Adam Smith or to the classics. 'The unifying element [...] is constituted by the identity of their author' (Brown 1994: 207) – if I may borrow a sentence out of context.... The common result reached by all these scholars is to identify an Adam Smith very different from the traditional view of him, although this tradition is not a unitary 'canon'. But, to my mind, the framework of these interpretations invents a degree of coherence which is too good to be true. To put it in very simple terms: while in *moral* philosophy Stoics and Epicureans do have some points in common, and it is possible, and right, to pick out traces of both doctrines in Smith, the same cannot be done in natural philosophy or science. Here the two philosophies diverge completely: to the cosmic order of Stoicism the Epicurean alternative was a chaos of atoms. Now in Smith's philosophy we find traces of the first, but not of the second; so the authors who wanted to find them had to force the argument to the point of regarding Smith as a very tortuous mind, attributing to him a precise philosophical position not simply *despite*, but *because*, he did not speak of it.[26]

The other trend, that of the 'paradigms', does not concentrate exclusively on Adam Smith, but takes in a whole range of political, institutional, jurisprudential and moral topics in the literature from the Renaissance onwards. Obviously it considers the classics, but is obliged to do it with a closer regard for the texts because it works on the Renaissance scholarship which mastered them thoroughly. The result is a picture which enlightens the cultural *humus* in which Smith lived, and its use of the classics. I think this approach is preferable, perhaps because of my historical and philological training.

Classical scholarship in Europe was built on the firm ground of the careful and unknown work of hundreds of editors and commentators of the classics. I recall that the commentaries were the basis of university teaching; and that many editions of the classics were done with the *recollectae*, that is, the lecture notes taken by students and collected by the printers when they had to prepare an edition (Lo Monaco 1990: 115–19). All this created a great deal of shared knowledge, of debated questions, of specialized issues, which began in the schools and universities and became the common inheritance of all learned people. Up to now, sources of this kind have scarcely been studied.

As regards Adam Smith, the influence of the classics on him has been studied mainly on a conceptual basis: what ancient philosophy (or part of it) is consistent with his thought, or with some of his concepts; what kind of inspiration he may have drawn from the authors he knew and loved best. It is, certainly, the most relevant part of the inquiry; but I think it could be more complete and accurate if we had a thorough knowledge of the works and interpretations that were available to Smith. Few scholars, for instance, have noticed that in his day the textbooks and the histories of philosophy gave less attention to Plato and Aristotle than to the Hellenistic philosophers (Vivenza 2001a: 21, 211).

I think that much of the exegetical work on the classics is the basis for many important modern writings. Obviously the main concepts are different, but it is possible to show that at least a part of modern arguments is derived from elaboration of classical topics. It is also possible to show that, while starting from the classical matrix, they came to saying something very different, even contrary. That happened, too, to the Scottish philosopher who is the subject of these pages.

Notes

1 The above sentence is perhaps too sweeping; Haakonssen (1988; 1989; 1996: 2–3; 1998: xvii) has demonstrated that the two paradigms coexist in the Scottish Enlightenment, although he draws a line between Hume, Smith and Millar on the one hand, and the other Scottish thinkers on the other. Also Winch (1983) has nuanced his civic-humanist position by recognizing the importance of the jurisprudential paradigm in Smith's thought. Evensky (1989: 126; 1992: 71) believes that there was a shift between the two paradigms in Smith's thought during his lifetime.

2 'The man whose whole life is spent in performing a few simple operations…has no occasion to exert his understanding…and generally becomes as stupid and ignorant as it is possible for a human creature to become'.

3 In LJ (Smith 1978) Smith seems to approve the classics' stance ('They considered, and *I believe with justice*, that every sort of constant labour hurt the shape and rendered him less fit for military exercises', LJA iv.82, italics added), while in WN his attitude was different, being more sympathetic with the labourer's privations (cf. Vivenza 1990: 582–5). This is understandable: in LJ Smith is teaching his students about the realities of the ancient world, while in WN he is dealing with present or, rather, future perspectives. This is a good opportunity to recall that Smith, here as in many other instances, although choosing a classical argument, is on a different position about the issue: he can envisage a problem for the modern working classes, while for Xenophon and other classical authors the problem simply did not exist.

4 The two paradigms are usually connected with a hierarchical structure (the jurisprudential) and with an egalitarian one (the civic humanist), but the civic humanist's egalitarianism applies only to the holders of political power.

5 The motif of 'Christian Stoicism' as being common in the Scottish Enlightenment is illustrated also in Sher (1985: 175–86).

6 This would indicate a further influence of Roman jurisprudence on Smith's philosophical-juridical thought; cf. Haakonssen (1996: 132–48). The phrase quoted in the text is at p.147.

7 There is no connection of the invisible hand with 'providential' or design arguments according to Rothschild (2001: 131–6).

8 '…Man, partly from the Instinct of Benevolence, but, chiefly, from Self-Love, in consulting his own Advantage, acts in many cases for the Good of others' (Cumberland

1727: 164). This kind of 'invisible hand', it is worth adding, is 'the Will of the Author of Nature' (*ibid*). The sentence is actually written by John Maxwell, the English translator of Cumberland's treatise; and was quoted also in the French translation by J. Barbeyrac (cf. for example Amsterdam edition of 1744, p.183 n. 2). Cf. Vivenza 1996: 34 with n. 60.

9 Fitzgibbons (1995) uses different phrases ('Stoic or Ciceronian philosophy', 'Ciceronian version of Stoicism', and the like) to define a 'Ciceronian virtue' of Stoical origin, which Smith accepted, modified, rejected. It is opposed to a 'Graeco-Christian virtue' corresponding, it would seem, to Aristotle and Scholasticism. My opinion on this book is expressed in Vivenza (1999a: 112–17).

10 At the beginning of the twentieth century, French and German scholarship recognized in Cicero's *De Republica* the idealization of a *princeps* and created the so-called 'republican theory of principate', to which, however, the excellent book of Lepore (1954) has done justice.

11 The true reason of Smith's rejection, in fact, was his awareness that Stoic morals was completely self-sufficient, cf. Vivenza (1999a: 99–102; 2001a: 74–5).

12 Smith's work has been connected with all these literary genres; for example, Andriopoulos (1999), Clark (1992), Heinzelman (1995). A different kind of analysis is that of Endres (1991, 1995) who tries to elucidate the rhetorical strategies of the WN by retracing them in the text. Cf. also the historical and methodological assessment of Skinner (1983).

13 Cf. however: 'The purpose is not to deny that economics is a science, as many critics have complained, but rather to emphasize that all discourse deploys strategies of persuasion' (Tribe 1999: 618).

14 This is incorrect, to my mind: it is true that in Smith's LRBL all the strategies, not only in poetry, epic, tragedy, but also in oratory, aim at moving sentiments – but they are precisely strategies. I mean that, when an author sitting at the writing desk weighs and chooses carefully what elements are likely to move the reader or spectator, and what others are better left out because they could not do so, it is difficult to believe that reason does not enter at all in this calculation.

15 Recent attention has been given to the idea of 'judgment', but in a different sense from Smith's (see n.19 below). I think it is derived from the attempt to use Kant's *Critique of Judgment* in order to analyze Smith's model of moral judgment, cf. for example Valihora (2001).

16 For the different kind of knowledge concerning epistemological and moral questions, see Raphael 1979: 91–2; Haakonssen 1982: 210–11, 1990.

17 About *moral* Scepticism, as far as I know, apart from Griswold's writings, there is only a short hint in Schneewind (1991: 299). Cf. Vivenza (1999b: 201 n. 32).

18 The minor virtues, together with the 'habits of economy, industry, discretion, attention and application of thought' (TMS VII.ii.3.16), are connected with the so-called bourgeois virtue; cf Minowitz (1993: 79–81).

19 If superior prudence is other-regarding, however, it is difficult to understand why it is defined as temperance and even 'just another name for self-command' (Den Uyl 1991: 131).

20 At Fleischacker (1999: 123) Smith's judgment is approximated to Aristotle's *phronesis*. I cannot understand what this author means exactly by 'judgment': 'commonsense' (136), 'lower kind of phronesis' (135), 'properly calibrated "sympathy" or "wisdom" ' (150). I cannot, however, criticize the work because Fleischacker compares Smith with Kant and it is beyond the scope of this paper to comment on that approach.

21 Which were, I recall, the same thing in Socratic morals; cf. Gauthier and Jolif 1959: 465).

22 I hope to be able to show, in a future work, that this possibly derives from reasoning worked out by sixteenth-century commentators, mainly Protestant but also Catholic, on the passage of Cicero's *De Officiis* I. 20–22. Up to now, I have only published some articles (Vivenza 1996: 22–37, 2001b).

23 Only Rosen (2000: 92), to my knowledge, has distinguished between the Aristotelian-Scholastic distributive justice, and that of the natural law theorists.
24 Brown (1994) is more interested in TMS and WN; Fleishacker (1999) in the latter.
25 Usually the whole analysis is centred around a single main concept: separation (Foley), dialogism (Brown), appearances (Griswold).
26 The most remarkable example is Foley; cf Vivenza (1982: 66–8). Griswold is mainly interested, as it has been said earlier, to moral scepticism; in any case he, too, maintains that '[Smith's] silence about scepticism is best interpreted as deliberate' (Griswold 1999: 157); cf Vivenza (1999b: 189–90, 200–1).

Bibliography

I hope that my drastic choice of reducing references to a minimum may be understood, although this means that important names and works have been left out.

Ancient authors

Aristotelis *Ethica Nicomachea*, rec. I.Bywater, Oxonii, e Typographeo Clarendoniano, 1962.

Cicéron, *Les devoirs*, texte établi et traduit par M. Testard, Paris, Les Belles Lettres, 1965–70.

M. Tulli Ciceronis *De finibus bonorum et malorum*, rec. J.N. Madvig, Hildesheim, Olms, 1965.

Epictetus, *The discourses as reported by Arrian (books I–II)*, with an English translation by W.A. Oldfather, Cambridge, MA/London, Loeb classical library, Harvard University Press, 1998, vol. I.

Epictetus, *The discourses (books III–IV). Fragments. Encheiridion*, with an English translation of W.A.Oldfather, Cambridge, MA/London, Loeb classical library, Harvard University press, 1998.

L. Annaei Senecae *Ad Lucilium Epistulae Morales*, rec. L.D. Reynolds, Oxonii, e Typographeo Clarendoniano, 1986.

L. Annaei Senecae 'De Providentia', in *Dialogorum libri duodecim*, rec. L.D. Reynolds, Oxonii, e Typographeo Clarendoniano, 1977.

Marc Aurèle, *Pensées*, texte établi et traduit par A.I. Trannoy, Paris, Les Belles Lettres, 1953.

Xenophontis 'Oeconomicus', in *Opera omnia*, rec. E.C.Marchant, Oxonii, e Typographeo Clarendoniano, 1962.

Modern authors

Andriopoulos, S. (1999) 'The invisible hand: supernatural agency in political economy and the gothic novel', *Journal of English Literary History*, 66: 739–58.

Backhouse, R.E. (1993) 'Rhetoric and methodology', *Perspectives on the History of Economic Thought*, IX, 3–17.

Bonar, J. (1922) *Philosophy and Political Economy*, London: Allen & Unwin.

Brown, V. (1994) *Adam Smith's Discourse: Canonicity, Commerce and Conscience*, London/New York: Routledge.

—— (1997) ' "Mere inventions of the imagination": a survey of recent literature on Adam Smith', *Economics and Philosophy*, 13: 281–312.

Brunt, P. (1975) 'Stoicism and the principate', *Papers of the British School at Rome*, XLIII: 7–35.

Buckle, S. (1991) *Natural Law and the Theory of Property*, Oxford: Clarendon Press.

Campbell, T.D. (1971), *Adam Smith's Science of Morals*, London, Allen & Unwin.
Clark, H.C. (1992) 'Conversation and moderate virtue in Adam Smith's *Theory of Moral Sentiments*', *The Review of Politics*, 54: 185–210.
Cole, Th. (1967), *Democritus and the Sources of Greek Anthropology*, Cleveland, Western Reserve University Press.
Colish, M. (1992) 'Stoicism and the New Testament: an essay on historiography', *Aufstieg und Niedergang der roemischen Welt*, II, 26, 1: 334–79.
Cremaschi, S. (1984) *Il sistema della ricchezza. Economia politica e problema del metodo in Adam Smith*, Milano: Franco Angeli.
—— (1989) 'Adam Smith: sceptical Newtonianism, disenchanted republicanism, and the birth of social science', in *Knowledge and Politics: Case Studies on the Relationship between Epistemology and Political Philosophy*, M. Dascal and O. Gruengard (eds), Boulder/London: Westview Press.
Cropsey, J. (1977), *Polity and Economy. An Interpretation of the Principles of Adam Smith*, The Hague, M. Nijhoff.
Cumberland, R. (1727) *A Treatise of the Laws of Nature, made English from the Latin by John Maxwell*, London: R. Phillips.
—— (1744) *Traité philosophique des lois naturelles*. Traduit du latin par Monsieur Barbeyrac, Amsterdam, chez Pierre Mortier.
Den Uyl, D.J. (1991) *The Virtue of Prudence*, New York: Peter Lang.
De Mattei, R. (1951) 'Sapienza e prudenza nel pensiero politico italiano dall'Umanesimo al sec. XVII', in *Umanesimo e scienza politica*, E.Castelli (ed.), Milano: Marzorati.
Endres A.M. (1991) 'Adam Smith's rhetoric of economics', *Scottish Journal of Political Economy*, 38: 76–95.
—— (1995) 'Adam Smith's advisory style as illustrated by his trade policy prescriptions', *Journal of the History of Economic Thought*, 17: 86–105.
Evensky, J. (1989) 'The evolution of Adam Smith's views on political economy', *History of Political Economy*, 21: 123–45.
—— (1992) 'Ethics and the classical liberal tradition in economics', *History of Political Economy*, 24: 61–77.
Fitzgibbons, A. (1995) *Adam Smith's System of Liberty, Wealth and Virtue*, Oxford: Clarendon Press.
Fleischacker, S. (1999) *A Third Concept of Liberty: Judgment and Freedom in Kant and Adam Smith*, Princeton: Princeton University Press.
Foley, V. (1976) *The Social Physics of Adam Smith*, West Lafayette: Purdue University Press.
Forbes, D. (1982) 'Natural Law and the Scottish Enlightenment', in *The Origins and Nature of the Scottish Enlightenment*, R.H. Campbell and A.S. Skinner (eds), Edinburgh: John Donald Publishers.
Gauthier, R.A. et Jolif, J.Y. (1959) *L'étique à Nicomaque*, tome II, deuxième partie, Louvain/Paris: Publications Universitaires de Louvain.
Giuliani, A. (1997) *Giustizia ed ordine economico*, Milano: Giuffrè.
Griswold, C.L. (1999) *Adam Smith and the Virtues of Enlightenment*, Cambridge: Cambridge University Press.
Guilhamou, J. (2000) 'De l'histoire des concepts à l'histoire linguistique des usages conceptuels', *Généses*, 38: 105–18.
—— (2001) 'L'histoire des concepts: le contexte historique en débat', *Annales ESC*, 56: 685–98.
Haakonssen, K. (1982) 'What might properly be called natural jurisprudence?' in *The Origins and Nature of the Scottish Enlightenment*, R.H. Campbell and A.S. Skinner (eds), Edinburgh: John Donald Publishers.

—— (1988) 'Jurisprudence and politics in Adam Smith', in *Traditions of Liberalism*, K. Haakonssen (ed.), Sydney: Centre for Independent Studies.

—— (1989) 'Natural jurisprudence in the Scottish Enlightenment: summary of an interpretation', in *Enlightenment, Rights and Revolution: Essays in Legal and Social Philosophy*, N. MacCormick and Z. Bankoski (eds), Aberdeen: Aberdeen University Press.

—— (1990) 'Natural law and moral realism: the Scottish synthesis', in *Studies in the Philosophy of the Scottish Enlightenment*, M.A. Stewart (ed.), Oxford: Clarendon Press.

—— (1996) *Natural Law and Moral Philosophy, from Grotius to the Scottish Enlightenment*, Cambridge: Cambridge University Press.

—— (ed.) (1998) *Adam Smith*, Ashgate: Dartmouth.

Harpham, E.J. (1994) 'Liberalism, civic humanism and the case of Adam Smith' (1984), *American Political Science Review*, 78: 764–74; reprinted in Wood (ed.) V: 18. (Quotations in the text are from the latter edition.)

Havelock, E. (1957), *The Liberal Temper in Greek Politics*, New Haven, Yale University Press.

Heinzelman, K. (1995) 'The last georgic: *Wealth of Nations* and the scene of writing', in *Adam Smith's* Wealth of Nations: *New Interdisciplinary Essays*, S. Copley and K. Sutherland (eds), Manchester/New York: Manchester University Press.

Heise, P. (1991) 'Stoicism in Adam Smith's model of human behaviour: the philosophical foundations of self-betterment and the invisible hand', *Oekonomie und Gesellschaft* Jahrbuch 9: 64–78.

—— (1995) 'Stoicism in the EPS: the foundations of Adam Smith's moral philosophy', *Perspectives in the History of Economic Thought*, XI: 17–30.

Henderson, W.R., Dudley-Evans, T. and Backhouse, R. (eds) (1993) *Economics and Language*, London: Routledge.

Hont, I. and Ignatieff, M. (1983) 'Needs and justice in the *Wealth of Nations*: an introductory essay', in *Wealth and Virtue: the Shaping of Political Economy in the Scottish Enlightenment*, I. Hont and M. Ignatieff (eds), Cambridge: Cambridge University press.

Kalyvas A. and Katznelson, I. (2001) 'The rhetoric of the market: Adam Smith on recognition, speech, and exchange', *The Review of Politics*, 63: 549–79.

Lagueux, M. (1999) 'Do metaphors affect economic theory?', *Economics and Philosophy*, 15: 1–22.

Lepore, E. (1954) *Il princeps ciceroniano e gli ideali politici della tarda repubblica*, Napoli: nella sede dell'istituto.

Lo Monaco, F. (1990) 'Alcune osservazioni sui commenti umanistici ai classici nel secondo Quattrocento', in *Il commento ai testi*, O. Besomi and C. Caruso (eds), Basel/Boston/Berlin: Birkhauser Verlag.

Macfie, A. L. (1967), *The Individual in Society. Papers on Adam Smith*, London, George Allen & Unwin.

Martin, J.P. (1982) *Providentia deorum. Aspects réligieux du pouvoir* romain, Rome: Collection de l'Ecole française de Rome n. 61.

Minowitz, P. (1993) *Profits, Priests and Princes: Adam Smith's Emancipation of Economics from Politics and Religion*, Stanford University Press.

Morrow, G.R. (1969) *The Ethical and Economic Theories of Adam Smith*, New York, Augustus M. Kelley (reprint).

Muller, J.Z. (1993) *Adam Smith in his Time and Ours: Designing the Decent Society*, Princeton: Princeton University Press.

Oestreich, G. (1982) *Neostoicism and the Early Modern State*, Cambridge: Cambridge University Press.

Pocock, J.G.A. (1983) 'Cambridge paradigms and Scotch philosophers: a study of the relations between the civic humanist and the civil jurisprudential interpretation of eighteenth-century social thought' in *Wealth and Virtue: the Shaping of Political Economy in the Scottish Enlightenment*, I. Hont and M. Ignatieff (eds), Cambridge: Cambridge University Press.

Raphael, D.D. (1972), 'The impartial spectator', *Proceedings of the British Academy*, 58, 335–54.

—— (1973), 'Hume and Adam Smith on justice and utility', *Aristotelian Society*, 73, 87–103.

—— (1979) 'Adam Smith: philosophy, science and social science', in *Philosophers of the Enlightenment*, S.C. Brown (ed.), London: Harvester Press.

—— (2001) *Concepts of Justice*, Oxford: Oxford University Press.

Robertson, J. (1983) 'The Scottish Enlightenment and the limits of the civic tradition', in *Wealth and Virtue: the Shaping of Political Economy in the Scottish Enlightenment*, I. Hont and M. Ignatieff (eds), Cambridge: Cambridge University Press.

—— (1985) *The Scottish Enlightenment and the Militia Issue*, Edinburgh: John Donald Publishers.

Rosen, F. (2000) 'The idea of utility in Adam Smith's *The Theory of Moral Sentiments*', *History of European Ideas*, 26: 79–103.

Rothschild, E. (2001) *Economic Sentiments: Adam Smith, Condorcet, and the Enlightenment*, Cambridge Mass.: Harvard University Press.

Salter, J. (1994) 'Adam Smith on justice and distribution in commercial societies', *Scottish Journal of Political Economy*, 41: 299–313.

—— (1999) 'Sympathy with the poor: theories of punishment in Hugo Grotius and Adam Smith', *History of Political Thought* XX: 205–24.

Schneewind, J.B. (1991) 'Natural law, scepticism, and methods of ethics', *Journal of the History of Ideas*, 52: 289–308.

Scott, W.R. (1940) 'Greek Influences on Adam Smith', in *Etudes dediées à la mémoire d'André M. Andréadès*, K. Varvaressos (ed.), Athènes: Pyrsos.

Sher, R.B. (1985) *Church and University in the Scottish Enlightenment: the Moderate Literati of Edinburgh*, Princeton: Princeton University Press.

Skinner, A.S. (1972), 'Adam Smith: philosophy and science', *Scottish Journal of Political Economy*, 19: 307–19.

—— (1974), 'Adam Smith: science and the role of the imagination', in *Hume and the Enlightenment: Essays presented to Ernest Campbell Mossner*, W.B.Todd (ed.), Edinburgh/Austin: The Universities of Edinburgh and Texas.

—— (1983) 'Adam Smith: rhetoric and the communication of ideas', in *Methodological Controversy in Economics: Historical Essays in Honour of T.W. Hutchison*, A.W. Coats (ed.), Greenwich Conn./London: JAI Press Inc..

Smith, A. (1976a) *The Theory of Moral Sentiments*, D.D. Raphael and A.L Macfie (eds), Oxford: Oxford University Press; Glasgow Edition.

—— (1976b) *An Inquiry into the Nature and Causes of the Wealth of Nations*, R.H. Campbell and A.S. Skinner (eds), Oxford: Oxford University Press; Glasgow Edition.

—— (1978) *Lectures on Jurisprudence*, R.L. Meek, D.D. Raphael and P.G. Stein (eds), Oxford: Oxford University Press; Glasgow Edition.

—— (1980) *Essays on Philosophical Subjects*, W.P.D. Wightman (ed.), Oxford: Oxford University Press; Glasgow Edition. 'History of Astronomy', pp. 31–105.

—— (1983) *Lectures on Rhetoric and Belles Lettres*, J.C. Bryce (ed.), Oxford: Oxford University Press; Glasgow Edition.

Sorabji, R. (1980) 'Aristotle on the role of intellect in virtue', in *Essays on Aristotle's Ethics*, A. Oksenberg Rorty (ed.), Berkeley: University of California Press.

Tribe, K. (1999) 'Adam Smith: critical theorist?', *Journal of Economic Literature*, XXXVII: 609–32.

Valihora, K. (2001) 'The judgment of judgment: Adam Smith's *Theory of moral Sentiments*', *British Journal of Aesthetics*, 41: 138–59.

Verburg, R. (2000) 'Adam Smith's growing concern on the issue of distributive justice', *European History of Economic Thought*, 7: 23–44.

Viroli, M. (1994) *Dalla Politica alla Ragion di Stato: la Scienza di Governo tra XIII e XVII Secolo*, Roma: Donzelli editore.

Vivenza, G. (1982) 'Adam Smith e la fisica antica', *Economia e Storia*, 3: 65–72.

—— (1990) 'Lavoro e attività politica: motivi classici e moderni nel pensiero di Adam Smith', in *Economia Stato Società: Studi in memoria di G.Menegazzi*, a cura di G. Gaburro, R. Molesti, G. Zalin, Pisa: IPEM edizioni.

—— (1996) 'Benevolenza pubblica, benevolenza privata e benevolenza reciproca: la virtù del dono e dello scambio dall'antichità al Settecento', *Studi storici Luigi Simeoni*, XLVI: 15–37.

—— (1999a) 'Ancora sullo stoicismo di Adam Smith', *Studi storici Luigi Simeoni*, XLIX: 97–126.

—— (1999b), 'Adam Smith e la filosofia scettica', *Nuova economia e storia*, V: 185–200.

—— (2001a) *Adam Smith and the Classics*, Oxford: Oxford University Press.

—— (2001b) 'The 'Northern' Cicero: on the fortuna of the *De Officiis* in central Europe', *Mésogeios*, 13–14: 201–27.

Waszek, N. (1984) 'Two concepts of morality: a distinction of Adam Smith's ethics and its Stoic origin', *Journal of the History of Ideas*, 45: 591–606.

Winch, D. (1978) *Adam Smith's Politics*, Cambridge: Cambridge University Press.

—— (1983), 'Adam Smith's "enduring particular result": a political and cosmopolitan perspective', in *Wealth and Virtue: the Shaping of Political Economy in the Scottish Enlightenment*, I. Hont and M. Ignatieff (eds), Cambridge, Cambridge University Press.

—— (1988) 'Adam Smith and the liberal tradition', in *Traditions of Liberalism*, K. Haakonssen (ed.), Sydney: Centre for Independent Studies.

Witztum, A. (1997) 'Distributive considerations in Smith's conception of economic justice', *Economics and Philosophy*, 13: 241–59.

Wood, J.C. (1994) *Adam Smith: Critical Assessments*, V, London/New York, Routledge.

Young, J. T. (1997) *Economics as a Moral Science*, Cheltenham: Edward Elgar.

—— (2001) 'Adam Smith's two views of the market', in *Knowledge, Social Institutions and the Division of Labour*, P.L. Porta, R. Scazzieri and A.S. Skinner (eds), Cheltenham: Edward Elgar.

Symposium on Emma Rothschild's *Economic Sentiments*

Introduction*

Ryan Patrick Hanley

Adam Smith's inquiries into the nature of society and into human nature are remarkable for their sensitivity to the perspective of 'the individual in society'. Rather than treat the individual and the community separately, Smith focuses on the reciprocal and mutually-formative aspects of their relationship. Such a perspective may prompt us to reconsider the proper relationship of the self and society. Perhaps we should expect nothing less from one who three times recalls us to the seemingly paradoxical claim that individual excellence lies in recognizing that we are each 'but one of the multitude in no respect better than any other in it' *Theory of Moral Sentiments* (TMS) (II.ii.2.1, III.3.4, VI.ii.2.2).

The question of nature of the ties that bind the self to others animates, at varying levels, both Emma Rothschild's *Economic Sentiments* and the four commentaries on it gathered here. Stephen Darwall's study of the metaethical and psychological foundations of Smith's political egalitarianism explores the ways in which sympathetic fellow-feeling presupposes an individual's capacity to recognize others as equals, and how this capacity for mutual respect is made manifest in both moral judgment and commercial transactions. Patricia Werhane develops this account in her comments on how Smith and Condorcet challenge utilitarian readings of enlightened political economy as founded on atomistic egoism by emphasizing sociable sentiment over fallible rationality. Samuel Fleischacker, also in the course of endorsing Rothschild's warmer and more romantic Enlightenment, likewise invites us to consider how Smith mediates the *prima facie* antagonistic claims of individual freedom and 'the social construction of the self' via careful analyses of the social roles of the invisible hand and of religion. Professor Rothschild's rich concluding statement addresses these concerns and more in the context of discussions of Smith's alleged non-foundationalism and his commitment to the preservation of human dignity. In so doing she returns us to the relationship of self and society via a consideration of the social and political institutions necessary to guarantee the recognition and preservation of the dignity of the individual.

The Adam Smith Review, 1: 127–64 © 2004 The International Adam Smith Society, ISSN 1743–5285, ISBN 0–415–27863–5

Note

* Earlier versions of the four papers were delivered on a panel sponsored by the International Adam Smith Society at the Annual Meeting of the Eastern Division of the American Philosophical Association (APA) held in Philadelphia on 28 December 2002 to discuss Emma Rothschild (2001) *Economic Sentiments: Adam Smith, Condorcet, and the Enlightenment*, Cambridge, MA: Harvard University Press. In accord with APA practice, the panel's official title took the form of 'Author Meets Critics: Emma Rothschild's *Economic Sentiments*'.

Acknowledgements

It is however a great pleasure to acknowledge that the panel's proceedings showed no trace of the shortcomings Smith thought characteristic of literary and critical enterprises, and were rather a model of that amiable 'good harmony' he associated with natural rather than with moral philosophers (TMS III.2.19–23). I thus take the opportunity to acknowledge again the generosity of our four contributors, and to express my thanks for the opportunity to participate in their conversation.

Equal dignity in Adam Smith[1]

Stephen Darwall

What I find most exciting about Emma Rothschild's *Economic Sentiments* is its detailed, convincing recovery of the profoundly egalitarian character of Adam Smith's (and Condorcet's) thought, the nature and significance of which began to be obscured by the conservative reaction to revolution in Europe, almost at Smith's death in 1790, as Rothschild also brilliantly illustrates, and has been insufficiently appreciated ever since. Smith's critique of regulation, corporation spirit and apprenticeship was concerned as much with equity and equal dignity as it was with economic efficiency. And Smith believed that the accumulation of British wealth itself depended 'above all [on] that equal and impartial administration of justice which renders the rights of the meanest British subject respectable to the greatest' (Smith 1976b, *Wealth of Nations* (WN) IV.vii.c.54).

As a commentator, I am in the embarrassing position of agreeing with virtually everything of substance that Emma Rothschild says about Smith. In what follows, I would like to explore how, as I read Smith, his ideas about equal respect and human dignity are grounded, at an even more fundamental level than Rothschild discusses, in the very framework of his theory of moral sentiments, as well as in his diagnosis of the distinctively human disposition to exchange in the WN.[2] Partly, I will be sketching how, according to Smith, the form that judgments of propriety and especially, equity, take both involve and presuppose a kind of equal respect. And I will suggest as well that exchange, as Smith conceives it, also presupposes and enacts equal respect. Exchange is a form of second-personal address that involves what Fichte and other German idealists would (not much) later call '*Anerkennung*', reciprocal recognition of one another as having equal dignity. These features give Smith a very different kind of sentimentalism than we find in Hutcheson or Hume. And it explains why, although Hume's and Hutcheson's metaethical views were naturally thought to support utilitarianism as a normative ethical theory, Smith's own normative ethical views would most naturally have taken the anti-utilitarian form that Rothschild so convincingly displays.

Before I discuss how equal respect is built into Smith's metaethics and moral psychology as I understand them, it will help to have before us some of the aspects Rothschild points to of Smith's substantively egalitarian moral and political views. Smith believed that social and political inequalities are almost never rooted in intrinsic human differences. The 'difference between a philosopher and a common street porter', he says, results primarily from 'habit, custom, and education', and inherent human differences are not half so great as those between a greyhound and a spaniel (WN I.ii.4–5; see also Smith 1978, LJA i.111–12). The only remedy to the disparities in ability and skill to which social arrangements give rise (including those that result from the division of labour that Smith thinks is necessary to national wealth), is a system of widely available public education. As Rothschild points out, both Smith and his conservative critics make an important implicit distinction between *education* and forms of training that are involved in apprenticeship and other socially-enforced hierarchy (Rothschild 2001: 97). Education, Smith believes, develops independence and makes people 'feel themselves, each individually, more respectable' (WN V.i.f.61). Smith's conservative critics, by contrast, condemn public education (Playfair: 'reading frequently leads to discontent, an ill-founded ambition, and a neglect of business') and praise apprenticeship for encouraging 'habits of industry', 'due subjection' and 'subordination' (Rothschild 2001: 99).

Like Condorcet, Smith is a sharp critic of domination and dependency in all its forms. He contrasts the 'servile and fawning attention' we and other animals can give when attempting to curry favour with the implicit mutual respect human beings distinctively can achieve in free exchange. (More on that presently.) And his description of what it is like to live with others on terms of mutual respect – 'breath[ing] the free air of liberty and independency' (Smith 1976a, *The Theory of Moral Sentiments* (TMS) VII.ii.1.40; see also Rothschild 2001: 70) – contrasts with what Condorcet calls the 'sentiment of oppression' (Rothschild 2001: 28). For both Smith and Condorcet, liberty is not simply the instrumentally valuable absence of obstacles to gaining other intrinsic goods. It essentially includes the intrinsically valuable relation of mutual respect.[3] In the 'free air of liberty and independency' individuals relate to one another on equal terms, as having a dignity as persons who may not be dealt with in the arbitrary and 'vexatious' ways that would-be superiors typically presume (Rothschild 2001: 28, 33). Finally, Smith believes that widespread poverty is not only a sign and cause of economic inefficiency. It is also *unjust*.

> It is but equity . . . that they who feed, clothe, and lodge the whole body of the people, should have such a share of the produce of their own labour as to be themselves tolerably well fed, clothed, and lodged.
>
> (WN I.viii.36)

But what underlies these liberal egalitarian normative claims or gives Smith the confidence that others should be convinced to accept them? Two things, at least,

I shall argue: first, Smith's account of the metaethics and psychology of moral judgments of propriety and equity, and second, Smith's understanding of the nature of free exchange. As Smith analyses both of these, equal dignity and mutual respect are built into their foundations. Let us begin with Smith's theory of the moral sentiment.

Sentimentalist approaches, such as Hutcheson's and Hume's, generally hold that moral judgments are made from an observer's or third-person standpoint. Motive and character are contemplated in a detached way, as part of the passing scene, and approved or disapproved from that point of view. So viewed, morality has nothing essentially to do with judgments we render from *within* the moral life as agents and patients who interact with and address one another, second-personally. It is not concerned, in any fundamental way, with reciprocity between equals or with any mutual accountability that expresses equal respect. It is akin, rather, to aesthetics, and moral value is like a kind of beauty, as Hume explicitly says.[4] It is an observer's, third-personal, rather than a participant's, second-personal, phenomenon.

It is ironic, therefore, that the term 'impartial spectator' originates with Smith, and not with either Hutcheson or Hume, since the perspective of moral judgment, according to Smith, is not strictly a *spectator's* standpoint at all. For him, the primary moral judgment concerns no form of beauty, but what he calls 'propriety'. Smith explicitly distinguishes between propriety and beauty, with an eye on Hume (TMS IV.2.1–3). And he holds that to judge whether a motive or feeling is proper, we must take up, not some external perspective, but that of the person who has the motive or feeling herself – the agent's standpoint, in the case of motivation, the patient's standpoint, in the case of feeling (TMS I.i.3–4). What we must have in view, is not the agent's motive or the patient's feeling itself, but the situation from which it arose, viewed from the perspective of the agent or patient. Of course, Smith does believe that the judgment must be impartially regulated. But impartiality disciplines the *way* in which we enter into the agent's or patient's point of view; it does not provide its own, external perspective. Moral judgment involves an impartial projection into the agent's or patient's standpoint. We imaginatively project *as any one of us* (TMS II.ii.2.1, III.3.5). The judgment that the agent's motive or the patient's feeling is proper involves what Smith calls '*sympathy*': an imaginative sharing of the motive or feeling from his point of view (as regulated impartially) (TMS I.i.1.3–5).

Smith's differences with Hume about the perspective of moral judgment relate to differences in their respective understandings of *sympathy*. For Smith, sympathy is a specific form of 'fellow-feeling' that involves a projection into the other's standpoint to see whether we can view his situation in the same emotionally- or motivationally-laden way he does. What the sympathetic person has in view is not the other's feeling viewed third-personally, but its object, viewed as the other would view it. Smithian sympathy thus implicitly recognizes the other as having an independent perspective. For Hume, on the other hand, sympathy is a psychological mechanism that transforms ideas of another's feeling or passion, viewed *third*-personally, into 'the very passion itself' (Hume 1978: 317). It stays resolutely outside the other's perspective, transforming ideas of his mental states, so viewed, into simulacra from an observer's point of view.

For Smith, when we judge an agent's motive, we do so from the agent's own perspective, viewing the practical situation as we imagine it to confront her in deliberation. And when we judge someone's feeling or reaction, we do so from her patient's perspective, viewing the situation as we imagine it to confront her as someone responding to it. Both judgments involve an implicit identification with, and thus respect for, the other as having an independent point of view. This already pushes Smith's thought away from the observer-based virtue ethics of Hutcheson and Hume. What takes him even farther is his metaethics of justice.

Injustice, for Smith, is essentially tied to warranted resentment. It is, in its nature, not simply improper conduct, but improper conduct to which the proper response is a second-personal reactive feeling (to challenge or hold the agent accountable in some way) that is appropriately *addressed* person-to-person. On Smith's view, we judge injustice, not from an observer's perspective, but by projecting ourselves impartially into the agent's *and*, crucially, into *affected parties*' points of view. Moreover, what we consider from the perspective of affected parties is whether to respond with a distinctive kind of feeling that itself presupposes mutual accountability between persons. We can only judge whether something is properly resented or resisted, by imagining being in the shoes of the affected parties and considering whether any of us, if reasonable, would feel a reactive, accountability-seeking sentiment that implicitly lodges some second-personal challenge or complaint.

For Smith, therefore, the implied framework of judgments of both equity and propriety is a moral community among independent equal persons. Judgments of both sorts involve an implicit intersubjectivity, a projection into the standpoints of independent individuals that is disciplined by a standard of one among equals, as 'one of the multitude, in no respect better than any other in it' (TMS III.3.4). Judgments of equity presuppose equal moral community even more vividly, since they give each person implicit standing as one among mutually accountable equals. 'A moral being', Smith tells us, 'is an accountable being...that must give an account of its actions to some other, and that consequently must regulate them according to the good-liking of this other'. Though Smith says that man is 'principally accountable to God', he quickly adds that each 'must necessarily conceive himself as accountable to his fellow-creatures, before he can form any idea of the Deity...' (TMS III.1.3[3]).

This egalitarian metaethics grounds a normative doctrine of equal dignity. What most 'enrages us against the man who injures or insults us', Smith says, 'is the little account which he seems to make of *us*' – 'that absurd self-love, by which he seems to imagine, that other people *may* be sacrificed at any time, to his conveniency' (TMS II.iii.1.5, emphases added). We resent disrespect of our dignity, our status as persons who *may not* be treated in certain ways. What resentment is 'chiefly intent upon', moreover, 'is not so much to make our enemy feel pain in his turn, as...to make him sensible that the person whom he injured did not deserve to be treated in that manner' (TMS II.iii.1.5). In other words, when we hold others accountable, we aim to have them feel and thereby acknowledge our equal dignity. We seek mutual respect as equals.

These same fundamental themes are at play also in Smith's analysis of free exchange, about which I shall have to be briefer. Although exchange's operative motive is personal gain, it is itself impossible without a presupposed second-personal normative infrastructure. Smith tells us that the disposition to exchange is distinctively human. But why? The reason is exchange's second-personal character and language's apparent indispensability in second-personal address.[5] 'Nobody', Smith says,

> ever saw a dog make a fair and deliberate exchange of one bone for another with another dog. Nobody ever saw one animal by its gestures and natural cries signify to another, this is mine, that yours; I am willing to give this for that.
> (WN I.ii.2)

As Smith thinks of it, therefore, exchange is a form of reciprocally recognizing, second-personal interaction. Both parties implicitly commit themselves in common to various normative presuppositions; for example, that the exchange is made by free mutual consent, that each has title to what he or she offers, and so on. Most significantly, both parties presuppose the normative standing each has to address each other in this reciprocally recognizing way. And both license the other in presuming that they are dealing fairly, not in the sense that what they offer is equal in value to what they are being offered (*caveat emptor* – self-interest and bargaining regulate that), but in the sense that they will actually deliver what they offer, that they will not seek to reacquire it through coercion, that the other is free to refuse the deal and walk away, and so on. Moreover, both presuppose their mutual accountability as equals, that each has standing to resist or resent violations of these norms. For Smith, therefore, exchange itself presupposes reciprocal recognition as mutually accountable equals.

Once we appreciate how deeply reciprocal recognition as mutually accountable equals is grounded in Smith's metaethics and his moral psychology, both in his theory of moral judgment and in his conception of exchange, the egalitarian character of his normative convictions is no surprise. They commit Smith to the positions that Rothschild so convincingly details, for example, that goals such as economic efficiency may be pursued only to the extent that these are consistent with mutual respect for all as free and equal persons.

Notes

1 Some of the ideas that follow are drawn from Darwall (1999).
2 It was an eye-opening presentation by Samuel Fleischacker (Fleischacker 1996), that first suggested to me the possibility of interpreting Adam Smith in this way.
3 For a contemporary expression of this idea see Pettit (1996).
4 Hume frequently uses 'moral beauty' to refer to virtue; see Hume (1978: 465, 479, 484). Although Hutcheson distinguishes beauty from virtue, he sees both as

corresponding to an observer's sense; see Hutcheson (1725). On the differences between Hutcheson and Hume, see Darwall (1994) and the chapters on Hutcheson and Hume in Darwall (1995).

5 Whether this propensity be one of those original principles in human nature, of which no further account can be given; or whether, as seems more probable, it be the necessary consequence of the faculties of reason and speech, it belongs not to our present subject to enquire. It is common to all men, and to be found in no other race of animals, which seem to know neither this nor any other species of contracts.

(WN I.ii.2)

'It is clearly the natural inclination everyone has to persuade' that is 'the principle in the human mind on which this disposition of trucking is founded' (LJA vi.56).

Bibliography

Darwall, S. (1999) 'Sympathetic Liberalism', *Philosophy & Public Affairs*, 28: 139–64.

—— (1995) *The British Moralists and the Internal 'Ought': 1640–1740*, Cambridge: Cambridge University Press.

—— (1994) 'Hume and the Invention of Utilitarianism', in *Hume and Hume's Connexions* M.A. Stewart and J.P. Wright (eds), Edinburgh: Edinburgh University Press.

Fleischacker, S. 'Adam Smith without self-interest: re-reading the *Wealth of Nations*', paper presented at the American Philosophical Association Central Division Meeting in 1996.

Hume, D. (1978) *A Treatise of Human Nature*, Oxford: Clarendon Press.

Hutcheson, F. (1725) *An Inquiry into the Original of Our Ideas of Beauty and Virtue*, London.

Pettit, P. (1996) 'Freedom as antipower', *Ethics*, 106: 576–604.

Rothschild, E. (2001) *Economic Sentiments: Adam Smith, Condorcet, and the Enlightenment*, Cambridge, MA: Harvard University Press.

Smith, A. (1976a) *The Theory of Moral Sentiments*, D.D. Raphael and A.L. Macfie (eds), Oxford: Oxford University Press; reprinted, Liberty Press (1982).

—— (1976b) *An Inquiry into the Nature and Causes of the Wealth of Nations*, R.H. Campbell and A.S. Skinner (eds), Oxford: Oxford University Press; reprinted, Liberty Press (1981).

—— (1978) *Lectures on Jurisprudence*, R.L. Meek, D.D. Raphael and P.G. Stein (eds), Oxford: Oxford University Press; reprinted, Liberty Press (1982).

...laissez-faire when it was new...

A comment on Emma Rothschild's *Economic Sentiments*

Patricia H. Werhane

I am pleased and honoured to be invited to comment on Emma Rothschild's new book, *Economic Sentiments: Adam Smith, Condorcet, and the Enlightenment.* Professor Rothschild begins her book with the provocative and propitious contention, 'This book is about laissez-faire when it was new', and indeed it is (Rothschild 2001: 1). Although the concept of laissez-faire precedes the eighteenth century, thinking through its actual practice is new and important for her two protagonists, Adam Smith and Marie-Jean-Antoine-Nicholas de Condorcet.

Rothschild enriches her analysis by placing the works of Smith and Condorcet within the context of the history of ideas in the eighteenth century, contextual detail often missing in history of philosophy. Schumpeter once said of Adam Smith, 'the *Wealth of Nations* does not contain a single analytic idea, principle, or method that was entirely new in 1776' (Schumpeter 1954: 184), and Rothschild demonstrates how every idea, even of great thinkers, is interdependent and woven out of the political and economic context and the networked history of ideas that preceded or is contemporary with that thinker. One regret is that the book is not titled, *Economic Sentiments: Adam Smith, Condorcet, Turgot and the Enlightenment*, since it is evident that Turgot was enormously influential in Smith's and Condorcet's thinking, as they were in Turgot's own development, and a great deal of the book is spent on Turgot. The reason for his exclusion is the book's focus on what Rothschild calls the 'disposition of enlightenment', the role of sentiment and dispositions in enlightenment thinking that was particularly evident in the works of Smith and Condorcet.

One of the striking features of *Economic Sentiments* is its preoccupation with the critical importance of sentiment to create a 'disposition of enlightenment'. Ordinarily tradition treats the Enlightenment as a period dedicated to the glorification of humanistic reason and rationality. Rothschild, on the other hand, taking cues from David Hume, finds that at least for Smith and Condorcet, '[s]entiments influence reasons in economic [and political] life, and reasons influence sentiments' (Rothschild 2001: 9). Rothschild defines sentiments as 'feelings of which one is conscious, and on which one reflects...[and] also events that connected an individual to the larger relationships in which he or she lived'. Thus during this period, at least in England and the Continent, 'the traffic of commerce of modern life was at the same time a traffic in opinions and sentiments'. (Rothschild 2001: 9). This leads Rothschild to read the *Wealth of Nations* (WN) as a 'history [and progress] of the human mind'. Smith's famous statement in Book I that each of us has a 'general disposition to truck, barter and exchange' is read as Smith's argument that this disposition is 'the source of opulence' (Rothschild 2001: 8). 'The history of the rise of commerce is, for Smith, an epic of the emancipation of the mind' (Rothschild 2001: 10). This emancipation in turn is the source of the ideal of free commerce for Condorcet. For Smith, the end of feudalism and the rise of commerce are critical factors in the development of the sentiment or understanding of idea of economic liberty, even for underpaid labourers, because they are now paid wages and thus are independent from bondage to land holders (Smith 1976b, WN III). It is, however, unlikely that Smith envisioned a broad-based political enlightenment. (I shall say more about political liberty later.) According to Rothschild's reading of Condorcet, on the other hand, this 'progress' was to change political as well as economic sentiments and dispositions, that is, become the enlightenment of everyone, not just leaders and intellectuals.

Rothschild argues that for Smith and Condorcet, and Hume as well, the enlightenment was a period of development and reform of self-conscious economic and political sentiments and dispositions. These sentiments challenged the status quo, and were crucial to the development of the ideal of individual liberty, which in turn provided the justification and impetus for free commerce as we know it today. In contemporary terms, the disposition of enlightenment introduced a new mindset, a new mental model with which to frame thinking about oneself as an independent free individual now able and responsible for one's own economic well-being, and about a less regulated, and later, industrial, political economy. For Turgot, the disposition of enlightenment was ideally to develop truly laissez-faire sentiments where each individual is on his or her own to make local and personal economic, political and educational judgments (Rothschild 2001: 20). Smith, and to a lesser extent Condorcet, were more cautious, and it would be a misreading of Smith to classify him as a laissez-faire economist. Condorcet even proposed a form of social insurance that would protect the poor against income losses and thus provide an economic base from which they could recover (Rothschild 2001: 172). Where the three agree is on the idea that each of us is, or should be, personally free to explore our economic opportunities with few restrictions and that governmental, social and political institutions tend to interfere with individual economic development. This is perhaps why, at least according to some commentators such as Charles Griswold, in the WN Smith focuses on political economy, not politics, where economic liberty is the crucial element out of which a just and economically stimulating political economy evolves or can evolve (WN V.ii.b.2; Griswold 1999: 301–10).

According to Rothschild, the disposition of enlightenment, as least as exhibited by Smith, Condorcet and Turgot, also introduces us to an age of uncertainty.

For Smith, there is no guarantee that free commerce will create economic well-being for everyone; rather, it is the least worst option. For Condorcet, the disposition of enlightenment 'is a discursive, disorderly condition' (Rothschild 2001: 218). It introduces progress and, with self-conscious reflection, dissatisfaction with that progress, less certainty about eternal truths, inconsistency in economic gains, political instability and both an empowering and questioning reflective self. Thus the alleged 'Heavenly City' of these eighteenth-century philosophers was neither exactly heavenly nor governed only by reason (Becker 1932).

In the history of ideas there is one interesting parallel between Smith and Condorcet that Rothschild does not fully exploit. The parallel is that they have both been misread and misinterpreted, and misinterpreted in such ways as to create commonly held but erroneous caricatures of their ideas. These caricatures, in turn, have affected our conception of the Enlightenment and the roles of their ideas in its development and influence. According to Rothschild, Sainte-Beuve and others misread Condorcet as a dogmatic cold atheistic rationalist. Even today Condorcet, like Smith, is sometimes read as an atomistic egoist, and as arguing that humans act, or should act, primarily in their own self-interest, particularly in affairs of commerce. Condorcet, like Smith, is also mistakenly depicted as a utilitarian, and as proposing a singular and fairly dogmatic view of the connectiveness of truth, reason and universal values (Rothschild 2001: chapter 7). Rothschild carefully dispels these misconceptions of Condorcet and creates a picture of a much more complex, and indeed, less dogmatically certain philosopher whose defense of political, religious and economic liberty precluded advocating the imposition of one set of rational or 'eternal' principles.

Smith, too, was widely misinterpreted, particularly by a number of nineteenth-century German commentators. Conjuring up what they called the 'Adam Smith Problem', in brief they saw a discrepancy between the Smith of *The Theory of Moral Sentiments* (TMS) who extolled the virtue of benevolence, and the Smith of the WN extolling only unmitigated self-interest as the primary virtue of economic exchanges, forgetting Smith's admonition that '[e]very man, *as long as he does not violate the laws of justice*, is left perfectly free to pursue his own interest…' (WN IV.ix.51, my italics). Even in the twentieth century no less than the Nobel Prize economist George Stigler proclaimed that the '*Wealth of Nations* is a stupendous palace erected upon the granite of self-interest' (Stigler 1971: 265). Smith has also been read, wrongly, as a utilitarian, despite his strenuous arguments to the contrary in TMS, and as a laissez-faire economist despite his cautions to the contrary in the WN. There are still commentators today who cling to various formulations of the Adam Smith Problem. The point is that historians of ideas themselves create sentiments and dispositions, interpretations of thinkers that then take over as representing what these thinkers actually said and wrote. The next generation of thinkers then refers to these interpretations, and sometimes we neglect to return to the original for verification.[1] Rothschild's book is an antidote for misreadings of Condorcet and the roots of the Enlightenment.

Economic Sentiments is much richer than these few ideas I have summarized. I now want to elaborate on three points having to do with Rothschild's reading of

Smith: the invisible hand, the question of the foundations of morality and the issue of political liberty. One of Rothschild's contentions that is both challenging and probably correct is that Smith 'did not take the invisible hand entirely seriously' and perhaps was using the term ironically (Rothschild 2001: 126). That certainly fits with a secular interpretation of the term, which, of course, is part of its ironical force. Previously, I had interpreted the invisible hand to be a reference to commerce, and in contemporary terms, to markets or 'the market' (Werhane 1991). Notice how we tend to personify 'the market' or the stock market as if it was a mega-person acting on its own. We say, for example, 'The stock market reacted to Bush's threat of war by doing x' or, 'The market's volatility affects my pension fund', as if the market was an independent player and thus a Someone we can blame for our unfortunate judgments, rather than an outcome of millions of individual and institutional trades. Sometimes in our use of these expressions we forget Smith's idea that the invisible hand is merely, at best, a metaphor or a way to generalize from individual actions to explain how these can produce unintended (negative as well as positive) consequences. Having read Rothschild on the invisible hand, I strongly suspect my reading of the invisible hand is a twentieth- and not an eighteenth-century interpretation. Nevertheless, the lesson that Smith implies is a foreboding about the personification of institutions or systems and an overdependence on them to interpret events or take the blame for untoward events. Similarly, Smith would worry about an appeal to a Designer or Universal Order as an explanatory mechanism to make sense of the world or to attribute blame. It is Rothschild's view that Smith (and Condorcet) admired human-created semi-order and the uncertainty that accompanies secular life.

My second set of comments has to do with Rothschild's reading of Smith through the thinking of Hume. I think it is a mistake to link Smith too closely with Hume's epistemology and moral philosophy. Smith is, at best, a poor epistemologist. It is as if he had read Hume, decided Hume was more or less correct and saw no further reason to either expound on that form of empiricism nor to critique or elaborate on it. Only in a couple of essays does Smith even attempt such a task. This may be a form of what Rothschild calls 'ontological modesty' (Rothschild 2001: 145) or simply disinterest in such philosophical details.

Smith is never as careful as Hume in his use of words or terms. For example, Smith uses the term sympathy, a critical idea in the TMS, in at least four ways. 'Self-interest' receives the same treatment (Werhane 1991), and Griswold argues that there are at least seven meanings of the terms 'nature' and 'natural order' in Smith's writings (Griswold 1999: 314–17).

I find, moreover, that it not altogether conclusive to assume that for Smith 'there is no fundamental principle of moral judgment. There is no foundation; all there is, is the correction and convergence of sentiments' (Rothschild 2001: 231). This describes what Smith calls the 'general rules', moral rules that individuals and societies create, edit and correct as we think about how others and we should act. However, in TMS Smith repeatedly refers to 'nature' and the 'natural order'. In many places in TMS and the WN, Smith uses the terms 'natural liberty' and 'natural jurisprudence'. While Griswold is correct that these terms are used in many senses, at least some of the time they appear to refer to what is given to us, to what is non-conventional, what is 'in nature', or what is teleologically purposive. In the *Lectures on Jurisprudence* (LJ) Smith explicitly adopts Pufendorf's theory of natural rights.[2] Later, in the WN, Smith elaborates to state, in language that is reminiscent of Locke, that 'the property which every man has in his own labour, as it is the original foundation of all other property, so it is the most sacred and inviolable' (WN I.x.c.12). I would conclude that although his ideas are not well developed, Smith is a foundationalist. Underlying morality, moral sentiments and moral judgments lurks an unquestioned natural rights theory and some vague notions of natural order. This does not necessarily make him a theist, but certainly his moral theory has humanist foundational roots.

Third, in comparing Smith, Turgot and Condorcet, Rothschild might have elaborated on what I take to be Smith's extremely slippery position on *political* liberty, at least as he explicates it in the WN. While Smith, Turgot and Condorcet are strong proponents of personal and economic liberty, it is, at best, unclear what Smith's position is concerning political liberty. Rothschild is careful not to ascribe a well-articulated theory of political liberty to Smith, but I would argue that this term is indeed problematic in his writing.

Condorcet identifies natural liberty with political as well as religious and economic liberty. This is less clear in the case of Smith. In the LJ and in the WN Smith focuses on economic life as driving the development and changes in government, government that arises not out of social contracts, but rather from needs for authority, utility and to protect property rights (Smith 1978, LJA v.119–27, LJB 12–15, 20–2; WN V.i.b.2). Most of us are fallible, small-minded and often preoccupied with our own interests,[3] so a legislative aristocracy or monarchy seem to be the least worst forms of government that will create authority to adjudicate rights and protect property. Smith is pessimistic that a purely democratic process would actually work to protect peace and order, both necessary for economic progress. Because of our parochialism, Smith also finds that few of us could govern wisely, taking the interests of all citizens into account. The best (or least worst) form of government is probably a limited monarchy in which executive, parliamentary and judicial orders are separate, with a divided parliament of Commons and Lords to prevent the tyranny of individuals or ideas. Human frailties being an issue, and fearing the tyranny of institutions and so-called 'systems thinking', Smith concentrates on the idea of a political economy where individual economic liberty underpinned by laws of justice rather than politics, and a complex political system is the foundation for the 'wealth of nations'.

In conclusion, the richness of Rothschild's approach helps us to understand how sentiments and dispositions and revisions of them can change, radically, the way we think about liberty, property, commerce, labour and political economy. These Enlightenment philosophers recognized that in real life we are emotional, sentimental, imperfect, fallible quasi-rational beings. They created new mindsets – new ways of framing experience – that postulated the importance of individuals and individual liberty and focused our attention on the role of commerce in changing, even improving, societal well-being. I read Rothschild as arguing that this change in mindsets, what we now call the Enlightenment, began with a change in sentiments and dispositions. Smith, Turgot and Condorcet were some of the important change agents. While she may overemphasize the role of sentiments and dispositions in the revolution of ideas of the Enlightenment, that theme is often ignored in our postulation of rationality as the fundamental explanatory mechanism. This book sets us straight on the history of ideas we call the Enlightenment, and on the importance of sentiments in the revolution of ideas.

Notes

1 In another place I have called this the *Rashomon* Effect, from the 1950 Japanese movie by that name (Werhane 1999).

2 While the LJ are compilations of student class notes, alone a testimony to their fallibility, as there are two sets of them, there are some parallels that likely reflect Smith's thinking.

3 In WN Smith writes, 'Though the interest of the labourer is strictly connected with that of society, he is incapable either of comprehending that interest, or of understanding its connection with his own' (WN I.xi.p.9). About landholders he concludes, 'That indolence, which is the natural effect of the ease and security of their situation, renders them too often, not only ignorant, but incapable of that application of mind which is necessary in order to foresee and understand the consequences of any publick regulation' (WN I.ix.p.8). Merchants and manufacturers fare somewhat better, but 'the interest of the dealers…is always in some respects different from, and even opposite to, that of the publick' (WN I.xi.p.10).

Bibliography

Becker, C. (1932) *The Heavenly City of the Eighteenth Century Philosophers*, New Haven: Yale University Press.

Griswold, C.L. (1999) *Adam Smith and the Virtues of Enlightenment*, Cambridge: Cambridge University Press.

Rothschild, E. (2001) *Economic Sentiments: Adam Smith, Condorcet, and the Enlightenment*, Cambridge, MA: Harvard University Press.

Schumpeter, J. (1954) *History of Economic Analysis*, Elizabeth Brody Schumpeter (ed.), New York: Oxford University Press.

Smith, A. (1976a) *The Theory of Moral Sentiments*, A.L. Macfie and D.D. Raphael (eds), Oxford: Oxford University Press; reprinted, Liberty Press (1982).

—— (1976b) *An Inquiry into the Nature and Causes of the Wealth of Nations*, R.H. Campbell and A.S. Skinner (eds), Oxford: Oxford University Press; reprinted, Liberty Press (1981).

—— (1978) *Lectures on Jurisprudence*, R.L. Meek, D.D. Raphael and P.G. Stein (eds), Oxford: Oxford University Press; reprinted, Liberty Press (1982).

Stigler, G. (1971) 'Smith's travels on the ship of state', *History of Political Economy*, 3: 621–38.

Werhane, P. (1999) *Moral Imagination and Management Decision-Making*, New York: Oxford University Press.

—— (1991) *Adam Smith and His Legacy for Modern Capitalism*, New York: Oxford University Press.

Smith's ambiguities

A response to Emma Rothschild's *Economic Sentiments*

Samuel Fleischacker

I want to begin by expressing a personal debt of gratitude to Professor Rothschild. When I began working on the *Wealth of Nations* (WN), about a decade ago, I found myself early on puzzled by the reception of the book and wondered whether there was any scholarly literature suggesting that the standard picture of Smith might be seriously mistaken, and that Smith's legacy might lie as much among what today we call 'welfare liberals' as among the so-called 'libertarians' or 'classical liberals'. I would probably have been happy to find *any* scholarly piece putting this suggestion forward; I held out only slim hopes that I might find a well-documented and persuasively argued critique of the conventional picture. So coming upon Rothschild's article, 'Adam Smith and conservative economics' (Rothschild 1992), was really like first looking into Chapman's Homer for me. After about a decade of further work on Smith, I still find that article about the best thing I know on the history of Smith's reception, and that it now constitutes chapter two of *Economic Sentiments* alone makes the book worth the purchase price.

There is a great deal that I find to treasure and admire in *Economic Sentiments* aside from its second chapter, but let me stick with that for a moment, since it gives me the opportunity to respond to certain complaints I've heard about the book as a whole. I believe I was originally led to Rothschild's 1992 article by the bibliography in Jerry Muller's book on Adam Smith. Muller, however, felt compelled to add that the article 'is marred by an image of Smith which is rather more radical than can legitimately be adduced from a balanced reading of his works' (Muller 1993: 260–1). Now Muller has a somewhat conservative 'take' on Smith, but I have heard similar complaints from people whose own politics are closer to Rothschild's own. The complaints mystify me, frankly, and this panel seems to me a good place to ask whether someone might help explain them. For it has always seemed to me that Professor Rothschild's argument about Smith's reception is a model of historical responsibility. In the first place, the image of Smith she presents – as sceptical of conventional religion, supportive of the rights of the poor and suspicious of war – seems hard to quarrel with. (I'll come back to this in a moment.) Second, to make her claims about Smith's initial reception – that at his death he was disliked by defenders of conventional religious beliefs and embraced by friends of the early French Revolution – she draws on a multitude of sources, including newspaper obituaries for Smith, which do indeed support her claims. Third, she fully allows that *both* what we might call, in retrospect, the 'rightwing' uses of Smith in the 1790s (William Pitt's, for instance, in the debates over wage rates and poor relief) *and* what we might call the 'leftwing' uses (Samuel Whitbread's, for instance, in those same debates) were legitimately able to draw on elements in Smith's texts;[1] far from reading a 'radical' image of Smith into his texts, she emphasizes the *ambiguity* of WN, in relation to later debates. Finally, she is careful to provide what philosophers call an 'error theory' for why Smith's later admirers might have seriously misunderstood him. If you want to say that a person is making a grave error about something that should be obvious, it is not enough just to give evidence that he or she is wrong; you also want to account for how a rational person could have made such a mistake. And if Smith was a great champion of the poor but came to be seen, by 1800, as indistinguishable from the Edmund Burke of the 'Thoughts on Scarcity' (Rothschild 2001: 64),[2] then a lot of people have made an enormous error about him. How might that have come about? Rothschild answers that question with a brilliant account of why, when Dugald Stewart produced the memoir that more than anything else defined the later view of Smith, he had strong political reasons to present as conservative a Smith as possible.

To return now to the first point, what is so shocking about suggesting that Smith was a religious sceptic and a supporter of the rights of the poor?[3] I want myself to raise some questions about the degree to which Smith's view of religion can be assimilated to Hume's, but surely there can be no doubt that Smith was critical of conventional Christian belief and practice and that his association with Hume brought great notoriety upon him. Smith himself remarked that the single sheet of paper that he wrote on the death of Hume brought upon him 'ten times more abuse than the very violent attack [he] had made upon the whole commercial system of Great Britain' (Smith 1987, *Corr.* Letter 208 to Andreas Holt, 26 October 1780: 251). Similarly, whether Smith was actually a republican or not may be a matter of debate, but he dropped some hints even in that direction (above all, Smith 1978, *Lectures on Jurisprudence* (LJA) v.123–27; and Smith 1976b, WN IV.vii.b.51),[4] and he criticized oppression of the poor by the government and by their employers all through WN. In any case, Rothschild doesn't claim that Smith was a republican,[5] merely that he supported popular instruction and political discussion, which he most certainly did (WN V.i.f.50–61). I find myself, therefore, wondering how any 'balanced reading' of Smith's work could arrive at conclusions *other* than Rothschild's.

I feel the same way about the arguments of chapters three and four, which draw out the complex correlations between Smith's views and those of Turgot and Condorcet on apprenticeship and the corn laws, and show what happened to views like Smith's in nineteenth-century debates over these matters. I found particularly useful Rothschild's comment that Smith's critique of government was directed at guilds, corporations and churches as well as at national governments (Rothschild 2001: 108), and her account of how Turgot and Condorcet aimed to deal with food scarcities by providing aid to the poor rather than by intervening with corn prices (pp. 75–81). I take it, by the way, that what she says in the latter respect constitutes a refutation of Istvan Hont and Michael Ignatieff's famous claim that '[b]y 1776, Smith remained the only standard-bearer for "natural liberty" in grain' (Hont and Ignatieff 1983: 18).[6]

Before turning to matters on which I want to raise some critical questions, let me note that I learned a great deal from the chapters in the book on Condorcet as well as the ones on Smith, and that I found the overall view that emerges from the book – of an Enlightenment that was more uncertain, warmer, more 'liberal and more romantic' (Rothschild 2001: 219) than the one we usually read about – extremely beautiful and inspiring. The material on Condorcet was especially illuminating to me, since I had, in my ignorance, until then accepted a standard sort of 'Smith vs. Condorcet' caricature, according to which Smith represents the good, tentative, common-sense-oriented version of Enlightenment rationalism while Condorcet represents the bad, over-confident, mathematically-oriented version of that same rationalism. As with everything else she takes up in this delicate and careful book, Rothschild does not entirely reject that picture – she acknowledges Condorcet's strong attraction to mathematical methods (p. 178) – but she complicates it greatly. I have never before seen the discursive, anti-utilitarian or moral sentimentalist sides of Condorcet, and upon seeing them I felt, as many other readers must have done, that he deserves far more attention than he usually receives.

Back now to Smith, and to some issues on which I have some questions for Professor Rothschild. I will raise two, which should be enough to fuel a discussion.

First, there is the matter of Smith's religious beliefs. I agree entirely that Smith was no Christian, by the end of his life at least, and that his commitment to Stoicism was qualified and less than whole-hearted – at least, again, by the end of his life.[7] We should certainly be very wary of attributing any of his scientific explanations to Stoic premises. But I don't see a reason to go as far as Rothschild does in assimilating Smith's view of religion to Hume's (pp. 130, 135, 231). I don't see why Rothschild says that 'It is most unlikely that [Smith] believed... in the existence of an all-ordering providence' (p. 135). After all, even in the 1790 additions to *The Theory of Moral Sentiments* (TMS) Smith describes the universe as 'that great society...of which God himself is the immediate administrator and director' (Smith 1976a, TMS VI.ii.3.3), and in the chapter from which this quotation comes, he makes clear throughout that belief in an all-benevolent and all-powerful God plays a valuable role in moral thought – it enables us to extend our sympathies beyond all local communities, to every sensible being in the universe – and implies that this moral function justifies the belief.[8] The line of thought here fits in with what Smith had said in earlier editions about rules of morality: that they are 'justly regarded as the Laws of the Deity' (chapter heading to TMS III.5), even if they can also be justified in a purely secular way. 'Religion enforces the natural sense of duty', he says (TMS III.5.13). Similarly, he is at pains in the last as in the first edition to explain how the moral sentiments may be regarded as 'viceregents of God within us' (TMS III.5.6) – pace Rothschild (p. 231), he here echoes, rather than rejecting, his teacher Hutcheson's belief that the moral sense is implanted in us by God – saying that, 'in this respect, as in many others', we are created after God's image (TMS III.2.31). This is a clever variation on the way Jewish and Christian philosophers had in the past interpreted Genesis 1:27,[9] and it allows Smith to give religious resonance to his view that the search for praise signifies a deeper search for praise-worthiness: the desire for praise is the 'image', in mundane social interaction, of the desire for an absolute, trans-mundane goodness. Religious belief thus serves a variety of moral functions, for Smith, and that itself gives us some reason to hold it. Smith anticipates the conception of religion Kant was to develop, by which belief in a providential God, and an afterlife, can help buttress and enrich morality, and is justified insofar as it does that.

Of course Hume never said anything like this. But why should we assume that Smith and Hume agreed on the reasonableness of natural religion? Rothschild says that the intimate 'tone of Hume's and Smith's correspondence,... is difficult to reconcile with the presumption of serious religious differences' (p. 301, n. 84). I don't see why. Smith disagrees strongly with Hume in both TMS (on sympathy, on justice, on beauty) and WN (on standing armies and, as it happens, on whether governments should establish churches); he indeed seems to enjoy arguing with Hume (as Hume did with him).[10] Theirs was a teasing and an argumentative friendship. And while it is true that Smith takes much the same tone Hume does towards orthodox *Christianity*, in their correspondence and in some of his work, Smith never gave any hint, privately or publicly, that he rejected *religion*. He certainly did share Hume's anti-clericalism, and delighted, with him, in the irreverence of a Voltaire. But Voltaire believed in a 'watchmaker' God of some sort, and it seems to me there is every reason to regard Smith as more like Voltaire, in this respect, than like Hume.

Second, and not unrelatedly, I'd like to hear a bit more about the invisible hand. I am not unsympathetic to Rothschild's approach to that famous metaphor. One should look out for irony in practically every passage of Smith, and the irony in many important passages has been missed. Besides, Rothschild's marshalling of other literary passages where some sort of invisible hand appears is extremely impressive, and it is of course likely that Smith was well-acquainted with the passages she quotes from Shakespeare, Voltaire and Ovid (p. 119). I agree also that Smith never treats economic phenomena in isolation from political circumstances, as modern economists often do, and that he would have disliked the assumption, characteristic of nineteenth- and twentieth-century invisible-hand explanations, that theorists have privileged knowledge of social systems (pp. 124, 136). Finally, it is certainly true that Smith places great emphasis on people judging for themselves and might therefore be expected to be suspicious of invisible hand explanations, in which the subjects of the explanations 'are blind' (p. 123).

So I was at least half-persuaded by the argument in Rothschild's chapter 5. But not fully so. For one thing, while the famous passage in IV.ii is the only place in

WN where Smith uses the *phrase* 'invisible hand', it is far from the only place where he expresses the ideas to be found in that passage. We are told many times that certain branches of trade, or the competition among them, will wind up being advantageous to the public even though all the participants aim only at their private profit (WN II.ii.106, II.v.7, II.v.37, IV.v.b.3). We are told explicitly that the decline of the feudal system, which Smith calls 'a revolution of the greatest importance to the publick happiness', was brought about by people 'who had not the least intention to serve the publick' (WN III.iv.17). Further, we are given, throughout both WN and TMS, invisible hand explanations of, among other things, how systems of justice come about (TMS II.ii.2.1–II.ii.3.6), the origin of conscience (TMS III.i), the origin of the division of labour (WN I.i), and the moral advantages of small religious sects (WN V.i.g.10–12). In all these cases, the engine of the explanation is the same: the invisible hand leading us to help society regardless of our private intentions is nothing more or less than the force of society itself, the impact of society on our conception of ourselves and on the circumstances making possible our individual activities. In TMS, we are shown in great detail how our sentiments are shaped by our desire to be approved of by our neighbours, and WN begins by explaining how the economic opportunities available to each of us so much as exist only because of the needs of other human beings. So the invisible hand is nothing mysterious – as Rothschild says, it is certainly not a Stoic God – but it is a pretty good metaphor for the fundamental principle behind both Smith's moral and his economic thought: the sociability of human beings, the fact that 'man, who can subsist only in society, was fitted by nature' (TMS II.ii.3.1) to assist his fellow human beings whether he will or not. Of course Smith also believes strongly in individual freedom; what is remarkable about him is that he combined a belief in what today we call 'the social construction of the self' with the belief that individual selves, once so constructed, are free and responsible beings. Indeed, for Smith, individual freedom and the social construction of the self depend on one another. Only the influence of society enables us to develop a self that *can* be free (TMS III.1.3), but only free individuals can constitute a true 'society', in which sympathy, and the moral forces it makes possible, can play themselves out.

Note that the invisible hand account I am offering does not make it any sort of necessary truth that unregulated markets will promote the good of society, as some twentieth-century libertarians would have it. To say that is to make (at least) two assumptions that Smith would have denied: (1) that the parties to market exchanges are always free and equal; and (2) that whatever contributes to the private good of individuals must, in the aggregate, always constitute the good of society. The former assumption overlooks the many ways in which parties to exchange can be unfree or (relevantly) unequal, which Smith, as regards workers and their employers, does not do. The latter assumption, which makes the good of society *tautologously* equivalent to the aggregate good of its constituent individuals, overlooks externalities, not to mention the ways that gross inequalities can corrupt society and government. For Smith, the good of individuals *generally* contributes to societal good because society has shaped the way individuals seek their own good. But the invisible hand of society will work to help society, as Smith himself says, only 'in many cases', not in all. Political action may be necessary to correct for its failures, and will always be necessary to provide the institutional background ensuring that the exchanges taking place in the marketplace really are free and equal ones.

It follows that the account I have offered of the invisible hand does not deny that political circumstances may structure economic ones, nor does it suggest that economic activities independent of political interference will always bring about beneficial results for society. As for Rothschild's two most powerful arguments against taking Smith's invocation of the invisible hand entirely seriously – that Smith objected to underplaying the intentions of individual agents and overplaying the wisdom of theorists (pp. 123–4, 141) – I don't think the sort of invisible hand explanation I am attributing to Smith is threatened by those arguments. In the first place, as I see it Smith allows for individual freedom to go *together with* a number of social forces playing themselves out 'behind each individual's back', as it were. And the fact that we are all led to some results by an invisible hand is meant, I think, to *enhance* our sense of our individual freedom, not to detract from it. When Smith uses invisible-hand explanations, and especially in the passages where he invokes that phrase, he means as much as anything to stress the degree to which apparently *powerful* agents do not control their own actions as fully as they think they do – which implicitly brings out the degree to which the *rest* of us, those without power, have more control over our lives than we think we do. Rothschild notes that Smith stresses the limits of 'the reason of the great[,]...the reason of the pretentious; of the state,...of powerful merchants' (p. 150). But the reason with which the invisible hand in WN is implicitly contrasted is precisely the reason of a powerful merchant and of the state. Surely the 'invisible hand' is a *part* of Smith's polemic against 'the reason of the great', then, and not itself a joke. In the invisible-hand passages of both TMS and WN, the person who doesn't know what he is doing is, respectively, a rich landowner and a powerful merchant, and in the latter Smith's express purpose is, as Rothschild says, to keep governments from exercising a more visible hand over the economy (pp. 138, 144). The target of WN IV.ii as a whole, moreover, is the 'merchants and manufacturers' whom Smith decries as a virtual 'standing army' intimidating the legislature of Britain (WN IV.ii.43; see also IV.ii.38) – it is they who claim, in the service of their own interests, that trade needs protection, needs the guidance of a visible hand. When he invokes the invisible hand, Smith makes the agency of these merchants look 'foolish', 'puny and futile' (Rothschild 2001: 123) – but that relieves the rest of us, a bit, from the sense that their agency has excessive power over our own.

And in the second place, for all that Smith the theorist may show 'what's really going on' as regards justice, the division of labour, and so on, in his invisible-hand explanations, there need be no implication that theorists know something about individual agents that those agents can't, or don't, know themselves.[11] All that this mode of explanation implies is that we can know certain things about society in *retrospect* that we cannot know in *prospect*. One thing Smith rarely does, in either

TMS or WN, is use an invisible-hand explanation to make *predictions* about where society is heading. On the contrary, he stresses how little we – all of us, theorists as well as ordinary people – know about the long-term, large-scale effects of our actions. That we are all quite ignorant of what effects our actions will have, especially on the large-scale or in the long-term, follows from the belief that each human being is free and therefore unpredictable – has, unlike a chess-piece, a 'principle of motion' of their own (TMS VI.ii.2.17). We don't know what effect our actions will have on the decisions of others, how they will react to what we do. But this ignorance, and the freedom with which it is linked, need not prevent any of us – again, whether theorists or ordinary people – from looking *back* on a course of human activity and finding unintended patterns in it. The cognitive advantage, in Smith's invisible-hand explanations, is held not by social-science experts vis-à-vis laypeople, but by those, expert or lay, who live after a series of events vis-à-vis those who participate in them. Retrospectively, we can see the workings of an invisible hand in many social developments; prospectively, we need each to judge for the best in our local situations, without worrying too much about what pattern, overall, our individual actions will form.

I therefore think Smith is more serious about the invisible hand than Rothschild suggests. Nevertheless, Rothschild has done something extremely important in prompting us not to take the metaphor for granted, to look out for the possibility of irony that can be found in so much of Smith's work. Here, and in general, Rothschild's book makes Smith more complex, and therefore richer, than he is often taken to be. *Economic Sentiments* will provoke, inspire and enliven the world of Smith scholarship for a long time to come.

Notes

1 Similarly, she says that Smith belongs to neither side in the pamphlet wars of 1790–2 (p. 55), and that there is no point to claiming him as a proponent or an opponent of the French Revolution (p. 66).

2 Rothschild's distinction between Smith and the later Burke should not be controversial at all: Gertrude Himmelfarb made a similar case; see Himmelfarb (1984: 66–73).

3 Let alone an opponent of war. Smith clearly detested war. He calls Britain's wars 'expensive and unnecessary' (WN II.iii.35), describes the crusades as a 'destructive frenzy' (WN III.iii.14), and characterizes the constant state of war in feudal times as 'a scene of violence, rapine, and disorder' (WN III.iv.10). He says soldiers are given to 'idleness and dissipation' and often to 'rapine and plunder' (WN IV.ii.42); see also I.viii.44). He never misses an opportunity to stress the 'waste of stock' caused by wars, the enormous expense that goes into waging them (WN II.iii.35, III.iii.14, III.iv.24, IV.i.20–30, IV.vii.c.63–4, IV.viii.53, V.ii.k.80, V.iii.50–1, V.iii.58, V.iii.88–92) – an important point in his debate with mercantilists who saw war as a *source* of wealth. Indeed, Smith treats war as the worst kind of government 'waste and extravagance' (WN II.iii.32–5, V.iii.49, V.iii.58), the worst enemy of 'the natural progress of things towards improvement', the great 'disease' that only 'the uniform... effort of every man to better his condition' can combat (WN II.iii.31). One of WN's main purposes, in promoting free trade, is to provide an alternative to the constant wars that went with mercantilism: 'Commerce... ought naturally to be, among nations, as among individuals, a bond of union and friendship' (WN IV.iii.c.9).

4 Joseph Cropsey argues that Smith's consistent praise for Holland in WN betrays a sympathy for republicanism; see Cropsey (2001: 75–6).
5 On the contrary: she says that 'Smith had no interest in doing without kings' (135), and that Condorcet, the other hero of *Economic Sentiments*, was far more 'interested and involved than either Smith or Hume in the philosophy and politics of democracy' (234).
6 Rothschild shows that Turgot too stood for 'natural liberty' in grain in 1776, and that Condorcet held that position in 1792.
7 He does not, however, quite call 'the Stoic concern with the "greatest possible quantity of happiness" ' in the universe a 'delusion', as Rothschild says (p. 133). Indeed he calls the idea of a Being who seeks to lead the universe towards such a goal 'by far the most sublime' of all objects of human contemplation (TMS VI.ii.3.5). What he objects to – here and at VII.ii.1.45–7, which Rothschild cites to support her reading – is the notion that *we* should seek to bring about this wonderful goal: 'The administration of the great system of the universe... is the business of God and not of man' (TMS VI.ii.3.6). *We* should attend to our local duties, and not try to solve problems for which we are unsuited. But the belief in God is important to this humble commitment: it is precisely because we can have confidence that God will take care of 'the big picture' that we can be content, ourselves, to carry out only small, local duties.
8 There is, moreover, no use of the word 'seems', or its synonyms, in connection with the existence of the Deity in this chapter (Rothschild notes that Smith often uses 'seems' when he expresses apparently religious beliefs; see p. 129). But he does not do so here.
9 The more standard reading of this verse sees the image of God in our intellect, not our emotions, but since Smith has shifted the emphasis in morality from intellect to sentiment, it makes sense for him, correspondingly, to see God's image in our sentiments.
10 For example, on the nature of sympathy, in TMS (see TMS p. 46 n.), and on rent, in WN (*Corr.* p. 186).
11 Here and in general, I think Smith resists attributing any special 'knowingness' to the theorist, just as Rothschild says (p. 124). But for that reason, it seems to me that Hayek's understanding of Smith is more on the mark than Rothschild suggests (p. 151). It is certainly true that Smith does not exalt 'the unconscious, the blind,... the imperfectly understood' (p. 149). But it is less true that Smith should be kept apart from Hayek's emphasis on local knowledge (p. 150). Certainly, the person who works on 'a few simple operations' all his or her life is said to be mentally 'mutilated and deformed' (WN V.i.f.50, V.i.f.61). But such a person is not a good example of someone with local knowledge – she or he, rather, has *no* understanding, *no* knowledge. Smith often speaks very highly of those with local knowledge – knowledge of 'their local situations' (WN IV.v.b.16) – insisting that their understanding of what is to be done, in their situations, will be superior to that of any legislator looking at the situation from above. *A fortiori*, surely, their knowledge will also be superior to that of any theorist. In many ways, Smith treats theory, the broad universal way of looking at society, as secondary to the knowledge of particulars. But this attitude towards theory is not significantly different from the Hayekian views, Rothschild describes at the top of p. 150. It may be important to distinguish between two aspects of Hayek: one that praises local knowledge and one that praises a lack of all knowledge, a blessed ignorance. I haven't read Hayek in a while, but as I recall, it is right to see both tendencies in his work. And if so, the first will be quite Smithian, while the second is something Smith would have abhorred.

Bibliography

Cropsey, J. (2001) *Polity and Economy*, South Bend: St Augustine's Press.
Himmelfarb, G. (1984) *The Idea of Poverty*, New York: Knopf.

Hont, I. and Ignatieff, M. (1983) 'Needs and justice in the *Wealth of Nations*', in *Wealth and Virtue*, I. Hont and M. Ignatieff (eds), Cambridge: Cambridge University Press.

Muller, J. (1993) *Adam Smith in His Time and Ours*, Princeton: Princeton University Press.

Rothschild, E. (2001) *Economic Sentiments: Adam Smith, Condorcet and the Enlightenment*, Cambridge MA: Harvard University Press.

—— (1992) 'Adam Smith and conservative economics', *Economic History Review*, 45: 74–96.

Smith, A. (1976a) *The Theory of Moral Sentiments*, D.D. Raphael and A.L Macfie (eds), Oxford: Oxford University Press; reprinted, Liberty Press (1982).

—— (1976b) *An Inquiry into the Nature and Causes of the Wealth of Nations*, R.H. Campbell and A.S. Skinner(eds), Oxford: Oxford University Press; reprinted, Liberty Press (1981).

—— (1978) *Lectures on Jurisprudence*, R.L. Meek, D.D. Raphael and P.G. Stein (eds), Oxford: Oxford University Press; reprinted, Liberty Press (1982).

—— (1987) *Correspondence of Adam Smith*, E.C. Mossner and I.S. Ross (eds), Oxford: Oxford University Press; reprinted, Liberty Press (1987).

Dignity or meanness

Emma Rothschild

It is a great pleasure to be here, and I am most grateful to the International Adam Smith Society for organizing this panel. It is an additional pleasure that it should take place in a city about which Smith had heard a great deal, and which was characterized, in his view, by a condition to which he attached the greatest importance, namely 'philosophical good temper and moderation' (Smith 1976b, WN V.i.g.8).

It is a tremendous honour for me to participate in this discussion with three such distinguished colleagues, and I am grateful to all of them for their illuminating comments. All of them are concerned, in different ways, with a double question which was at the heart of Smith's preoccupations for most of his life, as it was for many of his contemporaries. The question, in David Hume's words, is 'of the dignity or meanness of human nature', and of how we go about 'forming our notions of human nature' (Hume 1987). It is this elderly question on which I want to concentrate my own comments.

Professor Darwall, in his insightful remarks, describes the foundation or groundwork of Smith's ideas of equal respect and dignity in the 'very framework' of his account of human nature, both in respect of the psychology and metaethics of moral judgment, and in respect of the psychology and what might be called the meta-commerce of exchange. I find Professor Darwall's explanation of the second-person 'infrastructure' of exchange entirely convincing. Exchange is founded on the universal disposition to speech, which is characteristic of all individuals, and speech is founded, in turn (or so Smith speculates, in the *Lectures on Jurisprudence* (LJA), in the *Wealth of Nations* (WN) and again in the last additions he made to *The Theory of Moral Sentiments* (TMS)) on the disposition to persuade (Smith 1976a, TMS VII.iv.25; Smith 1978, LJA vi.56; WN I.ii.2). The foundation of commerce can be identified, thereby, in one of the respects in which all individuals are equal.

Commerce is also founded on equality in the different sense that a commercial society will only function well if individuals recognize themselves to be each others' equals, at least in some minimal respects. Smith's writings on commerce are full of illustrations of the ways in which civil inequality, or inequality before the law, can interfere with the progress of opulence. The fear which is a consequence of unequal power renders contracts void. The tradesmen who sell their upholstery to a rich landlord do not consider themselves to be indebted to him. The greatest of all England's commercial advantages consists in the 'equal and impartial administration of justice which renders the rights of the meanest British subject respectable to the greatest' (WN IV.vii.c.54; LJA, i.117–18, ii.131).

The connection to *Anerkennung*, or recognition, is profound. The words 'recognition' and 'recognise' are nineteenth-century innovations, in their principal modern sense, and Smith does not actually use them. But the idea of recognition is at the heart of Smith's account of human nature. The purpose of all the toil and bustle of the world, he wrote in a famous passage in TMS, is 'to be observed, to be attended to, to be taken notice of'. The dismal destiny of the poor man is that he 'goes out and comes in unheeded', and that he is 'out of the sight of mankind'. He is 'observed and attended to by nobody' (TMS I.iii.2.1; WN V.i.g.12). But exchange, which is of necessity the exchange of equal values, is a means of being observed. The poor man's exchangeable value is as good as the rich man's, and their engagement with each other is (as Turgot wrote) a 'debate between every buyer and every seller' (Turgot 1913–23, vol. 3: 326).

I was convinced, too, by Professor Darwall's account of the foundation of moral judgment in equal recognition. Curiosity about the sentiments and intentions of other people is in Smith's description, another of the universal dispositions of all individuals. 'In every age and country of the world men must have attended to the characters, designs, and actions of one another', he wrote in the WN; 'this passion to discover the real sentiments of others is naturally so strong', he wrote in the TMS, that it often degenerates into impertinent prying (WN V.i.f.25; TMS VII.iv.28). Morality, like commerce, is the expression of a disposition in which all individuals are equal, and similar.

The process of moral reflection, for Smith, is one in which the individual sees herself reflected in the eyes of other people, and reflects, herself, on what she would feel if she were someone else (including if she were someone else who was looking at her). Smith, like Condorcet and many others of their contemporaries, was preoccupied with trying to imagine what it would be like to be someone else. He succeeds in 'changing places in fancy' with Oedipus, Jocasta, a negro slave, a woman who is ashamed to go out in public without shoes, a murderer in dread of discovery; he is defeated, only, by the effort to imagine the pains of child-birth (TMS VII.iii.1.4). He was preoccupied, more generally, with other people. He indeed uses the phrase 'other people' eighty-four times in TMS; the large majority of these uses, interestingly enough, are in the new passages he added to the final, 1790 edition.

It is evident that the moral process Smith describes cannot function well if individuals do not conceive themselves, in some sense, to be like other people. If one is surrounded by beings whom one does not recognize, and in whom one cannot recognize oneself, then one cannot possibly engage in the sort of reflective, discursive correction of sentiments which is so important to Smith's (and to Hume's) account of moral judgment. Adam's complaint to God, in Book VIII of *Paradise Lost*, is that every one around him, or every living thing, is other, different, inferior. It is this that induces him to ask for someone like himself, with whom he can converse (Eve, in the event):

> Among unequals what society
> Can sort, what harmony or true delight?
>
> (*Paradise Lost*, VIII: 383–4)

Professor Darwall's account of the 'grounding' of Smith's ideas of equal respect seems to me to be compelling, for all these reasons. But there are two, related aspects of Smith's moral theory which do pose a number of difficulties for this interpretation, and on which I would very much like to hear Professor Darwall's comments. The first has to do with Smith's own conception (or lack of conception) of the ground or foundation or framework of moral thought, and the second with his account of the condition he describes, a little breathlessly, it must be said, as 'reason, principle, conscience, the inhabitant of the breast, the man within, the great judge and arbiter of our conduct' (TMS III.3.4).

There is little doubt that Smith thought of himself as 'endeavouring to establish' what he described as a 'system of moral philosophy', and in particular, a system which provided some account of the principles of moral approbation or judgment. It was a speculative system, in his description; a system of sympathy; and a different system of sympathy from Hume's (TMS VII.i.1, VII.iii.intro.3, VII.iii.3.17). In this respect he is indeed presenting himself as a spectator, or a man of system; a third-person observer of a second-person system. But what is striking, in his descriptions of this system, is how little he seems to be concerned with what we would call either foundational or metaethical questions.

Smith certainly refers to the universal dispositions or original principles of human nature (including the dispositions to persuade, have conversations, and reflect on other people's sentiments). He says very little, all the same, about the foundation or grounding of his own system in an account (an abstract science, or an anthropology, or what would later have been called a psychology) of human nature. His Victorian critics were unjust in accusing him of misplaced introspection, or of 'evolving from his own consciousness' the circumstances of social existence (Leslie 1879: 385, 387). He was an indefatigable observer (Jean-Baptiste Say's description), an incomparable writer about moral character (Kant's description), a magnificent assembler of historical or 'positive knowledge' (Jean-Baptiste Say, again). But he was not tremendously interested in the foundations of his own or other people's systems.

Smith was also somewhat less than interested in what would now be called metaethics, or the theory which is concerned with the status of normative or substantive claims about ethical life.[1] It is true that he makes a distinction, in Part VII of TMS, which is similar to that between ethics and metaethics.[2] He describes his own system as a contribution to the latter enquiry, and thereby as a 'mere matter of philosophical curiosity', of no practical importance and with little or no (or 'possibly' no) influence on actual notions of right and wrong. He denies any intention of putting forward a (normative) system of virtue (TMS VII.iii.intro.3). But he is by that token unconcerned to put forward his own (speculative) system as a support to or foundation of a normative theory. The bulk of TMS, and the overwhelming mass of his 1790 additions, is concerned, rather, with something close to what Bernard Williams has called 'think[ing] in ethics'. Its spirit, too, is reasonably close to what Williams describes as a form of philosophical scepticism, or a 'theory about the nature of ethical thought that *leaves open* the question of whether there could be [metaethical] tests' of ethical thoughts.[3]

The second and related difficulty has to do with the large number of passages where Smith does invoke the spectator's perspective, and the impartial spectator in particular. Professor Darwall comments on the irony that it should be Smith, the theorist of the second person and of the 'imaginary change of place with other men', who is so widely identified with the device of the impartial spectator. I am full of appreciation for the enterprise of freeing Smith from the preferences of his posthumous enthusiasts, and the impartial spectator, like the invisible hand, looms larger in *Smithianismus* than in Smith's own work. But Smith did have a fondness for concise and persuasive devices. He uses the phrase 'impartial spectator' frequently in TMS, and even more frequently in his last additions; Dugald Stewart, in his important biographical memoir of Smith of 1793, devotes considerable attention to Smith's ideas of the impartial spectator. (I will return later to the device of the invisible hand.)

The difficulty which the idea of the impartial spectator poses for the interpretation of Smith's moral theory in terms of equal dignity is that it seems to propose a different and more abstract foundation for moral judgment. It also introduces a third person, or the third-person perspective, into the innermost sentiments of individual existence. Smith is entirely explicit in making it clear that the impartial spectator is imaginary and not real (in either a secular or an unsecular sense); he refers seven times, in his last additions to TMS, to the 'supposed impartial spectator' (TMS III.2.32 (twice), III.3.1, VI.ii.1.22, VI.concl.1, VI.concl.2, VII.ii.1.34).[4] But his descriptions of the interiority or insideness of moral reflection are at the same time extraordinarily vivid. He speaks repeatedly of 'the man within the breast', 'the great inmate of the breast', 'the inhabitant of the breast, the man within', the 'eyes of this great inmate' which look into even our 'inward sentiments and feelings', the 'inmate who, in the evening, calls us to an account' (TMS III.2.32–5, III.3.5, III.3.25–9, VI.i.11, VI.ii.1.22, VI.concl.1, VII.ii.1.34, VII.ii.1.44–7).

My understanding of these passages is roughly as follows: that by sympathizing with other people – with 'you', as it were – and by observing your responses to her conduct, the individual can get a sense of what it would be like to be the impartial spectator of her own conduct. But there is a different understanding, which would have been far more natural to Smith's contemporaries. It is that the principle or conscience within the breast is put there by God. It is not a distinctive faculty, or a moral sense. But it is like the moral sense in that it is placed in nature by God. The equal dignity of all individuals is no more, on this view, than the equality of souls which was at the heart of so much Protestant theology, especially in England, from the seventeenth century onwards. It is the dignity of eternity, in the beautiful words of John Donne's sermon of 1627 on the sleep of death:

> There shall be no Cloud nor Sun, no darkness nor dazzling, but one equal light, no noise nor silence, but one equal music, no fears nor hopes, but one equal possession, no foes nor friends, but one equal communion and Identity, no ends nor beginnings, but one equal eternity.
>
> (Donne 1956, vol. 8: 191)

Even if my secular understanding is correct, Smith is open to the objection, which Dugald Stewart made in 1793, that he provides only a very non-chalant explanation of the origin of the inner and equal institution, the tribunal within us. 'Still he insists', Stewart writes, that our moral sentiments have some secret reference to the sentiments of others; 'still, he contends', that the jurisdiction of even the innermost conscience is derived from the turbulent outside world (Stewart 1980: 287). The comparison which I find intriguing here is indeed with the greatest of all theorists of equal dignity, namely Kant, and in particular with *The Groundwork of the Metaphysic of Morals*. Kant's account of the kingdom of ends, in which all rational individuals can be ends in themselves, is characterized by an elaborate economic imagery, of market prices, luxury prices and inner value, namely dignity. His account of the insideness of moral judgment also has a great deal in common with Smith's, as Professor Fleischacker has shown (Fleischacker 1991).

Kant's moral individual, like Smith's, sets out on an interior journey, in which she must travel deeper and deeper within her own conscience. But where Smith's individual is continually comparing her own judgments with the judgments of the world, Kant's seeks to leave the world behind her, or outside. She has an 'inner sentiment' or an 'inner sense'; she must find her way even inside this inner sentiment to the 'I' which is its foundation; inside the 'I' itself, or deeper and deeper within her, is the power of reason (Kant 1984: 110–11; 1964: 119). The moral journey leads even further into an innermost space which is cleansed of the empirical and which is thereby infinitely small (and also infinitely large).[5]

In the astonishing metaphor at the very end of the *Groundwork*, of the bird of reason, the limit of moral inquiry is constituted when reason is prevented from searching for morality in the empirical world, and also in a world that is empty: 'from flapping its wings powerlessly, without leaving the spot, in a space that for it is empty – the space of transcendent concepts known as "the intelligible world" ' (Kant 1984: 125–6; 1964: 130). But for Smith, all this preoccupation with grounds and groundworks is of apparently very little concern. I suppose one could say that Smith's individual also flutters, or oscillates; like Kant's great osprey, she floats back and forth (*herumschwärmen*), but from the world to the mind, and from the mind to the world.

Let me turn now to Professor Werhane's generous and stimulating comments. I certainly thought of *Economic Sentiments* as being about Hume and Turgot, as well as about Smith and Condorcet. Turgot was in some respects an even more profound theorist of economic life than Smith. His account of the process of exchange, as a series of transactions involving two contracting parties, each of whom estimates the value to himself of the commodities he has to sell and the commodities he wishes to buy, and who together arrive at an exchangeable value or price at which these two values are equal, is one of the truly brilliant insights of eighteenth-century economic thought. It is also, interestingly enough, a good illustration of the relationship between commerce and equality. The two contracting parties are not necessarily or in general equal. But in the instant of exchange, in a transaction which is not characterized by force or fraud, they exchange values which are for them equal. They do not recognize each other, in the sense that they know each other's history or social condition, but they recognize that they are each free to contract for an equal exchange. Their transaction is for Turgot as for Smith a form of conversation; a 'debate' (vol. 3: 89–98).

Turgot's generalization of these two-party transactions (or pairwise comparisons) to the 'entire society' is a remarkable tour-de-force. Prices and quantities in different markets 'are related to one another by a reciprocal dependence, and arrive at equilibrium themselves'. When commerce and competition are entirely free, this 'point of equilibrium' is also the point of greatest 'production, enjoyment, wealth and strength'. Prices change by imperceptible degrees, and 'the debate between every buyer and every seller is a sort of *tâtonnement* which makes known to everyone, with certainty, the true price of everything' (Turgot 1913–23, vol. 3: 315, 326, 334). I want to return in a moment to the invisible hand. But this vista of reciprocal and universal interdependence corresponds, far more than anything Smith himself wrote, to the conception of commerce which, as Professor Werhane rightly points out, is so closely connected to the idea of the invisible hand.

Turgot was deeply concerned, too, with sentiments and dispositions. Both he and Hume expressed, more eloquently than Smith, the fatal flaw of theories of universal self-interest, namely that they are either false or tautological. 'There is much of a dispute of words in all this controversy', Hume wrote in his essay on the dignity or meanness of human nature; the man who denies all public spirit and private friendship has either 'forgotten the movements of his heart', or 'calls not things by their proper names' (Hume 1987: 84–5). For Turgot, writing of Helvétius's postulate of universal self-interest, in a letter to Condorcet,

> in the sense that this proposition is true, it is childish, and a metaphysical abstraction from which there is no practical result to be drawn, because it is then equivalent to saying that 'man only desires that which he desires'. If he [Helvétius] is talking about a reflective, calculated interest by which man

> compares himself to others and prefers himself, then it is false that even the most corrupt men behave according to this principle.
>
> (Henry 1883: 143–4)

'It is false that moral sentiments do not influence their judgments, their actions, their affections', Turgot continued. The proof was that they need to make an effort to overcome their feeling when it is in opposition to their interest; that they feel remorse; that they are touched by novels and tragedies. A novel 'whose hero acted according to the principles of Helvétius', he added, 'would be most displeasing'. Turgot's recourse, like Hume's, is to a compendium of evidence. He invites the reader (Condorcet, in this case) to remember his own heart; to observe other people; to take an interest in what other people are interested in reading; to think about novels and tragedies. Sentiments, for Turgot, too, were at the heart of moral life.

Professor Werhane raises an important question about whether Smith was a 'foundationalist'. I have already touched on this question, and I want to return to it at the end. I certainly thought that the argument I tried to make in the last chapter of *Economic Sentiments*, about the similarity of Smith's theories of moral, political and commercial enlightenment, was the most serious part of the book. Smith's philosophical universe is in each case, I suggested, one of considerable insecurity.[6] It takes the form, in each case, of a multitude of individual sentiments, relationships, transactions and conversations, out of which the philosopher constitutes a system. Only these individual sentiments exist; they are the foundation or substance of the system. But they are not a bad foundation, in the end. The reciprocal correction of moral sentiments; civilized political discussion; free and good-tempered competition: these conditions, which are themselves interdependent, are together something to be valued, and something, even, of which one can be confident.

I certainly would not wish to deny that Smith was influenced by the natural rights theories of Pufendorf and others. He studied natural law, and he taught it, at length. He uses the words 'nature', 'natural', and their cognates about 600 times in TMS, in a dizzying variety of senses, as Professor Griswold has shown. Oddly enough, in all this profusion, he does not use the phrase 'natural order' (or indeed 'natural right'). But I do not think that the weight of natural jurisprudence, after a century of objections, with which Smith was well acquainted, as Professor Haakonssen has shown, is sufficient to constitute the foundation of his moral theory (Haakonssen 1981; Griswold 1999). He had a conception of natural and even of sacred rights, to which I want to return; he also had a conception of the natural and universal dispositions of human individuals. These together are not quite enough to make him a 'foundationalist'.

Smith was not so much a 'poor epistemologist', in my view, as a non-chalant epistemologist; someone who did not think a great deal, at least in the last thirty years or so of his life, about what it is to have a theory of knowing (or thinking). Hume, in the conclusion of Book I of the *Treatise*, writes of imagining himself, after many hours of thinking about scepticism, to be in the 'most deplorable condition', the deepest darkness of 'philosophical melancholy'. He then goes out to dinner, plays backgammon, 'I converse and am merry with my friends', and when he returns he finds his earlier speculations to be 'cold, and strain'd, and ridiculous'. Smith, too, had moments of philosophical melancholy, as we will see. But they were not, in general, about the nature of understanding (Hume 1978: 269).

I am not sure, too, that I would be as critical as Professor Werhane of Smith's views of political liberty. I tried to suggest, in the book, that the distinction between economic, political, personal and even religious liberty was much less clear in Smith's lifetime than it became soon after his death. Economic regulation, for Smith, could be an infringement of personal liberty, and political oppression could take multiple economic or commercial forms. Smith was not particularly interested in theories of democracy, although he did lecture at considerable length on voting procedures, on different ways in which what he described as the 'voice of the people' could be expressed in political processes, and on the duration of parliaments (LJA v.9–12, 51–3; LJB 78). He was not himself one of the selected men in eighteenth-century Scotland – 187 electors in the county of Fifeshire, towards the end of Smith's lifetime – who were entitled to a political life. (David Hume, interestingly enough, was offered the opportunity to become a voter or 'parchment baron' in the county of Renfrewshire in 1774, which he declined on the grounds that he disliked taking journeys, and living in other people's houses, 'at the most disagreeable time, that of an election'. See Adam 1887: xxi, xxxii; Hume 1969, vol. 2: 284; and Rothschild 2002).

But Smith was intensely interested in political life and political liberty in a larger sense. He had a distinct and capacious conception of what he described as a political society; 'servants, labourers, and workmen of different kinds, make up the far greater part of every great political society', he wrote in the WN.[7] The right to choose one's government was only one among several political rights. In free countries, as Smith pointed out, the security of government depends on 'the favourable judgment which the people may form of its conduct' (WN V.i.f.61). Political liberty consists, among other things, of the right to make and express political judgments. Smith also, interestingly enough, mentioned the right to information; 'the English nation think they have a right to information in political affairs by books and pamphlets', he said in 1763 (in a lecture on the jurisprudence of contempt for the sovereign) (LJA v.84). This distinction between political procedures and the larger political liberty within which they are embedded – or, in modern terms, between electoral democracy and liberal democracy – is of continuing importance. Smith believed, as Professor Werhane rightly points out, that liberty should be underpinned by laws of justice, and this applies at least as much to political liberty as to the liberty to buy and sell, or come and go. The separation of the judicial and the executive power, about which Smith writes so eloquently in Book V of the WN, is itself a form of political liberty (WN V.i.b.24–25).

Let me turn to the comments of Professor Fleischacker, to whom I am most grateful and from whom I have learnt a great deal about Smith and other philosophers, over many years, from *Kant-Studien* in 1991 to *William and Mary Quarterly* in 2002 (Fleischacker 1991, 2002). First, the invisible hand. I am at least half-persuaded by what Professor Fleischacker says. The chapter of *Economic*

Sentiments which is concerned with the invisible hand is unsatisfactory in several respects. One is that it is unsociably long, and that the end-notes are as long as the text. Another is that all this text and all these notes are concerned with a less than momentous proposition. I wanted to show that the invisible hand was not very important to Smith. I also wanted to show, and this is perhaps a less bathetic conclusion, that even ideas which were *like* the idea of the invisible hand were not of great importance to Smith.

The invisible hand chapter is the one chapter of the book which is concerned explicitly and extensively with twentieth-century political (and economic) theory. It is also concerned, implicitly, with twentieth-century politics. It would be foolish of me to deny a desire to provoke, at this point in the book (although not, especially, elsewhere). I wanted to give pause to the modern Smithians who identify Smith with a single great idea, and also to the political Smithians who see (or saw) in the invisible hand not so much an explanation as a clarion call, not so much a description as a prescription.

I should add, here, that I am grateful to Professor Fleischacker for having noticed at least some of what seemed to me to be a continuing drizzle of tentativeness in much of the book. I do not have an answer to his question, about the reception of the book as provocatively radical. In a sense, I suppose, the book seemed to me to be reasonably provocative for at least part of the left. It was an attempt to understand why the late eighteenth-century prospect of a free and commercial society, a society of market exchange, was so inspiring, so heroic, even, to people at the time. Of the twentieth-century theorists who play a role in the book, I would say that James Buchanan and Robert Nozick are identified as particularly perceptive; Hayek is clearly the theorist who is discussed at greatest length, and with very great respect. It is a book, really, about the possibility of liberalism. Its anti-heroes, who can be found on the right and the left, were the men of unquestioning confidence, in science or religion or the state; the men for whom 'interference with the freedom and openness of the understanding' was not, as it was for Condorcet, in John Morley's description, the 'worst kind of sacrilege' (Morley 1886, vol. 2: 255).

The unbathetic question, to return to the invisible hand, is, as Professor Fleischacker says, about the 'ideas to be found' in the famous passage, or about ideas which are like the idea of the invisible hand. I think that Professor Fleischacker's point about the invisible hand passage being part of Smith's polemic against the reason of the great – about the merchant in IV.ii.9 of the WN as himself a powerful and influential figure – is a very important one. This figure is less obviously foolish than the other subjects of the invisible hand, and Smith does, here, use an explicitly universalist language: 'As every individual, therefore, endeavours…every individual necessarily labours'. But the class of individuals about whom these universalizations are proposed are themselves privileged (the class of persons with their own capital to employ), and the distinctly privileged merchant of a few paragraphs earlier, the Amsterdam merchant with interests in Lisbon and Konigsberg, looms large over the entire passage (WN IV.ii.6–9; Rothschild 2001: 128).

It had not occurred to me that Smith might be encouraging 'the rest of us', the less than powerful, by pointing to the limits of the powers of the supposedly powerful, and I am grateful to Professor Fleischacker for the suggestion. I think that his point about individuals being in part free and in part the subject (or object) of social forces is also important. Kant comments, in another of his 'Smithian' passages – in which he talks about individuals who are 'unconsciously promoting an end which, even if they knew what it was, would scarcely arouse their interest' – on the circumstance that individuals are in part free, in their choices about marriage, for example, and in part subject to the laws depicted in demographic statistics, and this multiplicity of all our lives is of continuing importance (Kant 1970: 41).

I am less fully convinced by Professor Fleischacker's association of a number of passages in the WN and TMS as 'sort-of-invisible hand' explanations, of a particular, retrospective and agreeable sort. The WN is in substantial part an elegy to the freedom of commerce, and to the moderate pursuit of one's own self-interest, especially by the middling sort of people. It is not surprising that it should contain many illustrations of the happy consequences of the progress of opulence, some of which were unintended by the individuals involved. It is also not surprising that Smith should have observed that one can often, in retrospect, see patterns in events that were not visible at the time. This is, after all, the main point of philosophy, as he wrote in the 'History of Astronomy': 'to introduce order into this chaos of jarring and discordant appearances' (Smith 1980, II.12).

Everything that anyone does, more generally, has unintended consequences. (I described this observation as crushingly uninteresting.) The 'sort-of-invisible hand' passages that Professor Fleischacker discusses are of course far from uninteresting. But Smith also provides important illustrations of unintended consequences which are not good but frightful. The most dramatic of these is the discussion, in his last additions to TMS, of the 'piacular guilt' of Oedipus and Jocasta, who 'without design', or in 'undesigned violation', do things which would, if intended, have justly been seen as deeply wrong (TMS II.iii.3.4–5, VII.iv.30).

There is a serious, and unironic use of invisible-hand explanations which was very important to Smith, as I suggested in the book. It is a pre-emptive use, and it consists in pointing out that 'things may go on perfectly well' (the phrase was Samuel Clarke's, in his correspondence with Leibniz) without the intervention of the sovereign, or the all-ordering Minister of Finance. This sort of argument is particularly effective when it is retrospective, or historical, for the reasons that Professor Fleischacker gives; it is a demonstration that things have in fact, and on occasion, gone perfectly well without (for example) government regulation. But it is even more effective when it is combined with an explanation of why this should have been the case, and it is this explanation which Smith sometimes provides, and sometimes does not.

Professor Fleischacker gives an attractive, minimalist account of the invisible hand: it is 'nothing more or less than the force of society itself, the impact of society on our conception of ourselves and on the circumstances making possible our individual activities'. I like this; I am tempted to throw up my hands and say that I, too, believe in the invisible hand, if this is what it is. (I also like Professor

Werhane's invisible hand of commerce.) But I am not entirely sure that I know what it is, and indeed whether it is minimalist or maximalist. (To say that the force of society, or of sociability, is such that things usually turn out perfectly well, would be, for example, a strong or maximalist position.) I am also not sure – and this is the important point with which I want to end – why it is that Smith, or I, or Professor Fleischacker, should have such confidence in it.

I want to conclude, therefore, with some observations about religion, and about confidence. It is one of the most difficult of all enterprises, for the historian, to write about the religious convictions of individuals in the past. One has to think oneself not only into the interior of another, distant individual's mind, but also into a different and distant public world. Like the religious and irreligious thinkers of the sixteenth century, as described in Lucien Febvre's important book about religious disbelief, Smith and Hume and Voltaire were 'immersed, from their birth, in a bath of Christianity'. To say of them, as has been said so often of Rabelais, that they were 'people like us', who obscured their beliefs out of expediency, or fear, is to lose sight of what Febvre called a 'human conception' of the spiritual life, and of the human condition of triumph over fear (Febvre 1968: 18, 308).

Smith's friendship with Hume is only one of the reasons that I ended up being fairly convinced that he was uncomfortable with natural as well as organized religion. Smith certainly disagreed with Hume on many questions, some of them important; he said as much, in recommending his friend John Bruce, the author of an unmetaphysical book on moral philosophy, to his publisher, Thomas Cadell ('he and I differ a little, as David Hume and used to do') (Smith 1987, *Corr.* p. 296). My own sense, all the same, was similar to that of the younger John Sinclair, himself a distant observer, namely that 'his intimacy with Hume was of that fraternal character which seemed to intimate coincidence of opinion and identity of sentiment' (Sinclair 1837, vol. 1: 39–40). I was reassured in this view by Smith's literary interests, and especially his classical reading. I talk at considerable length about Lucian in the book, and Smith's esteem for Lucian – he said of Lucian that 'there is no author from whom more real instruction and good sense can be found', and he owned four separate editions of Lucian, including an *index verborum* – is difficult to reconcile in an eighteenth-century context, it seemed to me, with a confidence in providence (Smith 1983, LRBL 121–6). The obscure episode of Smith's published letter about the circumstances of Hume's death is moreover difficult to reconcile with a confidence in the importance of religion for virtue. Smith's letter was a description of the death of a perfectly unreligious man, who was also 'approaching as nearly to the idea of a perfectly wise and virtuous man, as perhaps the nature of human frailty will permit' (*Corr.* p. 221).

It is true, as Professor Fleischacker points out, that Smith refers frequently to God in TMS, including in the new passages he added at the end of his life. I see no reason to suppose that Smith was being ironic (it would be a detestable irony, in his own words) when he describes the agreeable consequences, both for the individual and for the world, of religious belief. But I cannot believe that his new descriptions of providence – for a writer who had taken such an interest in hyperbole, paranomasia and the mock heroic – were entirely serious. The 'all-wise

Author of Nature', the 'great, benevolent, and all-wise Being', determined to maintain 'at all times, the greatest possible quantity of happiness', the 'immediate administrator and director' of the world, the 'divine Being' charged with the 'administration of the great system of the universe', the 'great Conductor of the universe'; it is difficult for me to imagine Smith choosing these phrases to describe something in which he believed in any very comfortable way. They are too similar, for one thing, to his descriptions of Stoic doctrine: the 'great conductor and physician of the universe', the 'all wise Architect and Conductor', the 'great Superintendent of the universe', and so forth (also in his last additions to TMS) (TMS III.2.31, VI.ii.3.2–6, VII.ii.1.37). They are also too allusive of conditions which Smith did not, in general, esteem; being all-wise, for example, or being an administrator.

Smith took religion extremely seriously. In this he was unlike David Hume. I suggested earlier that he was non-chalant in his epistemology, which Hume was not. He was also non-chalant in at least some of his ontology. But he was not non-chalant in respect of the ontology of the existence of God. I tried to show in the book that he was proposing a subtle and profound description of the psychological difficulties of disbelief, and one that was both more profound than Hume's, and more sympathetic to the foundations of religious feeling. He says, again in the last additions to TMS, that 'the very suspicion of a fatherless world, must be the most melancholy of all reflections'; that the virtuous man 'who has the misfortune to doubt' the doctrine of an equal eternity (that there will be exact and equal justice in the world to come) 'cannot possibily avoid wishing most earnestly and anxiously to believe it' (TMS III.2.33, VI.ii.3.2). These are very moving sentiments. I do not think that they are the sentiments of a man who is not, himself, a man of doubt.

I am not sure that Adam Smith did not believe in God. How could I be sure? Intellectual history, like the rest of history, is in part a matter of doing something very Smithian, namely of trying to think oneself into the way of thinking of someone else. (It is also a matter of trying to find evidence of these individual or collective states of mind.) But I do feel reasonably sure that Smith's religious views, whatever they were, were very unlike Voltaire's. He had no desire, unlike Voltaire, to exasperate; the Christianity in which he grew up, in a small Fifeshire town which was a centre of religious dissent, and in Glasgow in the epoch of the Great Awakening that traversed the Atlantic world, was as different as was possible, in eighteenth-century Europe, from Voltaire's; he was not a man of easy conviction, or a man without anxiety.

The last point I want to make is about confidence, and it is a point about all the questions with which we have been concerned. I said at the very end of the book that Smith (and Condorcet) had confidence in the future of the human disposition, and in the odd condition of 'humanity'. Smith was extremely courageous, if I am correct in my understanding, in his willingness to construct theories with only incomplete or interim foundations. (A system, after all, is not a house.) In the last part of TMS, he criticized one foundation after another. He was unlike Kant, in spite of the awkwardness of the impartial spectator, in refusing the way out into the noumenal world. He was unlike Aristotle, in spite of his allusions to universal principles and original dispositions, in refusing to propose a substantial theory of human nature. He was unlike Hume, in refusing a universal principle of utility.

Smith was unscientific or unscientistic, in spite of his remarks about the progress of the abstract science of the mind; the Scottish science of man was very different from the scientific studies of morality which were so ubiquitous in the late nineteenth century (*La morale et la science des moeurs*, for Lucien Lévy-Bruhl, or the works of the 'English psychologists' with which Nietzsche was so fascinated) (Nietzsche 1994: 6, 11–12; Lévy-Bruhl 1906: i–xxxiv).[8] He succeeded in the brave enterprise of living without certainty; the enterprise which was more than anything else responsible for the revulsion against the ideas of the enlightenment in the 1790s, and for the determination, which continues, to see in enlightenment ideas the origins of terrifying revolution.

But Smith was still, I think, moderately confident about something. (Can one live without confidence, any more than the sceptic can live his scepticism?) He was confident, more or less, in the dignity, and the equal dignity, of all individuals, men and women and children. He thought that some rights, and some rules, were sacred. He believed that individuals were in general, and especially when they lived in families and in societies, moderately good-tempered. He believed that there were circumstances – Philadelphian circumstances, one could say, including prosperity, and being educated, and having a large number of competing identities, and having a good constitution, in which the independence of the judiciary is reasonably secure – under which things would be likely to turn out reasonably well. He was in this sense, at least, a foundationalist; he believed in something like 'the force of society itself'. This may be, I suppose, a part of the answer to the riddle of the sphinx.

Acknowledgements

I am most grateful to the chairman of the panel, Ryan Hanley, to the participants in the panel, Steven Darwall, Samuel Fleischacker and Patricia Werhane, and to Amartya Sen, for helpful comments.

Notes

1 On metaethics, see Williams 1985: 72–4.

2 There are two 'questions which ought to be examined' in moral philosophy, Smith writes; 'first, wherein does virtue consist... and, secondly, by what power or faculty in the mind is it, that this character, whatever it be, is recommended to us? Or in other words, how and by what means does it come to pass, that the mind prefers one tenour of conduct to another...?' (TMS VII.i.2).

3 These would be tests, for example, about the acceptability or coherence of ethical thought; Williams (1985: 73–4).

4 On conscience, dialogue and the impartial spectator, see Brown 1994: chapters 2 and 3.

5 'Wir begreifen aber doch seine *Unbegreiflichkeit*:' 'We do comprehend its *incomprehensibility*'. This is from the last sentence of the *Grundlegung* (Kant 1984: 128; 1964: 131). The metaphor is of a person who progresses deeper and deeper into her own breast, into a space which is more and more confined. This space is the infinitesimally tiny point of entry, into the infinitely extensive world of ends. By climbing inside her own 'I' she climbs out into the other world; she climbs through her own inner soul, as it were. This is the same metaphor, more or less, as that used by C.S. Lewis in his redemptionist children's book, *The Lion, the Witch and the Wardrobe*:

> This must be a simply enormous wardrobe!' thought Lucy, going still further in...'This is very queer', she said, and went on a step or two further...And then she saw that there was a light ahead of her; not a few inches away where the back of the wardrobe ought to have been, but a long way off. Something cold and soft was falling on her. A moment later she found that she was standing in the middle of a wood at night-time with snow under her feet and snowflakes falling through the air.
>
> (Lewis 1980: 13)

6 It is similar in some but not all respects to the conceptual systems of Hume, and of others of Smith's contemporaries, including Condorcet (Rothschild 2001: 228–46).

7 'No society can surely be flourishing and happy, of which the far greater part of the members are poor and miserable', he added (WN I.viii.36).

8 Smith's comment in the first edition of the TMS about the abstract science of mind – he refers to 'a time when the abstract science of human nature was but in its infancy, and before the distinct offices and powers of the different faculties of the human mind had been carefully examined and distinguished from one another' – is one of the moments at which the modern Smithian feels herself to be most distant from Smith's own intellectual world (TMS VII.iii.2.5).

Bibliography

Adam, C.E. (ed.) (1887) *View of the Political State of Scotland in the Last Century*, Edinburgh: David Douglas.

Brown, V. (1994) *Adam Smith's Discourse: Canonicity, Commerce and Conscience*, London: Routledge.

Donne, J. (1956) 'A Sermon preached at Whitehall, February 29 1627', in *The Sermons of John Donne*, Evelyn M. Simpson and George R. Potter (eds), Berkeley, CA: University of California Press.

Febvre, L. (1942; 1968) *Le problème de l'incroyance au 16e siècle: La religion de Rabelais*, Paris: Albin Michel.

Fleischacker, S. (2002) 'Adam Smith's reception among the American founders, 1776–1790', *William and Mary Quarterly*, 3rd series, 59(4): 897–924.

—— (1991) 'Philosophy in moral practice: Kant and Adam Smith', *Kant-Studien*, 82, Heft 3: 249–269.

Griswold, C.L. (1999) *Adam Smith and the Virtues of Enlightenment*, Cambridge: Cambridge University Press.

Haakonssen, K. (1981) *The Science of a Legislator: The Natural Jurisprudence of David Hume and Adam Smith*, Cambridge: Cambridge University Press.

Henry, C. (ed.) (1883) *Correspondance inédite de Condorcet et de Turgot 1770–1779*, Paris: Didier.

Hume D. (1987) 'Of the dignity or meanness of human nature', in Hume, *Essays, Moral, Political and Literary*, Eugene F. Miller (ed.), Indianapolis: Liberty Classics.

—— (1978) *A Treatise of Human Nature* L.A. Selby-Bigge (ed.), Oxford: Clarendon Press.

—— (1969) *The Letters of David Hume* J.Y.T. Greig (ed.), Oxford: Clarendon Press.

Kant, I. (1984) *Grundlegung zur Metaphysik der Sitten*, Stuttgart: Reclam.

—— (1970) *Ideas for a Universal History* in *Kant's Political Writings* Hans Reiss (ed.), Cambridge: Cambridge University Press.

—— (1964) *Groundwork of the Metaphysic of Morals*, H.J. Paton (trans.), New York: Harper & Row.

Leslie, T.E.C. (1879) 'Political economy and sociology', in *Essays in Political and Moral Philosophy*, Dublin: Hodges, Foster and Figgis.

Lévy-Bruhl, L. (1903; 1906) *La Morale et la Science des Moeurs*, Paris: Alcan.

Lewis, C.S. (1950; 1980) *The Lion, the Witch and the Wardrobe*, London: Lions.

Morley, J. (1886) 'Condorcet', in *Critical Miscellanies*, vol. 2, London: Macmillan.

Nietzsche, F. (1887; 1994) *On the Genealogy of Morality*, Carol Diethe (trans.), Cambridge: Cambridge University Press.

Rothschild, E. (2002) 'Adam Smith', Donald Dewar Memorial Lecture, University of Edinburgh, 24 April 2002.

—— (2001) *Economic Sentiments: Adam Smith, Condorcet, and the Enlightenment*, Cambridge, MA: Harvard University Press.

Sinclair, J. (1837) *Memoirs of the Life and Works of Sir John Sinclair*, Edinburgh: Blackwood.

Smith, A. (1976a) *The Theory of Moral Sentiments*, D.D. Raphael and A.L. Macfie (eds), Oxford: Oxford University Press; reprinted, Liberty Press (1982).

—— (1976b) *An Inquiry into the Nature and Causes of the Wealth of Nations*, R.H. Campbell and A.S. Skinner (eds), Oxford: Oxford University Press; reprinted, Liberty Press (1981).

—— (1978) *Lectures on Jurisprudence*, R.L. Meek, D.D. Raphael and P.G. Stein (eds), Oxford: Oxford University Press; reprinted, Liberty Press (1982).

—— (1980) *Essays on Philosophical Subjects*, W.P.D. Wightman (eds), Oxford: Oxford University Press; reprinted, Liberty Press (1982).

—— (1983) *Lectures on Rhetoric and Belles Lettres*, J.C. Bryce (eds), Oxford: Oxford University Press; reprinted, Liberty Press (1985).

—— (1987) *Correspondence of Adam Smith*, E.C. Mossner and I.S. Ross (eds), Oxford: Oxford University Press; reprinted, Liberty Press (1987).

Stewart, D. (1980) 'Account of the Life and Writings of Adam Smith, LL.D.' in *A. Smith's, Essays on Philosophical Subjects*, W.P.D. Wightman and J.C. Bryce (eds), Oxford: Oxford University Press.

Turgot, A.R.J. (1913–23) *Oeuvres de Turgot et Documents le Concernant*, G. Schelle (ed.), Paris: Alcan.

Williams, B. (1985) *Ethics and the Limits of Philosophy*, London: Fontana.

Book reviews

Luc Boltanski, *Distant Suffering: Morality, Media and Politics*

Translated by Graham D. Burchell, Cambridge University Press, 1999, xviii + 246pp.

ISBN Hardback 0–521–57389–0, Paperback 0–521–65953–1

Reviewed by Fonna Forman-Barzilai

And thus spoke the spectator: Adam Smith for humanitarians

The last twenty years have seen a veritable renaissance of interest in Adam Smith not only within the disciplines that have traditionally engaged him, but among philosophers, political and social theorists, anthropologists, psychologists and students of communication, of culture, of gender, of literature, among others. More recently, it has not been unusual to see Smith summoned in yet another debate, one that revolves around themes of cosmopolitanism and humanitarian action. For some, Smith's ideas of moral spectatorship and sympathetic imagination in *The Theory of Moral Sentiments* (TMS) provide a useful language for describing a human tendency to feel compassion for suffering people, even those at a distance, which might then ground a corollary duty to provide humanitarian relief. This casual appropriation may not sit well with those who are intimate with Smith's texts; but in times like ours, when millions in Africa are dying of AIDS, when displaced peoples roam the globe tattered and hungry in search of a home, when women, minorities, foreigners and the poor are often subjected to the most horrifying and dehumanizing forms of coercion and degradation, it is not surprising that Smith's thoughts on sympathy have seemed poignant and relevant for a good number of people.

Luc Boltanski, in this timely English translation of *La Souffrance à Distance* – now as *Distant Suffering: Morality, Media and Politics* – argues that Adam Smith's discussion of moral spectatorship in the TMS can help to ground a twenty-first century humanitarian theory of political commitment – what Boltanski calls a 'politics of pity'.[1] Boltanski, a French historical sociologist and Director of the Ecole des Hautes Etudes en Sciences Sociales in Paris, has written a deeply reflective and complicated book on the ways that distance in a world of speed and technology often distorts the relations between suffering and spectatorship, between

The Adam Smith Review, 1: 167–96 © 2004 The International Adam Smith Society, ISSN 1743–5285, ISBN 0–415–27863–5

observation and action, and between morality and politics. Boltanski offers strategies through which we might bring distant suffering into focus and humanitarianism back onto the political agenda. He wants to overcome what he calls a contemporary 'crisis of pity' in which so many of us have become cynical and suspicious of 'any form of political action oriented towards a horizon of moral ideals' (Boltanski 1999: xvi). Because the book is more reflective than argumentative, however, and because Boltanski in a manner characteristic of French social science moves freely across the disciplines of history, literature, psychology, politics, communications and sociology, one cannot possibly capture its richness and breadth in a short review. With the audiences of this journal in mind, therefore, I shall undertake the more limited task of isolating and engaging Boltanski's very timely appropriation of Adam Smith's moral psychology for a humanitarian political agenda.

Boltanski regrets that contemporary debate over humanitarian action tends to get stuck in the rigid binary languages of 'abstract universalism' and 'narrow communitarianism', the first of which sides 'with global solidarity against national particularisms and preferences', while the second 'unmasks the hypocrisy or, at best, naive eirenic idealism which ignores the primacy of interests and ties forged by history' (Boltanski 1999: xiii). Boltanski maintains that Adam Smith's theory of spectatorship sustains a theory of humanitarian political commitment that is unburdened by this tension since it provides an 'apparatus' capable of unifying sentiment from a distance, capable of establishing and nourishing genuine connections between people quite differently situated, 'without force' (Boltanski 1999: 36) and 'without recourse to communal identification or to an Edenic fusion' (Boltanski 1999: 38). Because Smith emphasized the 'radical distinction' between a detached, impartial observer and the individual whom he or she is observing, and did not seek to impose 'the same ethical values' upon them (Boltanski 1999: 54), his theory helps demonstrate that humanitarian impulses need not be censured as an arrogant (usually Western) assertion of partial understandings and preferences, a 'smug celebration of the return of kindness', a sort of narcissistic declaration of moral superiority.

Today, most of us get our information about distant suffering through televisual, Internet, audio and written news reports. Boltanski asks how such media representations of human suffering, projected visually and verbally across vast distances, might stimulate responsive commitment among the distant spectators who receive them. Like others, Boltanski is concerned that the distortion, sensationalism, repetition and fictionality that plague modern media have cultivated a deep and persistent cynicism among distant spectators that encourages retreat from normal humanitarian impulses. But, unlike many of his colleagues in the field of communications who argue that the humanitarian potential of modern media is overridden by its spectacular flaws, Boltanski insists that media, and particularly the spectacle of television, are essential for humanitarian action since they bring the distant nearer to the eye, shrink the world and spread knowledge. For Boltanski, humanitarian politics rests on the assumption that 'having knowledge points to an obligation to give assistance' (Boltanski 1999: 20). Indeed, 'nothing promotes the formation of a cause more than the spectacle of suffering' (Boltanski 1999: 30). But the question obviously turns on the sort of action we might expect from the spectatorial armchair. What can I do from La Jolla, California for those starving dark-skinned toddlers walking barefoot through raw sewerage, for the weathered mothers whose forlorn eyes plead ruefully with the camera lens, for that orphaned Iraqi boy whose bloody torso was recently broadcast hourly over Western television after his limbs were severed by an errant American cruise-missile? Boltanski asks: what form can [political] commitment take when those called upon to act are thousands of miles away from the person suffering, comfortably installed in front of the television set in the shelter of the family living-room? (Boltanski 1999: xv).

The novelty of *Distant Suffering*, and the insight that propels Boltanski's narrative forward, is that a distant spectator can commit himself or herself to moral action through an activity he calls *committed speech*:

> It is by speaking up that the spectator can maintain his integrity when, brought face to face with suffering, he is called upon to act in a situation in which direct action is difficult or impossible.
>
> (Boltanski 1999: 17)

Distant Suffering is primarily an extended reflection on what Boltanski means by 'committed speech' – its content, what qualifies speech as 'moral' and not 'merely spectacle' or 'just words', and finally, the ways that a spectator can deploy speech most 'effectively' to arouse others to action.[2]

We learn in *Distant Suffering* that committed speech 'must at the same time report to the other both what was seen and how this personally affected and involved the spectator' (Boltanski 1999: xv). In other words, though he must report accurately what he has seen, the distant spectator must not allow his report to become purely factual, 'just the facts', articulated in 'objectivist terms' without proper emotion. Boltanski thinks it is 'indecent' and 'inhuman' to give a purely factual account of distant suffering, for facts fail to convey the humanity of the sufferer (Boltanski 1999: 23–4, 43). Human bodies repel realism. Surely, as Boltanski puts it, arousing pity requires that 'suffering and wretched bodies…be conveyed in such a way as to affect the sensibility of those more fortunate' (Boltanski 1999: 11). And yet, the speaker must exercise restraint, for revealing too much can have a dehumanizing effect, in that we rob the unfortunate of her dignity, implying that she is only her suffering, reducible to her pain, and nothing more (Boltanski 1999: 33). So, committed speech calls for a delicate balance between objectivity and emotion, between reticence and eloquence, crafting emotionally inspiring narratives that humanize often horribly grisly facts.

For Boltanski, crafting such an 'acceptable report', striking the balance between reporting what happened and inspiring others to care, requires that spectators cultivate a capacity he calls 'reflexivity'. Reflexivity 'makes it possible to introduce a symmetry which reduces the tension between an aperspectival objectivism and moral involvement' (Boltanski 1999: 43). Like Smith, who described a dialogue between an actual spectator and the ideal spectator in his breast, Boltanski seeks to divide the spectator of distant suffering into a 'split self'

(Boltanski 1999: 39–44). The first Figure, the spectator, remains the impartial, detached, uninvolved individual who comes upon a scene of distant suffering. The second Figure, the 'introspector', 'enters within the person looking to consider the effect on him of what he is seeing, to become aware of his feelings and to inscribe them within the final account which is to be communicated to others' (Boltanski 1999: 43). Introspective reflexivity ensures two things: that the spectator will become aware of his own internal state upon observing a scene of suffering, and that he will then be able to communicate that state to others in a way that is sufficiently sensitive to the humanity, dignity and particularity of the unfortunate, and yet sufficiently passionate and eloquent to inspire those who hear the narrative to commit themselves politically. Boltanski concludes: 'This reflexive apparatus...reduces the tension confronting a politics of pity which cannot do without the conveying of distant suffering' (Boltanski 1999: 44).

But how well does this account map onto Smith's, which Boltanski explicitly claims as an influence? Boltanski reduces his 'empirical' spectator to excessive objectivity and factuality, and imbues the introspector with abounding emotion and tenderness. But this seems quite literally to invert the way Smith understood the relation between the actual spectator and the impartial spectator. Smith observed that spectators are quite often whipped passionately off-course into blind self-preference by a variety of pathologies and irregularities that threaten to undermine the certainty of moral judgment, something Smith was always seeking. For this reason (among others, surely) he invoked the impartial spectator, 'the inhabitant of the breast, the man within, the great judge and arbiter of our conduct' (Smith 1976, TMS III.3.4). The impartial spectator is a stabilizing force which Smith at one point associated with 'reason', often with 'conscience' and with God's plan. The impartial spectator brings order to a troubled mind, brings certainty into moral judgment, 'calls to us, with a voice capable of astonishing the most presumptuous of our passions, that we are but one of the multitude, in no respect better than any other in it' (TMS III.3.4). At one point, Boltanski seems to acknowledge that Smith's impartial spectator deployed a 'view of aperspectival objectivity' (Boltanski 1999: 49) – but it is difficult to square this perceptive observation with Boltanski's emotionally reflexive introspector. Clearly, he misses the implications of Smith's model of spectatorship when he offers up 'empirical' spectators that resemble Joe Friday and introspectors that resemble Barbara Walters.

I shall leave aside any further reflection on whether Smith's impartial spectator is capable of the 'reflexivity' that Boltanski attributes to it, having offered substantial remarks on similar themes in my recent review of Charles L. Griswold's *Adam Smith and the Virtues of Enlightenment* (Forman-Barzilai 1999). I should like instead to focus on the extent to which Boltanski appreciated Smith's own reflections on the relations between sympathy and distance.

For Boltanski, the inherent difficulty in a 'politics of pity' is how to motivate action from the perspective of distance. Indeed, he accepts the argument that moral responsibility survives distance, and that passivity in the face of knowledge often qualifies as a violation of duty (Boltanski 1999: 13). This assumption, he believes, lies at the heart of any humanitarian argument. And yet, he does not deny that distance creates many obstacles. For example, Boltanski resists the idea that 'nearness and distance make no moral difference', as Peter Singer (1972) suggests in claiming that we are all morally culpable for failing to assist children in Bengal dying of hunger (Boltanski 1999: 15). Nor does Boltanski accept Gerard Elfstrom's (1983) claim that 'moral constraints are in principle universal' and that intervention in response to a violation of human rights is therefore *always* justified (Boltanski 1999: 15). Boltanski acknowledges throughout *Distant Suffering* that distance renders moral responsibility increasingly uncertain and problematic since it diminishes the possibility of accurate and undistorted information, increases ambiguity concerning the kinds of action that are needed and makes it difficult to assess whether or not others have already responded to the same call. Furthermore, media projections of distant suffering are necessarily selective in what they show, producing much ambiguity about the intentions of the film-maker, broadcasting company, or the host state, uncertainty about which causes are most worthy of assistance, which parties in the drama are actually victim and persecutor and so on. And so, Boltanski is not sanguine about the problems created by distance. He concedes quite early on in the book that these problems, when considered collectively, 'provide support to arguments which rank obligation to help in accordance with a principle of distance (be concerned with those close to you first of all)' (Boltanski 1999: 16, 23).

In this he seems alas (and quite inadvertently) to strike a chord with Adam Smith, who argued quite explicitly that distance creates formidable barriers for the sympathetic imagination, which proximity and familiarity tend to relieve.[3] Although Boltanski never acknowledges it, assumptions about proximity pervade Smith's theory of sympathy, in particular the ways that distance tends to distort both our vision and our moral judgment. Proximity (and its sister concept, familiarity) improve the 'preciseness' with which we understand the circumstances of others when we imaginatively 'enter into' their circumstances (TMS VI.ii.1.2). We are better situated to understand the particular causes that motivate them and cause them pain. We are better situated to know how to care for them.

Given the very 'present' quality of Smith's account of sympathy, it is not surprising that he agreed with David Hume that 'sympathy... is much fainter than our concern for ourselves, and sympathy with persons remote from us much fainter than that with persons near and contiguous' (Hume *Enquiry*, 1948: 220). Indeed, Smith found it perfectly natural and appropriate that a spectator will tend to sympathize more actively with those 'upon whose happiness or misery his conduct must have the greatest influence' (TMS VI.ii.1.2). He characterized such activity as 'the proper business and occupation of our lives':

> To man is allotted a much humbler department, but one much more suitable to the weakness of his powers, and to the narrowness of his comprehension; the care of his own happiness, of that of his family, his friends, his country...
>
> (TMS VI.ii.3.6)

and again:

> By Nature the events which immediately affect that little department in which we ourselves have some little management and direction, which

> immediately affect ourselves, our friends, our country, are the events which interest us the most, and which chiefly excite our desires and aversions, our hopes and fears, our joys and sorrows.
>
> (TMS VII.ii.1.44)

An oddity of Boltanski's account is that he never mentions this dimension of Smith's moral psychology, in which our duties seem to radiate outward in concentric circles according to decreasing degrees of spatial proximity and familiarity.[4] He suggests that Smith failed to confront explicitly the problem of physical distance. He does acknowledge that Smith incorporated a 'kind of distance' into his theory by positing a spectator that was uninvolved, impartial, without ties or pre-commitments to the sufferer. And he praises Smith for invoking imagination as a way of traversing that distance (Boltanski 1999: 37–8). But aside from this nod to a *situational* or *positional* sort of distance, Boltanski suggests that Smith never really considered the impact of *physical* distance on his theory of spectatorship and that he overlooked:

> the tension between a necessarily local face to face encounter, as in the figure of compassion, and the conveyance over distance of a representation of suffering that is required by a general politics of pity, as if the second figure could be directly derived, smoothly and uninterruptedly, by extension of the first.
>
> (Boltanski 1999: 37)

But this cannot be right. Surely, Smith discussed the possibility of sympathy for distant strangers in terms that resembled his account of sympathy among locals. For instance:

> We can sympathize with the distress which excessive hunger occasions when we read the description of it in the journal of a siege, or of a sea voyage. We imagine ourselves in the situation of the sufferers, and thence readily conceive the grief, the fear and consternation, which must necessarily distract them.
>
> (TMS I.ii.1.1)[5]

But this does not capture Smith's explicit thoughts on the barriers that distance creates for the sympathetic imagination. I should like to close my discussion of Boltanski's *Distant Suffering* with the following passage drawn from the TMS, for I believe it best demonstrates Smith's vivid and somewhat surprising account of distance, the ways it affected his theory of spectatorship and consequently circumscribed his understanding of our duties:

> …extreme sympathy with misfortunes which we know nothing about, seems altogether absurd and unreasonable. Take the whole earth at an average, for one man who suffers pain or misery, you will find twenty in prosperity and joy, or at least in tolerable circumstances. No reason, surely, can be assigned why we should rather weep with the one than rejoice with the twenty.

> This artificial commiseration, besides, is not only absurd, but seems altogether unattainable; and those who affect this character have commonly nothing but a certain affected and sentimental sadness, which, without reaching the heart, serves only to render the countenance and conversation impertinently dismal and disagreeable. And last of all, this disposition of mind, though it could be attained, would be perfectly *useless*, and could serve no other purpose than to render miserable the person who possessed it. Whatever interest we take in the fortune of those with whom we have no acquaintance or connexion, and who are placed altogether out of the sphere of our activity, can produce only anxiety to ourselves, without any manner of advantage to them. To what purpose should we trouble ourselves about the world in the moon? All men, even those at the greatest distance, are no doubt entitled to our good wishes, and our good wishes we naturally give them. But if, notwithstanding, they should be unfortunate, to give ourselves any anxiety upon that account, seems to be no part of our duty.
>
> (TMS III.3.9, emphasis added)

Of course, it is slightly unfair to deploy a passage like this to challenge Boltanski's appropriation of Smith for a twenty-first century humanitarian agenda. What strikes the reader here is not merely Smith's rather cool attitude toward the suffering of others, but perhaps moreso, how vastly different Smith's world was from our own – the slowness, the difficulty of travel and communication, the paucity of information about the condition of distant peoples, the comparative insularity of state and corporate activity, the impotence of international law, the absence of international and transnational dialogue, as well as international and non-governmental agencies that might assist distant spectators in their desire to act, and so on.[6] For those of us interested in Smith's salience for today, we must pause to consider how our global condition might have changed Smith's mind about the proper scope of our duties. Surely ours is not the world described in the passage that precedes, where 'knowing' about distant suffering was unlikely or where assisting was beyond our capacity.

Notes

1 He borrows this from Hannah Arendt's (1963) discussion of Jean-Jacques Rousseau and his Revolutionary disciples.

2 Boltanski's reflections on the rhetorical 'forms' and devices available to the committed speaker (denunciation, sentiment and aesthetics) and the different literary genres through which they developed historically, are contained in Part II of *Distant Suffering*. These are wonderfully creative chapters, but since they are for the most part only indirectly implicated in Boltanski's reading of Smith, I shall leave analysis of them aside, draw upon them only when they shed light on Smith, and direct interested readers to a recent review by Robin Wagner-Pacifici (Wagner-Pacifici 2002).

3 For further discussion of distance in Smith's moral psychology, see Forman-Barzilai 2002.

4 See Forman-Barzilai 2002: 393–402.

5 Note also: 'Our joy for the deliverance of those heroes of tragedy or romance who interest us, is as sincere as our grief for their distress…' (TMS I.i.1.4).
6 See Forman-Barzilai 2002: 393–402, 411.

Bibliography

Arendt, H. (1963) *On Revolution*, New York: Viking.
Boltanski, L. (1993) *La Souffrance à Distance*, Paris: Editions Métailié.
Elfstrom, G. (1983) 'On dilemmas of intervention', *Ethics*, 93: 709–25.
Forman-Barzilai. F. (1999) Review of Charles Griswold's *Adam Smith and the Virtues of Enlightenment*, Cambridge, 1999, *Political Theory*, 28: 122–30.
—— (2002) 'Adam Smith as globalization theorist', *Critical Review*, 14: 391–419.
Hume, D. (1948) *Moral and Political Philosophy*, Henry D. Aiken (ed.), New York: Hafner Press.
Singer, P. (1972) 'Famine, affluence and morality', *Philosophy and Public Affairs*, 1: 229–43.
Smith, A. (1976) *The Theory of Moral Sentiments* D.D. Raphael and A.L. Macfie (eds), Oxford: Oxford University Press; Glasgow Edition. Reprinted, Liberty Press (1982).
Wagner-Pacifici, R. (2002) 'Pity has a human face', *Theory & Event*, 5, 4.

Kenneth E. Carpenter, *The Dissemination of* The Wealth of Nations *in French and in France, 1776–1843*

New York: The Bibliographical Society of America, 2002, lxiii + 255pp.

ISBN 0–914–93017–6

Reviewed by Henry C. Clark

The contemporary global significance of Adam Smith's masterwork in economics is seldom more vividly illustrated than in the story behind the book under review. By the author's telling, he had researched and written an essay on the French translations of the *Wealth of Nations* (WN) which appeared in Japanese for a bicentennial facsimile edition in Japan in the 1970s, but had then abandoned that research after leaving his post as curator of the Kress Collection of early works on economics in 1980. A Taiwanese scholar named Cheng-chung Lai visited him at his office in the Harvard library in the early 1990s about the possibility of publishing that essay (and one on Smith's broader Continental influence) in English. 'I agreed to do so', Carpenter tells us, 'primarily because Professor Lai's enthusiasm was contagious. Indeed, the cliché that he would not take no for an answer was almost literally true' (pp. x–xi). If so, then we are all in Professor Lai's debt, because the result a decade later is a study that will be of considerable interest to historians and students of Adam Smith, not unlike Ian S. Ross's *On the* Wealth of Nations*: Contemporary Responses to Adam Smith* (Thoemmes 1998).

The book is presented to us as a work of bibliographical reconstruction. It consists of descriptions of the physical characteristics and locations (not comprehensive) of the published, and some unpublished, editions of the translations of Adam Smith's work in France from 1776 to 1843; some textual material from the translations themselves; some statements by translators, editors, or publishers; transcriptions of full or partial texts of notices of the editions; and most interestingly for the historian, 'All reviews that have been identified are reproduced' (p. xvii). But the work is not a 'census of copies'; the author does not claim comprehensiveness, and the precise scope of the work is not as lucidly spelled out as it might be. The book is presented as a contribution to the publishing history of the WN, for example, but, citing recent work by scholars such as Jeremy Popkin (1990) and Carla Hesse (1991), Carpenter does not claim his work is a true 'publishing history'.

Carpenter's forty-page introduction entitled 'French transformations of *Wealth of Nations*: From Marginality to Centrality to Canonicity' makes a general argument that may be summarized as follows. First, from its first publication in 1776 until 1788, the WN was marginal to the intellectual life of France. This was not because the work went unnoticed on the Continent. The author observes that there was a German translation of the work already in 1776 (p. xxxiv). Rather, it seems to have arisen from publishing conditions that were quite specific to France. The capriciousness of the censorship apparatus there, combined with the sheer expense of publication, served as a powerful disincentive to undertake a large and controversial project such as this one. The free market *Abbé* Morellet, for example, who had begun his own translation of the work immediately upon its appearance, felt that only the royal printer could surmount such obstacles and bring the project to successful fruition (p. xxx).

The most striking evidence of Smith's marginality during this period concerns the important multi-volume *Encyclopédique méthodique* that began to appear in 1784. A sub-series entitled *Economie politique et diplomatique*, designed for the 'diplomat, administrator, and even the philosopher', began with a publisher's note (*avertissement*) to volume one in 1784 that bemoaned the lack of good studies in this field and indicated the works that would be drawn on in their encyclopedia: Montesquieu, Pufendorf and Grotius, but not Adam Smith. Starting in 1786, with volume two, Adam Smith is virtually the only source drawn on in the remaining three volumes. Thus, the emergence of Smith's work in the consciousness of this well-informed and influential community of scholars and publicists can be quite precisely dated to the mid-1780s (pp. 40–1).

A distinct second phase begins, according to Carpenter, in 1788 with the appearance of *Abbé* Blavet's translation, the first book-length translation of the work published in France (p. 57). It appears to be a mere coincidence that this edition was coming forth just as the old regime was collapsing in France, but there can be little doubt that the timing did much to shape its appropriation in that country. Throughout the revolutionary period, Smith's book was recommended to patriots and administrators alike as indispensable for solving the problems then facing the nation.

For example, the introduction to the *Bibliothèque de l'homme public*, a compendium of lengthy excerpts from important works on public affairs that began publication in 1790, promised to put 'the science of government and administration within the reach of everyone' (p. 82). The poet Jean-Antoine Roucher went further. When his translation of the WN appeared in 1790, he prefaced it by depicting Smith's work in architectural terms as a work that could provide a new plan, a new blueprint for the house of France then in such disarray (p. 90; cf. also p. 95). He also dedicated the work to Charles Marguerite Jean Baptiste Mercier Dupaty, recently deceased, who had been arrested in 1770 for 'insolent remonstrances to the king' and had subsequently become a self-styled moral heir to Voltaire. Finally, Roucher had promised on the title page a volume of forthcoming notes by the illustrious French intellectual Condorcet; the notes never materialized, but the notice is typical of the attempts at French appropriation then under way (pp. xlviii, 85–6). During the Reign of Terror in 1793, when the revolutionary government pursued policies that one might have thought quite inimical to Smith's 'natural system of liberty', Carpenter reports that the Minister of the Interior Garat sent the newly established 'observer delegates' (*commissaires observateurs*) to the provinces supplied with copies of Arthur Young's *Voyages in France* and of Smith's WN (p. 87). Looking back in later years, one French observer wrote, 'We all remember the sensation it [*Wealth of Nations*] produced in France when Roucher's translation appeared...all minds were in a state of ferment about political economy and about liberty... We read it with eagerness, we learned it by heart, we cited it as an authority' (p. 161). Throughout the upheavals of the revolutionary decade, in fact, Smith maintained his central status in French opinion.

A third phase, a transition from centrality to canonicity, begins, on the author's account, shortly after Napoleon's ascent to power, although that sequence of events is also evidently a mere coincidence. More important was the appearance of still a third major translation into French. In previous years, there had been a sometimes rather nasty dispute among the partisans of Blavet's and of Roucher's translations, over style and accuracy. But when the translation by Germain Garnier, completed in 1794, appeared in print in 1802, it fairly quickly superseded these earlier versions. Indeed, Carpenter is able to report that the last, 1794, edition of the Roucher translation had not sold out by the time of its reissue in 1806, partly due to its displacement by the Garnier version. That version also went beyond its predecessors' critical scope through the addition of a long introduction on Smith – including a comparison of Smith's doctrine with that of the Physiocrats and a 'Method for facilitating the study of Smith's work' that readers will be familiar with from the Ross volume cited earlier (pp. 214–25) – as well as a complete volume of notes on the work. No longer was the emphasis primarily on reaching the general public or would-be administrators; now the target would instead be those who wanted to understand economics as a science, and the expanded editorial apparatus would make this the ideal edition for scholars. A pre-publication announcement in the important *Moniteur universel* is typical in seeing the Garnier edition as constituting a 'complete course in this science' (p. 171). The process of canonization was completed in 1843 with the appearance of a reprint of Garnier's translation edited by Adolphe Blanqui that now included commentary on the work by some of the leading practitioners of this new science such as Malthus, Ricardo, Bentham and Sismondi. This version was volume five of the important *Collection des principaux économistes* that Guillaumin brought out in 1843; the next translation of the WN into French would have to wait until 1995.

One of the virtues of this book is that, although the author does not claim an expertise in intellectual history (pp. xxvii–xxviii), he nonetheless offers significant materials for those interested in seeing Smith in proper intellectual–historical context. There are a number of different ways in which the French appropriation of Smith's masterwork can be better charted with the help of the evidence marshalled here. One concerns the sheer nomenclature surrounding the work itself. How did French readers conceive of the WN in generic terms? What kind of a work was it? How did they perceive its purpose and scope? In fact, the answer to this question is not as easy as it may seem, and it is a mistake to assume, as is often done, that the work has always been viewed straightforwardly as a work in political economy.

The earlier responses, continuing through the revolutionary period, tend to be quite flexible and unspecific in their descriptions of the field or 'science' to which Smith's work belongs. Several saw him as a general theorist of social relations. Reverdil, writing in 1778, wrote, 'I don't believe that anyone before him has so well analyzed the mechanism of human society, and unfolded the supports that the various occupations of men have provided each other' (p. 19). The anonymous reviewer for the *Mercure de France* in 1788 seems to be groping for the terms to describe the Scotsman's enterprise. Smith, he writes, 'starts with a luminous fact [the division of labor] to then illuminate an immense horizon, that is, to unfold the principles and, so to speak, the contexture of the organization of civilized societies...' (p. 69). This notion of Smith as a general theorist of human development and of civilized society is a recurring one in the sources Carpenter has assembled (see the 1795 review in *La Décade philosophique, littéraire et politique* at 142 and the *Gazette nationale* review in 1802 at 188 for other examples). Sometimes, the science to which he is contributing is called that of 'political economy', sometimes it is 'social economy', and sometimes it is something else again, such as 'public economy' (see pp. 89, 92–7 and passim). It is more than a little intriguing to see, in the midst of the revolution that brought forth the modern world (1791–2), Xenophon's classic study of household management, *Oeconomicus*, appended to a Smith translation (pp. 117,119–20), with the remark, 'the *Oeconomicus*...is for domestic economy what the work of M. Smith is for political economy' (p. 122). Were these differences in nomenclature mere examples of loose thinking or did they mean something to contemporaries? Evidently, Garnier felt they were important enough to justify distinguishing at length between public and political economy (p. 189).

It is also instructive in this connection to find the ghost of Montesquieu haunting these pages (p. xlv). Right through the Garnier translation in 1802, French readers found one sprawling masterwork a useful reference point for the other, however different their scopes and contents may seem to us. A 1788 letter to the *Journal de Paris* that saw both works as useful for administrators remarked that Great Britain, in producing Adam Smith's work, had now repaid France for having produced that of Montesquieu (p. 74). A couple of years later, a reviewer for *Le Spectateur national* made the somewhat more specific point that the WN represents a new era in 'the history of political science, like *The Spirit of the Laws*' (p. 92). Only when Smith came to stand for the specific science of political economy – and not 'political science', 'social science', or other more generic entities – did Montesquieu begin to drop out of the picture as a viable reference point, as one sees in the critical comments Garnier makes about Montesquieu in his 1802 edition (p. 204).

The French school of free market, absolute monarchist theorists of the middle of the eighteenth century who called themselves Physiocrats, and who flourished in the 1760s and early 1770s, are also a frequent appearance in these pages. This contrast also casts light on the ways in which self-consciously French readers thought fit to appropriate the distinctively British writing of Adam Smith. As early as 1781, Smith's work was being preferred to the 'sect'-like works of the Physiocrats (p. 37), an argument that could only be carried so far, since another theme of French responses was that Smith was less stylistically and organizationally agreeable than were most French writers (the Physiocrats aside). The eighteenth-century French tradition of translation as popularization – seen, for instance, in Morellet's reworking of Beccaria's *On Crimes and Punishments*, a reworking that turned that work into an Enlightenment classic – seems to be at play in some of the material presented here (p. 38 and passim). Ian Ross' volume had already reproduced Garnier's argument that, whereas the Physiocrats strive for a natural science which must rest content with mere knowledge, Adam Smith more properly sees political economy as a moral science with a real capacity for improvement in the human condition (*Contemporary Responses*, 221). We are reminded by Carpenter, however, that Garnier had also contrasted the Physiocrats' abstract and absolute view of their science, a science that treats the human species as a single nation, with Smith's more concrete and relative view of the human species as being actually divided into different historically situated nations (p. 216). It is also noteworthy, though not surprising, that nowhere in Carpenter's volume does the name Condillac appear, despite the publication in 1776, just months before the WN, of his important and impressive work *Le Commerce et le gouvernement, considérés relativement l'un à l'autre* (*Commerce and Government considered in their mutual relationship*), which offered significant departures from the Physiocratic doctrine.

There are other topics on which Carpenter's material contributes to our understanding as well, such as the so-called Adam Smith Problem, the way James Steuart's *Principles of Political Economy* (1767) was compared to Smith's work, and the complex and controversial arguments by Emma Rothschild in her recent book *Economic Sentiments* (Harvard 2001) about the varying reception of Smith's doctrine after the French Revolution. The scope and organization of *The Dissemination of the* WN are not as transparent or as helpfully laid out as might be wished. The index is thin (no mention of Montesquieu, for example), and there is a noticeable though not extravagant number of errors in the transcriptions and printing, especially early in the book (pp. xxv, xxvii, 1, 6, 8, 83, 87, 238). But although the book will not be confused with beach-side reading, it nonetheless makes a real and welcome contribution to the study of Adam Smith and to his reception in what was at that time the leading country in Europe.

Bibliography

Hesse, C.A. (1991) *Publishing and Cultural Politics in Revolutionary Paris, 1789–1810*, Berkeley, CA: University of California Press.

Lai, C. (ed.) (2000) *Adam Smith Across Nations: Translations and Receptions of the* Wealth of Nations, Oxford: Oxford University Press.

Popkin, J.D. (1990) *Revolutionary News: the Press in France, 1789–1799*, Durham, NC: Duke University Press.

Ross, I.S. (ed.) (1998) *On the* Wealth of Nations: *Contemporary Responses to Adam Smith*, Bristol: Thoemmes Press.
Rothschild, E. (2001) *Economic Sentiments: Adam Smith, Condorcet, and the Enlightenment*, Cambridge, MA: Cambridge University Press.

AUTHOR'S RESPONSE

Kenneth E. Carpenter's response to review by Henry C. Clark

The author of this review has well described my study of Adam Smith in French and in France, has well summarized much of the introductory essay, and, what is more, has engaged with my book in an interesting way. Thus, Professor Clark has used the extensive quotations from contemporary documents to write about differing French perceptions about the basic subject of the WN. I am gratified, since I hoped that my book would be used in various ways and by scholars who do not consider themselves historians of economic thought.

Some quibbles I have. Professor Clark seems to equate my note that I have not produced a census of copies with an indication of lack of completeness. To set the record straight, every edition, every form of every edition, has been listed, and I feel confident that it is complete; but I did not produce a census of all exemplars. That might be an especially useful thing to do, if someone were to examine the notes of early readers. The copies that I saw show that WN did not merely sit unread on shelves.

Professor Clark indicates that there are some errors of transcription. No doubt there are, but it was my policy to follow the French text 'out the window' so to speak, without cluttering the pages with '[*sic*]'. Before assuming an error of transcription, especially before silently 'correcting' an 'error', the user of my book would do well to return to the original.

The reviewer discusses the numerous appearances of Smith in the *Encyclopédique méthodique* in a way that obscures my point that these extracts confirm the marginality of Smith in France during the 1780s. I believe they show marginality because these translated extracts generally appeared without identification of the author, or with the author identified only as 'Smith'.

I should, perhaps, have made clear the distinction in my mind between a notice and a review, since a notice was often only recorded, whereas reviews that I found were always transcribed. A notice was simply a listing of the book, and it seemed undesirable to clutter up a complex text by transcribing the exact form of that listing.

Professor Clark may be right that the structure of the book is not as clear as it might have been, perhaps a comment occasioned by the fact that my study took the form of successive entries for the various books. It had to be like this, because my goal was to produce a bibliography, not in the sense of a mere checklist of books, but rather a bibliography describing and analyzing each of the publications. A book directed solely at historians might have had a different structure, but I was addressing two audiences.

One was descriptive and analytical bibliographers, scholars who focus on the book itself, the material object. Bibliographers are accustomed to identifying different forms of a book, some even that the ordinary person would usually see as identical. The bibliographer then analyzes the relationships among the different forms, often with the goal of ascertaining authorial intentions among the textual variants. In the last decade or so bibliographers and book historians more generally have begun to examine the meaning inherent in non-textual elements, a part of what literary scholars have begun to call the 'paratext'. The paratext also has elements external to the book that also shape the meaning of the text for the individual reader, reviews being a major one. In a scholarly world in which the reader is seen as being, along with the author, a creator of meaning, I wished to encourage expansion of what bibliographers consider to be appropriate elements in a bibliographical description. Moreover, I found that paratextual elements are also immensely useful in understanding the book's various forms; hence that expansion helps the bibliographer to better carry out the traditional bibliographical task.

It has seemed to me, once curator of the Kress Library, that something of a mirror situation exists among historians of economic thought. My perception has been that such scholars tend to deal in ideas that are disembodied from the wider context in which they saw light. Thus, I believe that my book about context should ideally speak to historians of economics in two ways. One is that the contemporary prefaces and reviews provide textual evidence about the way a book was perceived at the time of publication. Second, the physical volume can also be 'read' for its messages to potential buyers and readers about the nature of the book and its intended audience. The two types of evidence, reinforcing each other, put the book in the context of the publisher and the buyer, that is, the market.

In effect, I have hoped that my methodology would help to make historians of economics more conscious of context and thus further a different kind of sophistication in the discipline. It can be argued that historians of science are in advance of historians of the social sciences in understanding the development of their field, and that that is to some extent because the historians of science are pursuing studies that are book historical. A notable example is Adrian Johns (1998), by a scholar whose dust-jacket blurb identifies him as a sociologist and a 'member of the Science Studies Program' at his university. Or, to cite another book that happens to be on my shelves: Marina Frasca-Spada and Nick Jardine (2000).

It seems clear to me that the unfamiliar form of my book – and, indeed, the unfamiliar part of its message – means that it will not easily and automatically be valued by historians of thought for its methodology. Thus, I am grateful to have had this opportunity, in responding to Professor Clark's gracious review, to add to the paratext of my book by pointing out what I considered to be its larger purpose.

Bibliography

Johns, A. (1998) *The Nature of the Book: Print and Knowledge in the Making*, Chicago: University of Chicago Press.

Frasca-Spada, M. and Jardine, N. (eds) (2000) *Books and the Sciences in History*, Cambridge: Cambridge University Press.

Gloria Vivenza, *Adam Smith and the Classics: The Classical Heritage in Adam Smith's Thought*

Translated by Clive Cheesman and Nicola Gelder, Oxford University Press, 2001, x + 240pp.

ISBN 0–198–29666–5

Reviewed by Peter McNamara

Back to the future

Gloria Vivenza's *Adam Smith e la cultura classica* was originally published in 1984. It now appears in English for the first time. Vivenza has revised the original book only slightly, but has added a postscript offering her reflections on some of the relevant Smith scholarship since 1984. Both the translation and the postscript are welcome developments. Vivenza's closely and carefully argued analysis of Smith's debt to the classics remains a valuable resource for all Smith scholars. Furthermore, the perspective of almost twenty years of Smith scholarship allows for some broad commentary as well as some incisive criticism.

Vivenza's procedure for analyzing Smith's relationship to the classics is straightforward. She distinguishes two types of influence. First, and to her the least interesting, is the way in which Smith consciously or unconsciously drew on the classics for felicitous words, phrases, or examples. The second kind of influence is where Smith drew on 'ideas, concepts, kernels, or trains of thought of classical origin which, passing through a lengthy process of transformation, adaptation, and "rediscovery" from century to century, had finally arrived, somewhat modified, in the Age of the Enlightenment' (p. 5). In addition, to the distortions time may bring to a doctrine or idea, Vivenza adds that the 'subjects he dealt with ...almost always display essential links with the contemporary world. As a result, even when their classical mould may be clearly discerned, their manifold connections with present day events are simultaneously evident, giving the classical author or thought a character quite different from the original one' (p. 5). Vivenza considers the classical influence in Smith's natural philosophy, moral philosophy, jurisprudence, political economy, and his studies in rhetoric and eloquence. With a sure and steady hand, she analyzes the possible sources for Smith's views and shows precisely the points of agreement and disagreement between Smith and the classical authors. Her conclusion, which is undoubtedly correct, is that the presence of the classics 'was more than just the "flirtation" of a man of great culture and many interests; it influenced not only his tastes but also his mind and his ideas' (p.189).

Vivenza shows that Smith not only relied extensively on classical sources but that he did so in a variety of quite distinct ways. Smith's treatment of the Roman law illustrates the point. The lasting influence of the Roman law (via the Canon law) in Scotland had given an impetus to Scottish legal scholarship that was historical and European in outlook. More significantly still, perhaps, the Roman law was a natural subject of study for someone like Smith working in the wake of Montesquieu's highly innovative insights into the connection between law and social circumstances. The historical record with respect to the Roman law was relatively full in comparison to other legal systems, thereby making it ideal for illustrating 'the evolution of a juridical system over time' (p. 111). In these respects, then, Roman law and history served as a reservoir of facts from which to make speculations about the nature and evolution of law and government. Beyond this use, Vivenza argues that the Roman law had an even greater significance for Smith in that it constituted a substantially successful attempt to establish a *system* of law. Writing to Lord Shelbourne, Smith observed that the Roman law was 'digested into a more regular System than the English Law' and concluded that its study was valuable for a law student because 'when he afterwards comes to study the law of any other country which is not so well digested, he carries at least the Idea of a System in his head and knows to what part of it he ought to refer everything that he reads' (p. 125). Roman jurisprudence thus serves as 'the best example of a legal system' in terms of structure and organization, even though Smith acknowledged there were problems with particular elements of that law (p. 186).

It is, perhaps, in the area of moral philosophy that the possible classical influences on Smith are most intriguing. Vivenza devotes substantial attention to Smith's relationship to the Stoics, a connection that has attracted the attention of many scholars. Smith frequently makes statements that evoke the Stoic idea of a providential order – a 'universal harmony' (p.185). The relevance of this particular Stoic idea to many of the broader themes of Smith's moral philosophy and political economy is manifest, but how far does Smith's agreement with the Stoics extend? Vivenza makes clear that Smith is far from accepting Stoic philosophy in its entirety. Unlike the Stoics, Smith 'does *not* consider evil to be a necessary part of the divine plan' and so Smith does not counsel 'complete resignation' in the face of evil (p. 69). Indeed, 'man has a natural aversion to evil' that shows itself in the sympathetic resentment we experience when we see another person harmed unjustly. This suggestion constitutes a 'decisive move away from the principles of the Stoa' (p.70). Similarly, Smith rejects in part the Stoic view that it is not whether we win or lose but how we play the game of life that matters. Smith believes we show a concern for the results of actions that is not, strictly speaking, moral but that has certain beneficial consequences. More generally, Smith presents 'a trenchant critique of apathy' (p. 75) – the Stoic (especially early Stoic) idea that we should live in absolute independence of pleasures and pains and from ordinary human attachments to family, friends and country. Again, Smith's break with the Stoics points in the direction of sentiment and action rather than autarchy and resignation. Vivenza detects an Aristotelian or late Stoic element to Smith's criticism that such independence is unnatural and inhuman.

Vivenza's analysis of Smith and the classics is not without a significant irony. Almost every time a classical source is identified, Vivenza adds, as I have noted, that Smith gives the source an unusual and sometimes unique interpretation, often jettisoning the original context and supporting ideas of the classical source. The result is that Vivenza's study of Smith and the classics yields – and I do not mean this as a criticism – what might be called a very conventional reading of Smith, especially in the degree to which it shows Smith emphasizing the centrality of economics as a determining force in human affairs. In this regard, it is worth observing that Smith's critical steps, mentioned earlier, away from Stoic doctrine are very much in keeping with the Enlightenment view that nature requires improving upon by human effort. Smith may differ from other Enlightenment figures about the best methods for making these improvements, but there is little disagreement about the end, namely, the Baconian goal of the relief of man's estate. Smith's political economy and his moral philosophy point away from doctrinaire and interventionist approaches in policy, politics and morality, but they, nevertheless, aim at a more prosperous and humane future for mankind. It is also worth observing that in the area of political economy – the subject of one of Smith's two great works and still the source of his fame – the classical influence and even references to the classics are, as Vivenza shows, rare and relatively unimportant.

Having said this, it would be wrong to conclude that the classical influence on Smith is not an important subject. Smith himself encourages us to take it seriously by placing his own thought – especially in *The Theory of Moral Sentiments* (TMS) – in the context of the history of philosophy. But just how should we approach this difficult subject? In the postscript, Vivenza takes to task a number of recent Smith scholars for a certain lack of precision in both translation and interpretation that has blurred important differences between Smith and the classics. Perhaps the most interesting and consequential of her criticisms is of Charles Griswold's widely and deservedly praised *Adam Smith and the Virtues of Enlightenment* and, specifically, his claim that Smith was influenced not only by Humean scepticism but also by ancient Pyrrhonic scepticism. Rather than a Stoic, Griswold's Smith is a non-dogmatic sceptic who seeks to preserve the insights and humanity of ordinary moral life from the theoretical hubris of philosophy, in general, and the Enlightenment, in particular. Griswold presents Smith as an Enlightenment thinker engaged in a critical dialogue with the Enlightenment itself and, therefore, as a powerful tool for thinking through the contemporary philosophical problems posed by the challenge of post-modernity.

According to Vivenza, this interpretation suffers from a flaw in its foundation because there is simply no basis for the idea that Smith embraced Pyrrhonism. Vivenza makes two points in support of this criticism. First, Smith never explicitly said or even suggested that he was a sceptic. Second, although Smith speaks sceptically in places about astronomical theories, this, Vivenza explains, was an entirely orthodox position among non-sceptics because astronomy was believed to be a mathematical or hypothetical endeavour, as opposed to physics, which was considered a truly philosophical pursuit aimed at finding ultimate causes. Vivenza suggests that Griswold has both misunderstood and illegitimately extended Smith's sceptical remarks in 'History of Astronomy' to Smith's corpus as a whole. The result is that Griswold over-emphasizes Smith's scepticism to the neglect of his attachment to the 'empirical and experimental' (p. 207) scientific method of his time and the strong elements of moral realism in his thought. One might disagree with this or other of the Vivenza's criticisms, but her postscript as a whole is a timely reminder of the difficulties inherent in linking Smith and the classics.

Is Vivenza too cautious in deliberately avoiding interpretations that do not have an explicit basis in what Smith said? Given the gaps in Smith's corpus and his conspicuous silences in his published works, her approach leaves us at a palpable loss on some very important questions – questions Griswold deals with at length – about Smith's stature as a philosopher, the relationship between the various aspects of his thought and his potential contemporary relevance. Furthermore, one must wonder whether the analytical framework used in *Adam Smith and the Classics* is itself adequate to the subject. Can Smith's relationship to the classics really be captured fully in terms of the two kinds of influences Vivenza distinguishes? Is it not possible, for example, that Smith was not only influenced by the classics but that he *uses* the classics – their authority, respectability and manner of writing – to advance his own agenda? Take the case of Stoicism. What purpose for Smith does volubly maintaining the Stoic idea that there is a God-governed providential order serve, when he shows empirically and without recourse to theology that in substantial respects nature exhibits such a harmony? To say that these inquiries were a confirmation of Stoicism would be to ignore Smith's many decisive departures from Stoicism. Might Smith's frequent references to Stoicism be opportunistic in that they provide a venerable moral and religious framework for what are essentially advances in social science – in political economy and in explaining moral behaviour – that otherwise might be controversial? Vivenza eschews these kinds of inferences, but in addition to its other advantages, her book serves both as an excellent place to begin to explore such possibilities and as a sounding board for any speculative inferences that such scholarship might suggest.

AUTHOR'S RESPONSE

Gloria Vivenza's response to review by Peter McNamara

I should like, first, to thank Professor McNamara for the kind things he has said in the main body of his review. I confine the rest of my response to some thoughts on his critical remarks, as he and other interested readers would no doubt expect.

He says that I have been too cautious in avoiding interpretations that are not based on Adam Smith's actual words. I think there is no need to go beyond

Smith's own words since they contain quite enough matter, more indeed than I discussed in the book. Professor McNamara says that, 'given the gaps in Smith's corpus and his conspicuous silences in his published works', my approach leaves the reader at a loss on three important questions: 'Smith's stature as a philosopher, the relationship between the various aspects of his thought and his potential contemporary relevance'. My book was not intended to be a study of all important questions concerning Adam Smith, but I did in fact say something about the second of those three, though of course only with reference to the classics. For instance, I discussed the ubiquitous structure of certain 'connections', as hinges of a system, that appear in each of Smith's fields of research, be it astronomy, law, ethics or literature.

But now I would reverse the argument. Is it not possible that Smith's 'gaps and silences' are (at least partly) responsible for stirring up so abundant a literature about his work? If so, this would be a destiny shared by Smith with Cicero, an ancient writer whom Smith does not admire but whose influence he cannot escape. Cicero almost never says what *he* thinks about the problems (of religion, for instance) on which he gives us the doctrines of the Stoics, Epicureans and Platonists. It is easy to ascribe to the 'silent' author very different ideas, sometimes opposed to each other, without being able to say which of the various interpretations has hit the mark. I have tried to avoid this.

Another problem is that, in dealing with classical influences on any aspect of thought, many scholars are too ready to draw analogies between ancients and moderns, analogies that are more apparent than real, arising from assonance, casual similarity, or association of ideas. This tendency has been much criticized, at least in Italy, being a kind of eagerness for forerunners, so that people find 'precedents' of this or that modern idea in Plato, Aristotle, the Stoics, etc. In many cases, the argument did not hold good, and this is why you get the complaint that the study of the ancient economic history and economic thought has been left to the classicists who, it is reasonably said, are ignorant of economics. But it is equally true that they alone are equipped to understand correctly the ancient texts: other scholars, however seriously committed, may be led astray, for instance by a translation, not necessarily an incorrect one.

So I have tried to avoid interpretations which could prove to be hazardous and ill-grounded. Perhaps I have run the risk of making too fine a distinction between Smith, the economist and Smith, the classical scholar; but I think I can counter the 'non-criticism' of my 'very conventional reading of Smith', and the observation that classical influences in the field of political economy are 'rare and unimportant' in Smith's thought. This is true of my book, but I could have shown (as I have in subsequent articles) that even in the WN there are echoes of classical sources used to illustrate modern arguments. They belong to what I have called the first type of influences, namely hidden memories that come to the surface, classical motifs often repeated, even after Adam Smith's time, because they reflect conditions that still have something in common with a modern situation, even though substantially the modern situation is different. Adam Smith describes the degradation of the modern factory labourer using classical arguments in a recognizable way because the ancient Greeks had believed, and put into theory, the idea that manual labour ruins body, mind and character. In similar vein A. Krupp, in the middle of the nineteenth century, advised his workers not to meddle in politics, for which they had neither time nor training. He was thereby reviving, though probably without being aware of it, an Aristotelian motif: Aristotle too had maintained that 'mechanical' workers should be kept away from political assemblies, because they lack both leisure and competence. To my mind these arguments were used almost automatically like instruments, so to speak: the ancient and customary argument could still suit the modern situation, or at least an aspect of it.

The classical influence on Smith's moral philosophy is what really has a structural function. Even in this field, obviously, important changes had taken place, but not a shifting of perspective and a change of status such as had happened in the field of economics, which became a new independent science, precisely with Adam Smith according to prevailing opinion. It became an autonomous science, adopting rules and criteria detached from morals and law, in which it had previously been embedded, and faced in practice with a completely different set of facts. Moral philosophy remained fairly similar to what it had been before, having had independent status for more than two thousand years and being concerned with much the same problems. Its most important change (though not as radical as the industrial revolution was for economics) was, I would say, the effect of Christianity; but, as is well known, Christian doctrine was able to find a compromise and to retain some part at least of classical philosophical thought.

My last comment is on Professor McNamara's final observation that some of Smith's references to Stoicism might be 'opportunistic' because they provided 'a venerable moral and religious framework for what are essentially advances in social science'. I had the same suspicion. My idea was that the references to Stoicism were especially appropriate for Smith's moral philosophy lectures, where the young teacher perhaps felt obliged to offer his young pupils an elevated and authoritative picture of problems that were certainly important for students mostly destined for the Church. Although I have more than once expressed the view (held by others too) that Stoicism and Christianity are basically incompatible, it is a matter of fact that an approach between them did take place and that since St Paul's time, Stoic arguments have been used to support Christian concepts.

Is it possible that Smith, mysterious about his own position on religion, might have preferred to use his beloved classics to say something on a topic on which he had to speak but was prevented by discretion from being too explicit? We shall never know.

All this I have thought, but have not written because, as Professor McNamara rightly says, I am too cautious to attribute to Adam Smith something which may be a reflection of my own feelings rather than his.

Jack Russell Weinstein, *On Adam Smith*

Wadsworth, 2001, 97pp.

ISBN 0–534–58384–9

Reviewed by Lauren Brubaker

Adam Smith's enduring relevance

A self-described 'introductory book' of only ninety-seven pages, Weinstein's *On Adam Smith* claims to present, if not wholly defend, a potentially controversial interpretation of Smith. The three claims constituting his approach are laid out in the Introduction: Smith is treated 'not as an economist who happened to write philosophy, but, rather, as a philosopher who wrote some economics', he is not merely a 'historical curiosity' but rather has a 'contemporary message', and finally, while 'most contemporary Smith scholarship' rejects the 'Adam Smith problem', 'suspicions' remain about the unity of his corpus, suspicions that Weinstein intends to combat by showing his work as a unified whole. He concludes the Introduction by asking his audience to put aside their preconceptions and prejudices in order to see that Smith 'has much to offer, and it is rarely what one expects'. With the partial exception of the claim about current relevance I find these claims unexceptional, even admirable. I suspect most readers of this *Review* would agree.

There are several levels to Weinstein's claim of relevance. At its most particular, he suggests that there may be guidance on capital punishment (p. 85) and on such questions as 'welfare, affirmative action, the privatization of education… and issues of diversity' (p. 92). He further asserts that Smith's counsel may be opposite to what we would expect from his reputation. He does not elaborate on any of these questions, however, and admits that Smith addresses such issues only 'obliquely' (p. 92). More generally he argues that Smith is a critic of 'self-interested, cold, libertarian capitalism' (p. 91) and even that Smith would 'challenge' any claim that 'capitalism is succeeding' (p. 2). The basis for the latter claim is not obvious. At times it seems to rest on empirical claims: 'the growth of world-wide capitalism has left many without access to most if not all necessities' (p. 67) or 'while some countries gorge themselves into obesity, others starve' and 'global cultural experience is becoming whitewashed in a money- and media-driven frenzy of homogeneity' (p. 2). Such assertions seem more an effort to flatter a contemporary prejudice than a serious argument. He fails to provide any evidence for the extent of such problems and, more importantly, never makes any effort to prove that even if true, Smith or we should find them unique to or aggravated by capitalism. We are left with the most general of his claims of relevance: that Smith 'spent his life endeavouring to show that economics must be presented alongside ethics' (p. 2), that he is 'concerned with the cultivation of morality and the needs of the poor' and that 'the free-market is only an acceptable structure when it is supported by institutions designed to negate the inherently divisive and exploitative character of capitalism' (p. 91). Despite the occasionally polemical phrasing, these boil down to the very Smithian claims that economics is properly a part of moral philosophy and that free markets in particular presuppose certain political or legal institutions. Aside from the admirable but vague claim that philosophy, political science and economics should 'communicate' with each other (p. 92), further lessons for our time would seem to depend on the more fundamental questions of the unity of Smith's work and the relation between his philosophy and his economics.

In addition to the short introduction, conclusion and a biographical summary, *On Adam Smith* contains four chapters: a discussion of *Lectures on Rhetoric and Belles Lettres* (LRBL) (Smith 1983) and 'Astronomy' (Smith 1980), of *The Theory of Moral Sentiments* (TMS) (Smith, 1976a), of *Wealth of Nations* (WN) (Smith 1976b), and of *Lectures on Jurisprudunce* (LJ) (Smith 1978). I will offer brief discussions of the last three.

The chapter on TMS argues that morality for Smith is 'contextual', 'perspectival' and 'communitarian' (pp. 40, 44). These terms have various, sometimes loaded, contemporary meanings and need some explanation. *Contextual* for Weinstein means that moral judgments must take into account the details of the actors and situation and thus are not easily or accurately made in general and abstract terms. This is a correct and important, although not unnoticed, aspect of Smith's moral theory.

What Weinstein means by *perspectival* is less clear. At times he bases this characterization on the fact that all moral judgments involve the imagination of the spectator and thus vary with the 'spectator's own experience' (p. 45). At other times he attributes it to the actor, arguing that 'who one is will greatly influence how one feels' and that the spectator must take into account 'the facts of the agents [*sic*] life' (p. 44). This latter may be no more than taking the agent's situation into account, in which case it collapses into 'contextual'. If a stronger meaning is given to the agent's distinctiveness, for example that the race or gender or religion of the agent changes the moral judgment, then 'perspectival' takes on more debatable connotations. By arguing that 'we must learn their stories, we must learn their histories, and we must understand their personhood' (p. 73), Weinstein seems to want to at least start down this road. For Smith, while these differences in the agent may explain differing reactions, they would not allow a spectator to approve significant violations of impartiality. The closest Smith comes to sanctioning different standards based on the characteristics of the agent is his allowance for greater benevolence (but adamantly not for violations of equal justice) based on degrees of familiarity (TMS VI.ii; see Otteson 2002: chapter 5). A similar argument can be made concerning the spectator's 'perspective', but again partiality, in this case of the spectator, is not a feature of Smith's theory but rather would be a clear indication a corruption of moral judgment. 'Perspectival' then either means 'contextual' in the limited sense discussed earlier, or if meant in a stronger sense, is a violation of Smithian impartiality. The use of a loaded contemporary term fails to aid our understanding of Smith.

Communitarian is another term with contemporary baggage. For Weinstein, it is the opposite of liberal: 'communitarian is understood as acknowledging some priority of the community and liberal is understood as a commitment to the priority of the individual' (p. 40). Here again Weinstein's meaning is ambiguous. He is absolutely correct to argue that for Smith 'moral adjudication and the formation of identity is a social process' (p. 54). But this tells us nothing about the relative priority of the individual or community when making actual moral judgments. Later he assets as Smith's position 'that humans are communal creatures, and that one must cultivate all people if one is to cultivate any one person' (p. 67). Depending on what one means by *cultivate*, this could mean each individual should have equal opportunity (a classic liberal as well as Smithian position) or that the community has a responsibility to ensure the success of every individual (perhaps a kind of communitarianism, but not Smithian). In context he seems to mean that every person in a community should be equally the objects of sympathy and equally free from oppression. This is both Smithian and liberal: impartial justice is based on sympathy with all individuals who are victims of injustice (as Weinstein points out elsewhere). Its relation to 'communitarian' is, however, dubious.

Even if we return to the most plausible understanding of Smith as 'communitarian' – that our natural sympathy both extends to all in our community and leads to common moral judgments – I think there is an important tension in Smith's account of sympathy. Do we naturally extend sympathy to others, or do we desire the sympathy of others? Put another way, does sympathy guarantee this sort of 'community'? (Weinstein astutely recognizes a tension between prudence and benevolence, but he does not develop it in this direction (p. 53)). Smith at different times emphasizes both our sympathy as spectators with an agent and our desire for the sympathy of spectators when we are the agent (TMS I.i.5.1). What happens when these two are in conflict, say in the case of slavery, or in the case of religious or political faction (TMS III.3.43)? If we put ourselves in the position of the slave, or in the place of a member of the opposing and perhaps oppressed faction or religion, we are moved to impartial justice based on this imaginative sympathy. If, on the other hand, we are primarily concerned with the desire for the sympathy of others, we seek the approval of our peers – the other members of our, perhaps oppressing, class, religion or party. Sympathy is at war with sympathy, partial community ('those like us') with impartial community (the liberal goal of equal justice for each individual, regardless of class, race, religion). Far from ignoring this problem, Smith insists that civil and ecclesiastical factions are 'by far the greatest' causes of the corruption of our moral sentiments (TMS

III.43; see also III.6.12). The ambiguity in the relation of sympathy and community highlighted by Smith offers food for thought, although not any clear partisan guidance, about several significant contemporary issues. Calling Smith a 'communitarian' only obscures this fruitful tension.

Weinstein credits sympathy both with generating community standards and with providing the ground to critique them. Occasionally he seems oblivious to any tension here, arguing that 'sympathy is self-correcting' (p. 77) or 'identity is itself a product of sympathy' (p. 65). At other times he properly emphasizes the fallibility of sympathy and the impartial spectator when embodied in particular human beings (p. 50). He then argues that moral corruption can be cured 'through sympathy and through education' (p. 47). Having discussed sympathy we now turn to his discussion of the requirements for a free market and specifically the role of education in his chapter on WN.

In the broadest sense Weinstein correctly insists that Smith was a practitioner of political economy, aware of the constant and inevitable interplay of politics and economics. At other times he less plausibly attempts to make Smith the political mentor of contemporary social democracy. This attempt at 'contemporary relevance' leads to a few egregious misreadings of Smith. Commenting on Smith's argument that the disposition to admire the rich and the great leads to ambition, with the result that 'candidates for fortune too frequently abandon the paths of virtue' (TMS I.iii.3.1,8), Weinstein inverts the argument, concluding that 'poverty and its consequent subordination are the major cause [*sic*] of the corruption of the sentiments' (p. 66)! Discussing natural price, he correctly says it 'incorporates profit in regards to material necessary for production' but incorrectly believes that it does not include 'profit received by the sale of the finished product' (WN I.vii.54–5). He uses this supposed omission to argue that 'one is forced to wonder whether profit is somehow "unnatural"' for Smith (p. 74)!

On surer ground, Weinstein argues that the free market 'is only acceptable to Smith when society is structured to promote justice, rights and morality' (p. 69). What structures do this? One of the welcome themes of his chapter on WN is that the market itself encourages virtue. As the market replaces the dependence characteristic of feudal relations, greater freedom is accorded to most citizens and the spread of liberty promotes prudence (pp. 64, 70). Smith recognizes as well that there are some negative consequences of increasing commercialization. Education, both secular and religious, is the main mechanism Weinstein sees for remedying these defects and supporting morality: 'The market could not exist without the virtue that comes with knowledge and belief' (p. 73). Looking closely at a few examples shows that Smith is considerably less optimistic than Weinstein about education. Discussing the proposals for the education of youth in WN V.i.f, Weinstein argues these are designed to 'bridge the gap between the classes' (p. 72). What he fails to make clear is that the education of the masses is very minimal, in sharp contrast to that of the 'superior rank', thus arguably contributing to class divisions (WN V.i.f.54, V.i.g.14). Smith's discussion of religious 'education' in WN V.i.g is primarily a discussion of a hypothetical disestablishment that would lead to a 'great multitude of religious sects'. This political arrangement is the real antidote to religious faction since it would leave 'each of them consequently too small to disturb the public tranquility'. The role of religion in preventing 'profligacy and vice' among the poor also bears little relation to education or 'belief'. Membership in a small religious sect means that individuals, rather than being lost in the anonymity of the city, are closely observed by their fellow sectarians. Desiring their sympathy, each will keep to the straight and narrow. The only 'religious education' discussed here consists of 'science and philosophy' for the elite, and the suggestion that the state should encourage the 'frequency and gaiety of public diversions' in order to mitigate the 'melancholy and gloomy humour' and too strict virtue characteristic of the religions of the poor, characteristics which lead to 'superstition and enthusiasm' (V.i.g.12–15). While certainly an advocate of education, Smith was more aware of its limitations as a guarantor of virtue and relies more on other institutional arrangements than Weinstein suggests.

A final theme of Weinstein's discussion of WN is his implausible claim that for Smith 'political and economic liberty are necessary conditions for each other' (pp. 58, 76). Perhaps this is merely a matter of imprecise phrasing on Weinstein's part, since in the next chapter on justice he makes the more reasonable claim that 'economic and political considerations require one another' (p. 89). That Smith, like Hume, certainly hoped that the progress of commerce and of economic liberty would promote political liberty has been noted before (see Cropsey 1957: chapter III). Weinstein's main concern, however, is to argue that Smith thought certain political institutions were necessary preconditions for the full realization of his system of natural liberty, which brings us to the chapter concerning justice.

Weinstein begins his chapter on justice with a discussion of the last paragraph of the *Advertisement* to the sixth edition of TMS. Here, as in the last paragraph of TMS itself, Smith explains the relations of the various parts of his moral philosophy. Natural jurisprudence or the 'general principles of law and government' is an important subset of moral philosophy, one that he promised to treat in a separate book. WN is a partial fulfillment of that promise 'at least so far as concerns police, revenue, and arms'. His book on economics is intended to be understood as merely a part of a part of his moral philosophy, an account of an important but subsidiary aspect of human life. This gives solid support to Weinstein's claim in his Introduction that Smith never intended his economics to be independent of his ethics.

He then makes use of the traditional division between distributive and commutative justice to argue that WN concerns the former and TMS the latter. The first problem with such a characterization is that distributive justice seems to mean benevolence in the sense of laws that have a welfare or redistributive impact, although he properly emphasizes that Smith is primarily concerned to foster 'equality of opportunity' (p. 82). Redistribution may be the contemporary meaning of distributive justice, but it is a meaning that turns on its head the traditional understanding (shared by both Aristotle and Smith; see TMS VII.ii.1.10) as the giving of unequal honours based on merit. The second problem is that even in the sense of benevolence or redistribution WN has surprisingly little to say on the question, beyond the redistribution in favour of consumers and workers that would naturally occur if the system of natural liberty were established.

Benevolence often has a negative connotation, as when he argues in the famous butcher, brewer, baker passage that the appeal to the self-interest of others in commercial society replaces a 'fawning attention' to the benevolence of superiors (WN I.ii.2). WN is primarily oriented to the production, not the redistribution, of opulence. The final problem here is that WN is very concerned with commutative justice. Time and time again Smith emphasizes that only if there is liberty and security can the market mechanisms he describes work to their full extent. Liberty and security for individuals is the pre-eminent concern of impartial justice understood as 'protecting every member of the society from the injustice or oppression of every other member of it' (WN IV.ix.51; see also Werhane 1991). The primary explicit connection between Smith's ethics and his economics is his contention that justice, not benevolence, is the one virtue necessary for society, particularly for free markets, as well as the primary virtue that can properly be compelled by law (TMS II.ii.1.8, II.ii.3.1–4).

The maintenance of impartial justice is not in any sense a minimal or trivial requirement, and Weinstein is right to emphasize that Smith's political economy requires constant state intervention (p. 71). It is the nature of that intervention that is in question. In his more social democratic and 'relevant' moments, he suggests that Smith's message is that we need institutions to educate us that 'we must care for each other' (p. 91). While not opposed to benevolence, Smith is far more concerned on a political level with institutions that guarantee that we do not harm each other. This is particularly relevant to his economics. Smith considers the establishment of complete natural liberty utopian since it is opposed by both 'the prejudices of the publick' (which are perhaps amenable to education) and the 'private interests of many individuals' (which are 'much more unconquerable'). He is quite specific: 'merchants and master manufacturers' have 'generally an interest to deceive and even to oppress the publick' by manipulating the market or restricting perfect liberty (WN IV.ii.42, I.xi.p.10). To prevent such distortion of the market and to encourage perfect liberty is a matter of impartial justice, not benevolence. It is clearly a political question of utmost concern to Smith, and to us.

Any book, particularly an introductory one, that encourages readers to put aside their preconceptions and consider seriously the relation between Smith's moral philosophy, politics and economics is to be welcomed. This particular book would be better if it did not let a desire for frequently partisan contemporary relevance to colour or obscure the effort to understand Smith. Yet if it induces its readers to actually read Smith they will find plenty of food for thought about Weinstein's themes of sympathy, community, education, benevolence and justice. Much of Smith is undoubtedly relevant to the world in which we live today, although rarely in a simple, direct or partisan manner. Weinstein is correct to conclude: 'It is just possible that Smith has more to say' (p. 92).

Bibliography

Cropsey, J. (1957) *Polity and Economy: An Interpretation of the Principles of Adam Smith*, The Hague: Martinus Nijhoff.

Otteson, J. (2002) *Adam Smith's Marketplace of Life*, Cambridge: Cambridge University Press.
Smith, A. (1976a) *The Theory of Moral Sentiments*, D.D. Raphael and A.L. Macfie (eds), Oxford: Oxford University Press; Glasgow Edition. Reprinted, Liberty Press (1982).
—— (1976b) *An Inquiry into the Nature and Causes of the Wealth of Nations*, R.H. Campbell and A.S. Skinner (eds), Oxford: Oxford University Press; Glasgow Edition. Reprinted, Liberty Press (1981).
—— (1978) *Lectures on Jurisprudence*, R.L. Meek, D.D. Raphael and P.G. Stein (eds), Oxford: Oxford University Press; Glasgow Edition. Reprinted, Liberty Press (1982).
—— (1980) *Essays on Philosophical Subjects*, W.P.D. Wightman (ed.), Oxford: Oxford University Press; Glasgow Edition. Reprinted, Liberty Press (1982).
—— (1983) *Lectures on Rhetoric and Belles Lettres*, J.C. Bryce (ed.), Oxford: Oxford University Press; Glasgow Edition. Reprinted, Liberty Press (1985).
Werhane, P.H. (1991) *Adam Smith and His Legacy for Modern Capitalism*, Oxford: Oxford University Press.

AUTHOR'S RESPONSE

Jack Russell Weinstein's response to review by Lauren Brubaker

I am grateful to Lauren Brubaker for taking the time to review my book and for responding adroitly as a scholar. Introductory books often get short shrift in the specialist literature, at least in part because they are projects of a different type. Although I tried to both write for lay people and make an original contribution to the field, the book is destined to be unsatisfying to specialists. Ninety-seven pages leaves little room for sustained argument or for emphasizing nuances of contention. I warn that, 'the reader should not be tempted into thinking [this book] is uncontroversial' (pp. 2–3). But, of course, lay people do not know enough of the debate to identify controversy when they encounter it. Thus Brubaker's frequent request for more information is inevitable. I too wish the book could have been longer.

His discussion emphasizes two types of claims: those he regards as obvious, and those he sees as mistaken. What he fails to see is that introductory books must emphasize the obvious, but what he considers obvious is not always so, and what he considers mistakes are, often, the consequence of the obvious. Consider his assertion that most readers of this *Review* would agree that rejection of the Adam Smith Problem is unremarkable. I wish it were so, but it is not. Otteson (2002), Brown (1994), Minowitz (1993) and Lux (1990), for example, each confer upon the problem significant legitimacy. Their struggles to cope with its various nuances lead necessarily to my focus on communitarian ideas.

Although no one disputes that Smith is a part of the liberal canon, many question identifying his work as liberal, see Khalil (2002), Letwin (1988), Winch (1988, 1978). Nevertheless, I do not claim that Smith is communitarian, only that, 'in many ways, TMS is', especially its discussion of sympathy (p. 40). Brubaker objects to the term *communitarian* because of its 'contemporary baggage', but an introductory text that is not immersed in contemporary discourse would be severely lacking. Primers must summarize both primary and secondary material without overburdening the reader with details, and that means not shying away from contemporary terminology with multiple meanings. Political philosophy is drowning in the liberal/communitarian debate, and part of Smith's appeal is that he bridges the two extremes.

Smith espouses certain communitarian ideas, even in Brubaker's wider interpretation of the term. In TMS, for example, Smith argues that humans are by nature social (Smith 1976a, TMS II.ii.3.1, III.2.6). He asserts that morality is the product of social processes, arguing explicitly that morality, even self-identification, is impossible in isolation (III.i.3–4). He is also insistent that general moral rules are after-the-fact constructs developing from social interaction (III.4.7–8), and that the most basic of these are enabled by education (III.5.1). In WN, Smith argues that the state should foster both secular and religious education (Smith 1976b, WN V.i.i.5), and the sympathetic foundation of morality functions best in small communities (Nieli 1986). Smith famously opposes the social contract (Khalil 1998). An introductory audience is helped by pointing out the 'non-liberal' nature of these claims, and as specialists, we would all be better served if we could get past this destructive dichotomy.

Brubaker also criticizes my approach to Smith's economics, beginning with the complaint that I offer no evidence for the tensions between poverty and contemporary capitalism. This baffles me. There is a vast amount of literature on this topic ranging from the scholarly to the popular, not to mention the daily reminders on television; the world has many ghettos. My point, however, is to counter the fact that 'Smith has become an icon for greed and self-interest…and serves as a convenient enemy' (p. 1). I challenge this fact; I do not condemn Smith for it. I am writing specifically against the partisan flattery of contemporary prejudice Brubaker accuses me of, precisely because Smith addresses the 'human cost' of these issues so 'bluntly' (Griswold 1999: 17).

Brubaker dismisses as obvious my assertion of Smith's connected understanding of economics and morality but rejects my association of poverty as a cause of the corruption of the sentiments. Smith makes these claims through his assertions that we admire the rich too much (TMS III.3.10), that the poor man's son's attempts at success do not make him more virtuous (TMS IV.1.7), and that this ultimately corrupts the imagination. Smith also asserts that our vanity glorifies our own riches and thus causes us to misjudge propriety (TMS I.iii.2.1). He writes that our disposition to admire the rich and powerful is, 'the great and most universal cause of the corruption of our moral sentiments' (TMS I.iii.3.2). Then, he argues that a labourer learns a trade 'at the expense of intellectual, social, and martial virtues' and that the torpor of his mind 'renders him, not only incapable of relishing or bearing a part in any rational conversation, but of conceiving any generous, noble, or tender sentiment, and consequently of forming any just judgment…' (WN V.i.f.50). For Smith, poverty and class difference severely impact access to material and social goods; this necessarily affects the sentiments.

Space allows me only one more response. Brubaker is correct in his assertion that Smith accounts for the role of profit in natural price; here the mistake is mine and he is right to call attention to it. My discussion is meant to draw parallels between price and the impartial spectator; both are ways in which agents manage large amounts of information to make correct judgments about what is appropriate. This is an important bridge between the two works. I hoped, and still hope, readers will 'wonder' about the nature of profit (p. 74), but this is not an argument against its being natural as Brubaker asserts. It is merely an open-ended question. More than anything else, I had hoped to inspire curiosity in my readers. Whereas Brubaker seems uncomfortable with such questions, I hoped to saturate the book with as many as possible. *On Adam Smith* sought to provide only a glimpse of what Smith's unified corpus might look like. It is up to its readers to seek out the details for themselves.

Bibliography

Brown, V. (1994) *Adam Smith's Discourse: Canonicity Commerce and Conscience*, London: Routledge.

Griswold, C.L. (1999) *Adam Smith and the Virtues of Enlightenment*, Cambridge: Cambridge University Press.

Khalil, E.L. (2002) 'Is Adam Smith liberal?', *Journal of Institutional and Theoretical Economics*, 158: 664–94.

—— (1998) 'Is justice the primary feature of the state? Adam Smith's critique of social contract theory', *European Journal of Law and Economics*, 6: 215–30.

Letwin, W. (1988) 'Was Adam Smith a liberal?', in *Traditions of Liberalism*, K. Haakonssen (ed.), Australia: The Centre For Independent Studies.

Lux, K. (1990) *Adam Smith's Mistake: How a Moral Philosopher Invented Economics and Ended Morality*, Boston, MA: Shambhala.

Minowitz, P. (1993) *Profits, Priests, and Princes: Adam Smith's Emancipation from Politics and Religion*, Stanford: Stanford University Press.

Nieli, R. (1986) 'Spheres of intimacy and the Adam Smith Problem', *Journal of the History of Ideas*, 47: 611–24.

Otteson, J.R. (2002) *Adam Smith's Marketplace of Life*, Cambridge: Cambridge University Press.

Smith, A. (1976a) *The Theory of Moral Sentiments*, D.D. Raphael and A.L. Macfie (eds), Oxford: Oxford University Press; reprinted, Liberty Press (1982).

—— (1976b) *An Inquiry into the Nature and Causes of the Wealth of Nations*, R.H. Campbell and A.S. Skinner (eds), Oxford: Oxford University Press; reprinted, Liberty Press.

Winch, D. (1988) 'Adam Smith and the liberal tradition', in *Traditions of Liberalism*, K. Haakonssen (ed.), Australia: Centre For Independent Studies.

—— (1978) *Adam Smith's Politics*, Cambridge: Cambridge University Press.

Conference report

Christel Fricke

An International Kolloquium on *Adam Smith as a Moral Philosopher* was held at the *Internationales Wissenschaftsforum der Universität Heidelberg in Heidelberg*, Germany, from 19 June to 21 June, 2003. The Kolloquium was initiated and organized by Christel Fricke (University of Heidelberg; now University of Oslo, Norway) and Hans-Peter Schütt (University of Karlsruhe, Germany).

Fifteen invited speakers explored and discussed the philosophy of Adam Smith in both historical and contemporary perspectives, focusing on the *Theory of Moral Sentiments* (TMS) but taking his other works also into account, the *Wealth of Nations* (WN) in particular.

James Otteson (University of Alabama, United States) presented Smith's strategy of justifying the objective validity of moral judgments as a 'middle way' between a more ambitious strategy relying on transcendent authorities and a more modest strategy relying exclusively on historically contingent factors like customs and habits of a given society as sources of moral normativity. He drew attention to a significant parallelism concerning the way in which Smith deals with moral normativity in the TMS and with economic normativity (like values and prices) in the WN.

Christel Fricke (University of Oslo, Norway) suggested a reading of the TMS in terms of a constructivist and procedural moral realism: humans who, by nature, have both selfish and social or sympathetic needs and desires constitute moral principles in the course of a process of learning by doing. This process is interactive in a two-fold way as humans interact with each other as well as with their environment and thereby learn how to react (both emotionally and as actors) to events in the world in a proper way. She saw the main problem for Smith in his having to take for granted that all participants in this process have to respect each other as equals from the very beginning, thus before any constitution of morality or moral education has taken place.

Georg Lohmann (University of Magdeburg, Germany) suggested a reading of TMS as concerned with both descriptive and normative issues. He explored the interrelations between sympathy and impartiality, feelings and reasons in practical deliberation and motivation to action, pointing out how Smithian moral subjects pay respect to the freedom of moral agents (including themselves). He raised the question to what extent moral judgments of the impartial spectator are apt to ground any positive duties for moral agents.

Charles Griswold (Boston University, United States) took up the so-called 'Adam Smith problem' in a new way, raising the question of how the conceptions of impartiality and justice of TMS relate to the economic theory of WN in general and to Smith's view that a free market is just and most efficient in producing wealth. He rejected the view that TMS provides a moral foundation for WN and defended instead a systematic conception of the way these works are interrelated. He argued for the impartial spectator's having to rely on much of the economic knowledge provided by WN and connected this line of thought to the prospect of supplementing the conception of commutative justice in TMS with a conception of distributive justice.

Aaron Garrett (Boston University, United States) approached the TMS in terms of the debate on moral luck, as most prominently engaged between Bernard Williams and Thomas Nagel. He pointed to a certain irregularity in Smith's emphasis on the importance of particular sentimental motivations for judgments of justice, an irregularity which arises from the fact that the moral merit and the justice of an action are judged with reference to the underlying intention of the actor whereas the feelings that an action arouses in spectators relate also to the consequences of the action. The moral judgment of an action, even though it should focus on the underlying intention, thus depends partly on its consequences and therefore on moral luck.

Samuel Fleischacker (University of Chicago, United States) raised the question of the extent to which Smith in TMS (where he is sensitive to both anthropology and the contingencies of human life and interaction) defends a universalistic conception of moral judgments and of the standards these judgments rely on. He rejected a relativist reading of Smith, defending instead a pluralist reading and pointing out how dependence on cultural contingencies is an essential part of moral standards as conceived by Smith; from a more modern point of view this strand of cultural tolerance should be seen as an advantage rather than as a weak point in Smith's moral philosophy.

Carola von Villiez (University of Bremen, Germany) underlined, much in agreement with other participants in general and with Georg Lohmann in particular, that there are both descriptive and normative claims on morality in TMS. She focused on similarities and differences between Smith's and Rawl's accounts of moral judgment. Even though their strategies of providing impartiality for the moral judge differ to a considerable extent, one should not overlook the similarities between their approaches to moral theory: They both provide means to reconstruct a given moral culture, intending to discover the basic moral (essentially normative) convictions which provide its foundation.

Stephen Darwall (University of Michigan, United States) explored Smith's theory of the judgment of propriety, focusing on the way in which it provides a foundation for equality of respect and human dignity. He pointed out how these values are fundamental for human interaction in general (as presented in TMS) and for their economic interaction in particular (as presented in WN). On this background, he argued that it could not be surprising to see Smith rejecting the utilitarian conceptions of the morally good held by Hutcheson and Hume; instead of understanding the morally good in terms of utility for the common good, Smith proposed an understanding of it in terms of the interaction of humans as equals.

Vivienne Brown (The Open University, United Kingdom) showed how moral judgments of an action as accounted for in TMS required different imaginative transpositions of the subject: he imagines how he himself would respond if he were in the position of the agent and how an impartial spectator of the action would respond (in terms of sympathetic feelings). As none of these imaginative transpositions can ever be fully effected, this leads to a 'dialogic' model of moral agency and moral judgment: the moral subject is split into different imagined characters who enter into a dialogue. Brown argued that this dialogic conception of moral deliberation provides a framework within which the possible presence of moral dilemmas and moral remainders can be made plausible, illustrating this with Smith's reference to Voltaire's Orphan of China.

Georg Mohr (University of Bremen, Germany) compared Smith's conception of moral sentiments to those held by Shaftesbury, Hutcheson and Hume. He explored the reasons why Smith rejected the different ways in which they had defended the attribution of a genuinely moral sense to human beings. But as Smith did not give up the view that moral judgments are grounded in feelings, he had to admit some kind of moral sense as a basic faculty of human beings. Finally, Mohr explored the pros and cons of a moral sense from the point of view of current debates in moral philosophy.

Kate Abramson (University of Illinois, United States) explored both proto-Kantian and neo-Aristotelian strands in the TMS in terms of two conflicting models of ideal virtue: the conception of virtue as perfect self-command and the conception of virtue as identification with the impartial spectator. She analyzed in detail the many ways in which a moral theory, that does not reject one of these, gets into serious trouble both in its account of moral motivation and in its account of the standard of morality. But instead of blaming Smith for not having chosen just one of these models, she suggested that we learn from him that neither of these models can be rejected without substantive loss and that the construction of a moral theory that overcomes the inconsistencies of these two models is still on the agenda for moral philosophy.

Robert Solomon (University of Texas, United States) analyzed Smith's conception of sympathy as a natural emotion and distinguished it from Hume's.

He defended a Smithian view, holding that the basis of morality and justice is to be found in the realm of affect rather than in theory and principles alone, and relying on contemporary thinking in psychology and philosophy to support this argument. His reading of Smith underlined the proximity of Smith to virtue ethics rather than to Kant's objectivist conception of the moral good.

Allan Gibbard (University of Michigan, United States) looked at Smith's theory of the emotions and sentiments underlying moral judgment by adopting the perspective of recent developments in evolutionary psychology. He defended the view that, even though Smith's theory needs supplementing and revising, crucial aspects of it can still be read as an insightful analysis of the role of emotions in social and moral life. In particular, he offered a close reading of Smith's account of sympathy and explored how to make sense of it in evolutionary terms, discussing the role of propriety, governing emotions and co-ordination processes on both an individual and a social level.

Karl Graf Ballestrem (University of Eichstätt – Ingolstadt, Germany) took a new look at the widely acknowledged friendship between Smith and Hume, arguing that even though they had much in common and shared many views, there were also points of substantial disagreement between them which should lead us to see their friendship in a different light. Not only did Smith reject (though in polite terms) Hume's moral philosophy in the TMS, he also refused to fulfill Hume's last wish that he publish his *Dialogues Concerning Natural Religion* after his death. Ballestrem suggested explaining this in terms of a profound disagreement between the two on matters of religion, pointing to the role that Smith attributed to religion in his moral theory. Given his views on morality and justice, Smith could not but consider these *Dialogues* as dangerous for the morality of society.

The proceedings of the conference will be published (in German) by de Gruyter in Berlin in spring 2005.

Notes for contributors

Submissions to *The Adam Smith Review* are invited from any theoretical, disciplinary or interdisciplinary approach (max. 10,000 words, in English). Contributors are asked to make their arguments accessible to a wide multidisciplinary readership without sacrificing high standards of argument and scholarship. Please include an abstract not exceeding 100 words.

Please send all submissions, suggestions and offers to edit symposia to the Editor, Vivienne Brown, Faculty of Social Sciences, The Open University, Walton Hall, Milton Keynes, MK7 6AA, UK; v.w.brown@open.ac.uk. Email submissions are welcomed. Alternatively please send three hard copies in double-spaced type.

Please prepare your manuscript for anonymous refereeing and provide a separate title page with your name. Interdisciplinary submissions will be sent to referees with different disciplinary expertise. Submitted articles will be double-blind refereed and commissioned articles will be single-blind refereed. All contributions must be in English; it is the author's responsibility to ensure the quality of the English text. Where quotations in languages other than English are required, authors are asked to provide a translation into English.

Final versions of accepted papers will need to conform to the ASR Guidelines for Authors (Harvard reference system), but submitted papers are accepted in any format.

Submission to *The Adam Smith Review* will be taken to imply that the work is original and unpublished, and is not under consideration for publication elsewhere. By submitting a manuscript, authors agree that the exclusive rights to reproduce and distribute the article have been given to the Publishers, including reprints, photographic reproductions, microfilm, or any other reproductions of a similar nature, and translations.

Book reviews

Books relating to Adam Smith or of more general relevance for Adam Smith scholarship will be reviewed in *The Adam Smith Review*. It is editorial policy to invite authors to respond to reviews of their work. Offers to review works published in languages other than English are welcomed. Please send books for review to the Book Review Editor: James R. Otteson, Department of Philosophy, University of Alabama, USA; jotteson@tenhoor.as.ua.edu.

CPSIA information can be obtained at www.ICGtesting.com
Printed in the USA
BVOW012004130613

323280BV00004B/16/P